FIVE
WORDS

FIVE
WORDS

* * * * *

Roland Greene

Critical Semantics in the Age of
Shakespeare and Cervantes

THE UNIVERSITY OF CHICAGO PRESS   *Chicago and London*

Roland Greene is the Mark Pigott KBE Professor in the School
of Humanities and Sciences at Stanford University. His most recent
book, *Unrequited Conquests: Love and Empire in the Colonial Americas*,
was also published by the University of Chicago Press.

The University of Chicago Press, Chicago 60637
The University of Chicago Press, Ltd., London
© 2013 by The University of Chicago
All rights reserved. Published 2013.
Printed in the United States of America

22 21 20 19 18 17 16 15 14 13   1 2 3 4 5

ISBN-13: 978-0-226-00063-3 (cloth)
ISBN-13: 978-0-226-00077-0 (e-book)

The University of Chicago Press gratefully acknowledges the generous
support of Stanford University toward the publication of this book.

Library of Congress Cataloging-in-Publication Data

Greene, Roland, 1957– author.
Five words : critical semantics in the age of
Shakespeare and Cervantes / Roland Greene.
pages cm
Includes bibliographical references and index.
ISBN 978-0-226-00063-3 (cloth: alkaline paper)—
ISBN 978-0-226-00077-0 (e-book) 1. Semantics,
Comparative—History. 2. Comparative literature. I. Title.
P325.5.C6G74 2013
412—dc23
2012029170

♾ This paper meets the requirements of
ANSI/NISO Z39.48-1992 (Permanence of Paper).

CONTENTS

ACKNOWLEDGMENTS

Five Words has gained a great deal from imaginative readers and thoughtful audiences. Many friends and colleagues offered observations and criticisms that improved the book, notably Albert Russell Ascoli, Vincent Barletta, Harry Berger Jr., Gordon Braden, George Hardin Brown, Philippe Buc, Kathryn Burns, Theodore Cachey, Kenneth Calhoon, Anthony Cascardi, Patrick Cheney, Margaret Cohen, Barbara Correll, Jorge Cañizares Esguerra, Anne J. Cruz, John Dagenais, Maria DiBattista, Heather Dubrow, Lynn Enterline, J. Martin Evans, Elizabeth Fowler, Barbara Fuchs, Hester Gelber, Denise Gigante, Linda Gregerson, Jay Grossman, Sepp Gumbrecht, Jean Howard, Heather James, Nicholas Jenkins, Victoria Kahn, William J. Kennedy, Seth Kimmel, Jo Labanyi, Clare A. Lees, Seth Lerer, Barbara K. Lewalski, David Loewenstein, Jenny C. Mann, Annabel Martín, Jeffrey Masten, Stephanie Merrim, Steven Mullaney, Eric Naiman, Stephen Orgel, Ricardo Padrón, David Palumbo-Liu, Patricia Parker, Marjorie Perloff, Charles A. Perrone, Curtis Perry, Nancy Ruttenburg, Kathryn Schwarz, Jennifer Summit, Wendy Wall, Christopher Warley, John Watkins, Julian Weiss, William West, Susanne Wofford, and Susanne Woods. Paula Blank, Claire Bowen, Ruth Kaplan, Joseph Lease, David Marno, and Ramón Saldívar generously read chapters or the entire manuscript; their responses enriched *Five Words* immensely, not to mention the confidence of the author. Two anonymous readers for the University of Chicago Press both understood the project and made searching criticisms. As always I appreciate the good sense of my editor, Alan G. Thomas, and the staff at the Press. Kathy Swain copyedited the manuscript with tact and authority. For all sorts of counsel and inspiration I am indebted to my Stanford and San Francisco circle, especially Lucy Alford, Frederick Blumberg, Lauren Boehm, Christopher Donaldson, Caroline Egan, Harris Feinsod, Christina Galvez, Fabian Goppelsröder, Kathryn Hume, Jenna Lay, Rhiannon Lewis, Talya Meyers, Noam Pines, Luke Parker, Virginia Ramos, Stephanie Schmidt, Alexandra Slessarev, Bronwen Tate, and Ema Vyroubalová. Jennifer Cameron was an enterprising research assistant. At one time that I believed the work at a dead end, my late colleague Jay Fliegelman offered encouragement that made a difference.

Portions of the chapters were delivered as the Reinhard Kuhn Memorial Lecture in the Department of Comparative Literature at Brown University, the Paul Gottschalk Lecture in the Department of English at Cornell University, the Renato Poggioli Lecture in the Department of Comparative Literature at Harvard University, the Leonora Woodman Lecture in the Department of English at Purdue University, and the keynote address to the Northern California Renaissance Conference at the University of California, Berkeley. Excerpts were also presented as lectures at the Center for Medieval and Renaissance Studies and the Center for Seventeenth- and Eighteenth-Century Studies, both at the University of California, Los Angeles; the Department of Spanish at Dartmouth College; the Department of English at Gonzaga University; the Faculty of Humanities at the University of Huelva; the Department of Spanish and Spanish American Studies at King's College, London; the Center for Early Modern History and the Department of English at the University of Minnesota, Twin Cities; the Newberry Library; the Early Modern Colloquium and the Department of English at Northwestern University; the Devers Program in Dante Studies and the Department of Romance Languages at the University of Notre Dame; the Department of Comparative Literature at the University of Oregon; the Department of Comparative Literature at the Pennsylvania State University; the Department of Comparative Literature at Princeton University; the Department of

English at Rice University; the Shakespeare Association of America; the Department of English at the University of Southern California; the Department of English at Vanderbilt University; the Department of Spanish, Italian, and Portuguese at the University of Virginia; the Northeast Milton Seminar at Wheaton College; and the Department of English and the Early Modern Studies Group at the University of Wisconsin, Madison. I was honored by these invitations, each of which gave me the opportunity to rethink elements of the project with an attentive audience.

Early versions of some of this book's arguments appeared as follows: a portion of "Invention" as "Ann Lock's *Meditation*: Invention versus Dilation and the Founding of Puritan Poetics," in *Form and Reform in the English Renaissance: Essays in Honor of Barbara Kiefer Lewalski*, ed. Amy Boesky and Mary Thomas Crane (Newark: University of Delaware Press, 2000), 151–68; a portion of "Resistance" as "Colonial Becomes Postcolonial," *Modern Language Quarterly* 65 (2004): 423–41, and "Resistance in Process: On the Semantics of Early Modern Prose Fiction," *Prose Studies* (2010): 100–109; a portion of "Blood" as "Shakespeare, Cervantes, and the Project of Early Modern Blood," in *Entre Cervantes y Shakespeare: Sendas del Renacimiento*, ed. Zenón Luis-Martínez and Luis Gómez Canseco (Newark, DE: Juan de la Cuesta, 2006), 141–60; and portions of "World" as "Island Logic," in The Tempest *and Its Travels*, ed. Peter Hulme and William H. Sherman (London: Reaktion Books, 2000), 138–45, and "The Global I: Rethinking an Early Modern Convention," in *Stories and Portraits of the Self*, ed. Helena Carvalhão Buescu and João Ferreira Duarte (Amsterdam: Rodopi, 2007), 161–74. All are reprinted with permission.

My best interlocutor is my wife, Marisa Galvez, whose judgment and encouragement have seen the book to its conclusion. *Five Words* is for her and our daughter, Eleanor.

Acknowledgments

ix

INTRODUCTION

An Experiment in Early Modern Critical Semantics

Stubborn and imperishable, words precede everything. Before literature represents, philosophy argues, or history records, there are words—protagonist words, complex words, keywords, and, not least, everyday words.[1] This book is an experiment in tracing some worldviews of early modern Europe and the Americas through five words that were manifestly, unremarkably in action during the sixteenth century and remain available today. *Invention. Language. Resistance. Blood. World.* The proposition that these words are literally the same then and now but profoundly different in their semantic purchase— that cultural change comes to us in the language of life, work, and the body—is perhaps the main insight of the following pages, commonplace and yet startling.

The first constraint of the project is the five words themselves. The next is the historical period, a notional century that starts about 1525, with the first publications of the French physician and fabulist François Rabelais and the Spanish philologist Juan de Valdés, and runs through the mature writings of the Peruvian mestizo historian known as the Inca Garcilaso de la Vega, the Portuguese priest António Vieira, and the English philosopher Margaret Cavendish. At its inception, this period of about one hundred and fifty years embraces the establishment of humanism in Europe beyond Italy, the first sustained attention to the vernaculars as vehicles of art and knowledge, and a wave of explorations and conquests in the Americas; at the distant end, it includes the mature writing of the two figures who appear in the book's title, the appearance of the Baroque as a reflection on humanism, and the beginnings of experimental science. This period is the heart of the Renaissance everywhere but Italy, the origin of modernity, and the principal era of European imperial expansion. Neither an interval between two intellectual ages as that term has been applied to the later eighteenth and early nineteenth centuries, nor a scene of coincident change across entire fields of meaning such as the age of modernism, this Renaissance absorbed new ideas according to patterns probably unique to the age. Emergent worldviews stood alongside waning ones (and anachronistically, still older, classical ones), while disciplines such as history, medicine, and astronomy came to accept different relations to discovery, power, and the past; the challenge of assimilating New World perspectives into European understandings persisted and even increased throughout the period, even as the wealth obtained by some rulers and their agents unsettled old hierarchies; and the religious schism within the Christian polity contributed active principles of interpretation across the range of human knowledge.

We know the story of the period by ideas and events, and we know of its literary history through authors and works. Instead, my approach is oblique. I want to see the century in five words—not as essence or epitome, for these are illusory, but as a representation of what a great number of people in Europe and the Americas believed within an experiential field bounded by everyday ideas. How did they conceive their relation to past and present? How did they imagine their place in the culture? How did these words and the culture change together? Now and then my story obliges me to trespass out of this historical range, but for the most part the argument concerns semantic and cultural change that can be seen within about one hundred and fifty years. Moreover, while I invoke several terms for the period provisionally—*Renaissance*, *early modernity*, *Baroque*—the project of *Five Words* is to build an account of this long era elementally, from the words themselves. Each word offers an array of meanings and associations out of which, in dialogue with heuristic reflection on the period, I attempt to tell a coherent story; the work of each chapter is to dispose the semantic elements in a way that illuminates both word and period, foreground and background, each in relation to the other. Further, an elemental history is not much concerned with the disciplinary implications that trail these period terms. Whether the adjective *Renaissance* was once displaced by *early modern* but has recently been revived, or *Baroque* was deeply out of fashion for many years but is now current again in the languages other than English, is not urgent to the book's argument. All of our periodizing words are themselves available for examination according to the tenets of this approach—and they should look different to us after *Five Words*, where they resound against each other in the several national and linguistic contexts under exploration. *Five Words* uses them to redefine them.

This project's resolutely elemental approach to the period should find a counterpart in its view of intellectual history. Humanism drives the age, but it is a profoundly unstable concept: wide-ranging in its investments (from philology to educational reform to jurisprudence and much more), highly variable by location and differentiated by generation, and relentlessly critical of itself as an ideology. As much as this book is about a period often called the Renaissance, it is about an array of doctrines and practices often gathered under the rubric of humanism.[2] To our profit, the study of humanism has often been concerned with big ideas, notable figures, or vivid networks. An elemental approach is something else again, an attempt not to retell the history of humanism in intellectual, heroic, or social terms but to capture the elusive character of the movement at the cellular level, where its values and contradictions are embodied in semantics. Accordingly, my argument returns often to the term *humanism* as a marker or a measure—to consider, for example, how two opposed senses of *invention* might be humanist in their own ways or how some notions of *resistance* should be understood in the context of humanism. The harvest of this approach is a humanism seen not from above or below but from an angle, where ideas meet language. As I do with the period, I aim not to reify but to remake the term.

What is a word in the sight of this project? Like several forerunners in a tradition of considering semantic change as an index of society and culture at large, when I name words such as *blood* or *language* I mean both the semantic integers that one finds in a dictionary—not incidentally, dictionaries are a product of the period addressed here—and the concepts that shadow them. Just as literal words when followed through a work suddenly and often indistinctly turn into concepts, my argument moves between words and their not only semantic but intellectual implications to trace congruities and divergences. Like most studies of words, this one aims at representativeness. While much of my argument is informed by my general reading in the period, *Five Words* reaps the benefits of digital publishing, especially now that for all the vernaculars I am concerned with, substantial databases of early modern works as well as contemporaneous archives are available online. Notions that I conceived by observation, about both local instances and general processes of semantic change, were refined by a more systematic program of reading. And yet representativeness does not entail that all usages of a given word matter the same, and as a literary critic I give considerable credence to luminous usages that may alter a semantic history all at once. The kind of change explored here is uneven, sometimes widely distributed but sometimes achieved in one time, one place, or one work.

In tracing concepts, I move among English, French, Spanish, Italian, and Portuguese to follow the intellectual currents that bring implications to the same idea in different languages. Even when the words at issue are cognates, they are sometimes configured semantically in culturally particular ways. Here is a brief example. *Invention*, I will argue, develops generally from a medieval term for the discovery of something extant, the Latin *inventio*, to an early modern concept for the making of something new. (The old sense survives in the English word *inventory*, while the new sense is strongly connoted in the term *inventor*: why, after the sixteenth century, is someone who carries out an inventory not an inventor?) And while this shift is unmistakable in several European vernaculars over the sixteenth century, it is far more equivocal in Portuguese, where the sense of *invenção* as evoking the ambiguous power of matter—the power to be discovered, to exist in a reality alongside human purposes—is never quite overcome by the emergent sense of the human power over matter, or the power to create. The discovery of Brazil in 1500, on the day of the Invention of the Holy Cross, is often called an *invenção*, and that equivocal Portuguese word gives the concept a flexibility that is not as often seen in French, Italian, or English after about 1600. (In Juan de Castellanos's compendious volume of tributes to distinguished men of the Indies published in 1589, the dedicatory poem in Latin refers to the Americas as "invented" or discovered by Spain, while in the Spanish translation the corresponding word is rendered as a form of *hallar* or to find.[3]) While we often think of discovery and creation as discrete capacities, early modern thinkers and readers saw one concept shade into the other, and they likely knew through the words themselves what we believe we have interpreted—for instance, that events such as Columbus's "discovery" of America are as much about inventing as finding.[4] An early modern conversation about *invention* across several languages, such as the one I reanimate between the English scholar Roger Ascham and the Portuguese historian Jerónimo Osório, contains semantic traces peculiar to their languages as well as to their disciplinary, religious, and national outlooks. Assembling some of the semantic complexity in which their work was saturated enriches our understanding. But sometimes one need not span languages or cultures. Such a conversation may take place within a single work if we listen for it: so I read Joachim Du Bellay's *Déffence et Illustration de la Langue Française* (1549) as it has evidently not been read before, allowing his two principal terms, *langue* (tongue) and *langage* (language), to jostle each other in search of differentiation instead of replacing *langue*, mentally or in translation, with the modern concept of language. The emergence of that concept is one of the outcomes of Du Bellay's project, but if we treat it as already given, we miss its unfolding.

In electing to follow these five words, I turn away from others that might seem more conventional to a study of the Renaissance: *human*, *faith*, *virtue*, *individual*, *sovereign*, and so on. To me it is salutary to concentrate on those terms that do not carry obvious ideological marks but instead seem natural, neutral, and quotidian. *Invention, language, resistance, blood,* and *world* are words that early modern people not only thought through but lived with.[5] A rich tradition of criticism across several generations has examined what might be called canonical early modern words.[6] But for many of those studies, the words are inseparable from doctrines and ideologies we have already encountered through other points of entry; that is, the words themselves are often treated as metonymies for ideas conspicuously in play during the period. I want to try something else. Of course, some of my terms are closely involved with the history of ideas. By some lights, the word or concept of *blood* for early modern observers was largely explained through the humoral theory of Galen and his successors until William Harvey proposed the circulation of the blood in 1628; and some scholars might argue that the term *resistance* is adequately elucidated in view of the theories of rebellion against authority developed by George Buchanan, Hubert Languet, and others in the later sixteenth century. These words and the others in this book, I believe, have more at stake than what we can recover through the relations between a given term and a corresponding set of philosophical, scientific, or political principles.

In the first place, the office of these particular words as equipment for living allows that their meanings flow not only from the intellectual discourses of the moment but from past ideas still in dissemination, new senses under development, and custom, to mention only three empirical factors.[7] Words that maintain a disciplinary purchase but are also used in everyday life tend to be complex semantic events, and *Five Words* is an experiment in describing some of that complexity. Accordingly, I propose for each one an interpretive anecdote, a hypothesis about the changes that take place over the sixteenth and seventeenth centuries. The succeeding argument gives body to the anecdote while confronting its limits and contradictions. I am especially interested in how these words enter and depart the period, how they move between languages, how their meanings shift over time, and how their usage reflects their definitions in particular contexts such as medicine, law, or rhetoric. Each of these words is more adaptable than any one or two of those contexts allow us to see. *Five Words* explains how they work in the world.

While the project was conceived in a spirit of deliberate constraint and the chapters written in alphabetical order, I realized once they were completed that a reader would entertain the story of *Five Words* better if the chapters appeared in the order in which they fall out across the period. So I disposed them in this sequence—*Invention, Language, Resistance, Blood, World*. For readers who are concerned with only one or two of these terms, the chapters can stand apart; but taken together they propose to tell a story about the Renaissance from semantics alone, in five words.

As it turns out, these words have a rich presence in the imaginative literature of the sixteenth and seventeenth centuries. Except for *world*, I have my doubts whether any of them is an especially literary word. *Blood* is not *heart*, and *invention* and *language* belong more to speculative writing about literature than to poems and plays. These words figure in literature not because they evoke mental images or stock associations but because for writers of fiction who wanted to represent how it was to live and think in early modern society, they were powerful carriers of often ambiguous or contradictory meanings. Not simply one discourse among others, literature is the kind of writing in which semantic complexities, which are finally inseparable from the unresolved issues of the age, are rendered into figure, person, and story. The questions about which historians, cultural theorists, and others speculate are reified in literature and made more equivocal and provocative, more powerful as an instigation to thinking, than in any history or treatise. While other discourses may be compromised by ambiguity, literature is drawn to it—and can fashion it into something new, granting the premium of fresh perspective to old problems. Philip Sidney's *Arcadia*, for instance, thinks openly about the possibility of resistance to absolute authority, but from standpoints and with emotional colorations that are unavailable to the observers and theorists who write about resistance outside fiction. William Shakespeare gathers from contemporaneous European thought an incoherent array of ideas about blood and in *The Merchant of Venice* demonstrates the differences among them in speech and action. We ought to recognize these and other literary works as interventions in intellectual and cultural history, with a special franchise to compose what is disordered and trouble what is settled. Poets such as Du Bellay and Luís de Camões are not extraneous to the life of knowledge in their time, as some modern poets may be. They change its course. Accordingly, I make it part of this project to treat literary and other works together, following the criterion that where a word and a concept are under revision I will engage them, whether in a poem, a history, or a sermon. Each chapter collates several authors' works in demonstration of the properties of the relevant word and concept, observing but not deferring programmatically to literature except where, as in *The Merchant of Venice* or Cavendish's *The Blazing World*, the process of plot, character, or spectacle is inseparable from the semantic constructions I follow.

Placing change in the foreground of my argument, I turn to several conceits to distinguish among the semantic operations of the five words. Obviously I am not charting semantic developments as a linguist would, but trying to make tangible what is often abstract and obscure. Further, I want to propose models for semantic change that can be applied to words other than the five discussed here. *Invention* figures in what I call a semantic palimpsest, in which new meanings replace but never entirely overwrite older ones, so that in many early modern contexts the term is a living history of its usages. Like a literal palimpsest, in which one inscription is brighter and more immediate than others, a semantic palimpsest shows meanings in different degrees of availability. Palimpsests suggest one fashion of meanings coexisting with one another, with older ones showing through what comes later. By contrast, *language* is something else: a pendent, or one term among two or more (in English, for example, *tongue, speech, discourse*, and so on) that are often present together, equally available and often interchangeable, and that allow distinctions to emerge spontaneously as a vehicle for critical thinking (and, sometimes, to disappear again once they have served their end). Early modern people were preoccupied with the differences between kinds of language, whether classical and vernacular, European and Amerindian, Ciceronian and Senecan, or formal and demotic, and the pendency of the terms for the phenomenon of language enabled them to entertain such distinctions for as long as they were useful. Even the genre of the dialogue, in which treatises about linguistic communication (among many other topics) were often conceived as conversations between two barely marked, often interchangeable speakers, is an expression of pendency in action. Unlike the other chapters in which a semantic project tends to resolve over the period, my discussion of language shows the terms exchanging meanings promiscuously at all times.

Resistance, I suggest, might be understood as a *cartone*, or an early modern cartoon, that is, a sketch on plaster to be developed later or left in its raw state, such as Leonardo da Vinci and Michelangelo executed for their lost paintings of battles in the Palazzo Vecchio in

Florence. Some words come into the period with a shock, as counterintuitive notions that make a kind of visceral sense before they are developed into ideas. *Resistance* is like that, a recognition that in some circumstances kings and other rulers should be neutralized or even actively resisted—but when? Why? By whom? Early in the period the term appears from the margins of what is thinkable, in a fugitive and not entirely legible moment in *La Celestina*, the liminal work of medieval and early modern Spanish literature. By the generation of Sidney *resistance* is a live concern, and in the era of Cavendish and John Milton it has become a concept with a body and a history, some of which I observe by stages. In *The New World of English Words* (1658) by Milton's nephew Edward Phillips, we witness *resistance* among several other terms that enter the period as *cartoni* but live on as they are revised into ideas:

RESISTENCE, (Lat. as it were a withstanding) a Term in Philosophy, taken for the property of a solid body, which resisteth and opposeth whatsoever comes against it.

REVOLUTION, (lat.) a rowling back, the turning back of cælestial bodies to their first point, and finishing their circular course.

SUBVERSION, (lat.) an overturning, or overthrowing.[8]

Each of these terms in its political sense comes to seem natural to early modern culture, but for *resistance*, as a specimen of the others, I want to consider how it became the word we know in later colonial and postcolonial thought, as in Thomas Jefferson's motto "Resistance to tyrants is obedience unto God."

If the cartone of *resistance* is a kind of blank that must be filled in over time, *blood* is almost too heavy with information and significance. *Blood* figures in what I call a conceptual envelope, in which a phenomenon known through direct experience moves within several intersecting planes of received knowledge, as we know (say) the weather by both observation and science. When a reader of the sixteenth century encounters *blood* as a term, he or she finds it in the open space at the center of this imaginary envelope, surrounded by conventional understandings of it in physiological, genealogical, and heroic terms; these notions must fit with one another and with what the reader knows by experience. For the envelope to cohere, these understandings must complement one another; for the envelope to be reconstructed, these notions must be revised discretely and in relation to each other. As I tell it, the story of *blood* in the sixteenth century is about the slow remaking of a received conceptual envelope with religious, chivalric, and cosmological values into a new one with scientific, social, and racial ones.

Finally, there is *world*. Perhaps the most challenging term to interpret across this period, *world* is everywhere, but has been scarcely examined closely, on its own terms. In fact, the concept has a bit of all the others to it—pendent with *earth*, perhaps, and a palimpsest of several uneasily contemporaneous cosmologies, and certainly a cartoon that can be either crudely drawn or elaborately filled. The conceit I apply to *world*, however, is an engine, because when it changes—turning from unitary, singular, and divinely created to partial, multiple, and man made—a number of other concepts change with it, in correspondence and reaction. Semantic engines such as *world* are metonymies not for a particular idea or doctrine but for a range of developments occurring across the human sciences. Early modern semantic engines are uncommon because they depend on terms that are implicated across many disciplines and contexts, such as *history* and *science*. *World* is unusual in that its revision signals not a particular disciplinary development—the way that *history*, for example, changes from fabulous to empirical—but a general shift in perception, as much phenomenological as intellectual.[9] Multifarious in meanings and results, *world* tends to thwart representativeness in critical semantics; what remains an attainable principle in the other chapters becomes all but impossible to hold in the final chapter, where the argument does not fully map the word but visits some of its stations in the period. If the power of a semantic engine is in its outcomes, many of which are distant or contingent, alternative versions of this final chapter by other scholars or by me could (and perhaps should) tell a substantially different story for this word.

Like the five words, the five conceits—palimpsest, pendent, cartone, envelope, and engine—are native to the long sixteenth century as objects that are devised or become especially visible in the period. Holding their own mysteries (why does *envelope*, as both noun and verb, rise in usage for the generation of Sidney, Spenser, and Shakespeare?), they could be the subjects of their own books. My interest, I hardly need to say, is not with the material culture to which these objects belong but with the impressions they evoke as we see and feel them moving, occupying space, maintaining their components, and fulfilling the intentions of human beings. Their import here is that they encourage us to imagine the relations among semantic elements in three dimensions and in time: old and new, side by side, one over the other, and so on. Not by accident, the conceits are drawn from objects that are either aesthetic while observing a public aspect or useful but with a certain beauty. That is how I approach the words themselves, as operating in a field of play that is aesthetic and social at once (and thus only intermittently rather than exclusively in other fields to which some critics might well assign them—philosophical, scientific, or psychic).[10] I lend a conceit to a given word to render thinkable what might otherwise seem a highly abstract story of semantic change and to provoke conjectures about other words. If *invention* is a palimpsest, can we say the same of *wit*? Do the counterparts of *wit* in the other vernaculars—*agudeza*, *ingegno*, *esprit*—entail the same semantic conceits? If *tongue* and *language* are pendents, what are some others we might recognize in mutable but regular relation to each other—such as, in English, *human* and *humane*? Questions such as these are more readily posed when words are provisionally imagined as equipment, and semantic change becomes legible in the terms of historical objects. Further, I like to suppose that this is to reconstruct some of the often unspoken ways that early modern people kept meanings in counterposition to one another, much as in the present day we may dispose meanings in terms of boxes or bandwidth. My project is finally about the meanings in motion, not the conceits or, for that matter, the works or writers.

An argument (or five arguments) involving separate areas of knowledge, a range of primary works, and distinctive processes of semantic change must condense a great deal of contextual information on the way to the conceptual events that form the core of each chapter. Having been mindful of this risk, I have chosen in the end to emphasize the stories of words in revision that are unique to this book rather than historical or philosophical accounts that can be found elsewhere. Neither intellectual history nor etymological analysis, the project finds its central purpose as literary criticism with words, rather than authors or works, as the primary objects of investigation. I call the approach of this book "critical semantics" in tribute to the models of historical, cultural, and other kinds of semantic investigation acknowledged in my first note. Still, this work is different from such antecedents because these five words are implicated in an intellectual fabric different from that of the modern period: more pragmatic than theoretical, less homogeneous across languages, and far less certain about which words are "key" and which are not. At the same time, this study is starkly different from various past specimens of historicist scholarship, such as books that followed broad networks of ideas across history without much attention to the distinctions among terms, or treated literary works as organs for thought through singular words, or dwelled at the borders between works of art and a surrounding culture in search of the exchanges that produce meaning.[11] All of these approaches are illuminating, but I am after something different again, a sense of words and concepts as holding in themselves the negotiations and contradictions that others find in received doctrines, intellectual trajectories, and cultural appropriations.

I want to recover some of the wonder with which early modern people regarded particular words that crossed eras (from the ancients to their own time) and languages (across Europe and the Atlantic). No doubt this is to court futility. One feels that if five men and women of letters of the middle sixteenth century—in London, Paris, Lisbon, Florence, and Mexico City—were to embark on their own studies of five words, perhaps in the manner of Erasmus's *Adagia* or Jean Bodin's *Colloquium heptaplomeres*, either the words (*honra, sprezzatura, wit*) or the analyses of them (the meaning of *faith*) would be unimaginably more diverse than for modern scholars and readers. Bringing these cultural regimes into a single conversation is a risky enterprise, but it reminds us of the complexity of the age, whether we call it the Renaissance or something else. I believe that a critical semantics adapted to early modern conditions ought to produce a fresh and compelling version of the period and of the poems, plays, and prose fictions discussed here. We should see in the words the stages and reactions of the given period, how early humanism was inflected by the age of discoveries, for instance, or how the Baroque emerged out of the blind spots and loose ends of high humanism. We should see literary history, refracted.

Since conceiving *Five Words*, I have sometimes been asked whether the words were chosen because they have a collective logic or appear together somewhere. My choosing them was almost arbitrary in that I wanted to see only whether something meaningful about the period could be recovered through words of an everyday character that nonetheless opened onto different disciplinary problems: *invention* onto rhetoric and technology, *language* onto linguistics and ethnology, *resistance* onto politics and imperialism, *blood* onto medicine and race, and *world* onto astronomy and philosophy—and all of them onto literature. As long as they were not redundant in these coalitions, I was not especially concerned about which words I chose. There are many more words and concepts that could stand in for the ones I discuss; what matters is that they are at work everywhere in the period, with unpredictable outcomes. (There are also several terms that shadow the project because they move across the chapters without getting sustained attention: *conquest, matter, imagination, rebellion*, and the richest, *experience*. Most of them have been treated somewhere else, even often.[12]) The project treats the instances of the words across languages and phases, from literary genres such as epic, lyric, and romance to histories, sermons, and treatises of many sorts. Moreover, I aim to resist the disciplinary superstition that often installs a few major figures—such as Shakespeare in English or Cervantes in Spanish—as the test of ideas in the period. Obviously these writers are part of the book's title and the argument—because their involvement with these terms is unusually searching—but not at the expense of others, such as Marguerite de Navarre, Vieira, or Cavendish, whose work with ideas and feelings in words is indispensable to the events I chart.

In the end, the nearly arbitrary character of my five words should serve as a reminder that many of the words in early modern writing, literary and otherwise, would seem as dense with semantic and cultural implications as these if only we knew how to think about them. The words treated here are not especially philosophical or political; at the same time, they are not the most ordinary. Rather, these five words, important within local fields of knowledge such as rhetoric or political theory, tend to appear in general discourse as though they were ordinary, their capaciousness taken for granted. They are the working terms on which worldviews are established, and there are many more of them than the canonical words with which literary and historical studies have often been preoccupied. Many words are like these words. I have sometimes envisioned extending this sort of project to every word on a given page by Rabelais, Sidney, or the Inca Garcilaso, distributing the terms to scholars with the injunction not only to explain their semantic changes over time but to set each discrete word in motion with the others: which belong to its field, which are undergoing change in correspondence with it, which are in dialogue with their counterparts in other languages, and so forth. The ensuing discussion might resemble what I have tried to do in this book, though with more granular attention and a complex set of conceits for how words change over time—such as a conceptual envelope assembled from several directions at once, or a palimpsest seen from two sides, or a cartone described by layers. It would be informing to see the kinds of conceits I have sketched here instead developed by readers working in concert, challenging one another's assumptions as they go. While this kind of critical reading entails a different sort of integer than we customarily follow through works of literature, it ought to be no less compelling than the interpretation of other integers—works, forms, doctrines, careers, motifs, ideologies—that have been naturalized by professional literary studies. Whenever the project seemed about to turn into one of these conventional studies, I was haunted by what Gertrude Stein wrote about one of her experiments: "I really do know that it can be done and if it can be done why do it."[13] I really do not know that the project of *Five Words* can be done. But I know why do it. What follows is an experiment in a sort of literary criticism that is new and old at once and that offers stories about the past that are fresh, deep, and worth developing further. I favor any approach that reacquaints us with literature as advanced, speculative thinking about the world we live in.

Introduction

14

INVENTION

Near the end of Rabelais's *Third Book of Pantagruel*, the protagonist prepares to sail, in a fleet of ships, in search of the Oracle of the Bottle. He takes aboard sailors, pilots, interpreters, and soldiers, as well as food, ammunition, money, and other provisions for a long sea voyage. "Among other items," writes the narrator, "I saw that he had loaded a great store of the herb Pantagruelion, raw as well as preserved and prepared."[1] Thus begins a curious episode in Rabelais's vast, digressive fiction. For the account of Pantagruelion consumes the rest of the *Third Book*, four chapters, including the herb's physical and botanical properties, its lifespan, and its uses. One of the enduring questions about this *Third Book* is why Rabelais interrupts his much-interrupted story to pay tribute to an herb—Pantagruelion is an imaginary amalgamation of plants such as hemp, cotton, and flax as well as minerals such as asbestos—at such length, postponing the narrative of the voyage until the *Fourth Book*. Pantagruelion refracts the nature and concerns of the protagonist to whom it refers: it is to Pantagruel what the iris is to the Virgin Mary or the laurel is to Petrarch.[2] And yet we are continually reminded in Rabelais's fiction that the early modern world is cut off from the pasts inhabited by such figures; that objects that once would have been legible in classical or Christian terms are now often parodies of those vanished or threatened idealisms; and that a Pantagruelion is more likely to embody the incongruities of the sixteenth-century present than the correspondences of any earlier time.

In that spirit, the account of Pantagruelion is striking because from its first mention, the narrator is at pains to anticipate a distinction that often becomes important in narratives of voyages of discovery. On the one side is the plant as the object of discovery, in its natural state, and on the other is the same plant as the object ("conficte et præparée") of human disposition or even creation. In this preposterous voyage, the ships are laden with an herb that already demonstrates what is usually developed through experience, namely, all of its possibilities— medicinal, culinary, practical—as seen in both natural and artificial uses. It is as though the crew plans to run backward through a voyage of encounter, bringing Pantagruelion to the rest of the world as an array of usages as well as a raw discovery. "In Pantagruelion I recognize so many virtues, so much vigour, so many perfections, so many admirable effects," writes the narrator, "that if its full worth had been known when, as the Prophet tells us, the trees elected a wooden king to reign over them and govern them, it would no doubt have gained the majority of their votes."

Si promptement voulez guerir une bruslure, soit d'eaue, soit de feu, applicquez y du Pantagruelion crud, c'est à dire tel qui naist de terre, sans aultre appareil ne composition. . . .

Sans elle seroient les cuisines infames, les tables detestables, quoy que couvertes feussent de toutes viandes exquises, les lictz sans delices, quoy que y feust en abondance or, argent, electre, ivoyre et porphyre.

Sans elle ne porteroient les meusniers bled au moulin, n'en rapporteroient farine. Sans elle, comment seroient portez les playdoiers des advocatz à l'auditoire? Comment seroit sans elle porté le plastre à l'hastellier? Sans elle, comment seroit tirée l'eaue du puyz? Sans elle, que feroient les tabellions, les copistes, les secretaires et escrivains? Ne periroient les pantarques et papiers rantiers? Ne periroit le noble art d'imprimerie? De quoy feroit on chassis? Comment sonneroit on les cloches? D'elle sont les Isiacques ornez, les Pastophores revestuz, toute humaine nature couverte en premiere position. Toutes les arbres lanificques des Seres, les gossampines de Tyle en la mer Persicque, les cynes des Arabes, les vignes de Malthe ne vestissent tant de persones que faict ceste herbe seulette. Couvre les armées contre le froid et la pluye, plus certes commodement que jadis ne faisoient les peaulx; couvre les theatres et amphitheatres contre le chaleur, ceinct les boys et taillis au plaisir des chasseurs, descend en eaue, tant doulce que marine, au profict des pescheurs. Par elle sont bottes, botines, botasses, houzeaulx, brodequins, souliers, escarpins, pantofles, savattes mises en forme et usaige. Par elle sont les arcs tendus, les arbelestes bandées, les fondes faictes. Et, comme si feust herbe sacre, verbenicque et reverée des Manes et Lemures, les corps humains mors sans elle ne sont inhumez.[3]

(If you want quickly to heal a scald or a burn, apply some Pantagruelion raw; that is to say just as it comes out of the earth, without any preparation or treatment....

Without it kitchens would be a disgrace, tables repellent, even though they were covered with every exquisite food, and beds pleasureless, though adorned with gold, silver, amber, ivory, and porphyry in abundance.

Without it millers would not carry wheat to the mill, or carry flour away. Without it, how could advocates' pleadings be brought to the sessions hall? How could plaster be carried to the workshop without it? Without it, how could water be drawn from the well? What would scribes, copyists, secretaries, and writers do without it? Would not official documents and rent-rolls disappear? Would not the noble art of printing perish? What would window-screens be made of? How would church-bells be rung? It provides the adornment of the priests of Isis, the robes of the pastophores, and the coverings of all human beings in their first recumbent position. All the woolly trees of Northern India, all the cotton plants of Tylos on the Persian Gulf, of Arabia, and of Malta have not dressed so many people as this plant alone. It protects armies against cold and rain, much better than did the skin tents of old. It protects theatres and amphitheatres against the heat; it is hung round woods and coppices for the pleasure of hunters; it is dropped into sweet water and sea-water for the profit of fishermen. It shapes and makes serviceable boots, high-boots, heavy boots, leggings, shoes, pumps, slippers, and nailed shoes. By it bows are strung, arbalests bent, and slings made. And as though it were a

Invention

17

sacred plant, like verbena, and reverenced by the Manes and Lemurs, bodies of men are never buried without it.)[4]

Rabelais's parody mocks the earnest enumerations of origins, properties, and uses of plants—and many other things, from wine to musical instruments to magic—found in compendia such as Giannozzo Manetti's *De dignitate et excellentia hominis* (1453), Alfonso de Toledo's *Invencionario* (circa 1467), and Polydore Vergil's *De inventoribus rerum* (1499), which belong to an early humanist tradition that celebrates *operosità* or constructive activity.[5] And the crude joke of the passage is that we are often unable to tell which of the uses of Pantagruelion is being celebrated. Does it grace kitchens as food, implement, or tablecloth—or all of these? In which forms does it make beds pleasurable—as pillow, blanket, or rope?

When the narrator insists that Pantagruel was the "inventeur" of Pantagruelion and then corrects himself—"je ne diz quant à la plante, mais quant à un certain usaige" ("I do not mean of the plant, but of a certain usage of it")—we are reminded that what concerns this episode as much as the herb is *invention*. The word is ripe for parodic but critical treatment because of how it changes at the threshold of the sixteenth century, under the pressure of the first wave of humanism and its enabling forces, such as the rise of print, the availability of classical learning, and the discovery of new societies.[6] When Rabelais's *Third Book* speaks of the natural herb as well as rent-rolls, church-bells, and leggings, we hear through the narrator's ostensible subject, Pantagruelion, the cultural and semantic implications of *invention* itself. And when Pantagruel "invents" Pantagruelion, that process brings to mind Rabelais's "invention" of the fiction itself, introduced in the prologue to the *First Book* as among several "books of our invention such as *Gargantua, Pantagruel, Throw-pint, The Dignity of Codpieces, On Peas and Lard Seasoned with a Commentary*, et cetera."[7] Hard though it is to keep in mind a plant of many uses, it may be more challenging to absorb a notion of *invention* that encompasses many senses from discovery to adaptation to application to conception.

Invention is perhaps the signal concept of early modernity. Not only is the term largely adapted into its modern semantic configuration during the sixteenth century—with a common core of meaning across languages as well as striking differences from language to language—but it is impossible to think about the early modern period without *invention* in all of its senses together. When one sense overwrites another, the word registers the changes that lend the Renaissance some of its complexity. In western European and transatlantic societies after the Middle Ages, *invention* is not only what it seems to be, a rhetorical process received from classical antiquity, but a figure that represents the confrontation between two factors, the human capacity to touch reality and that reality itself.[8] How we understand those two factors depends on the moment, the place, and the position of the observer. The nature of both the capacity (whether recording, altering, or creating) and the enveloping reality (whether divine, secular, or material) is negotiated throughout the century in strikingly new ways. When in the Middle Ages for instance, the reality at issue was understood to be Holy Scripture, as it was for Saint Augustine, invention became a procedure as much for exegesis as for argument. In that era the confrontation between human capacity and its reality was suspended within the precinct of hermeneutics, where a *modus inveniendi* was adapted into a *modus interpretandi* concerned with a matter that cannot be gainsaid, the *graphē* of God. The episode has been amply narrated and is not my concern here.[9] Rather, I am interested in what Rabelais and his contemporaries find intriguing and perplexing: an invention that is under revision throughout the sixteenth century as both human capacity and the surrounding reality are seen to change. *Invention* is thus a sort of figure that I call a palimpsest. Across the century, every usage of the word not only assumes a certain configuration of these elements but evokes other configurations; the word carries within it the history of its changes as well as its present balance of factors.[10] When early modern thinkers and readers encountered the term *invention*, they saw it as though written on a palimpsest or tablet held in common across languages, religions, and ideologies. To put it another way, the tension built into the word does not compromise its meaning; it is that meaning.

One might say there are two *inventions* at large in the European and transatlantic worlds, as discovery and as conception:

Invention as	Discovery	Conception
Object	Matter, Things	Experience, World
Medium	Memory	Utterance
Site of Authority	Original Writer → Present Reader	Present Writer
Temporality	Past to Present	Present to Future

Although in bold outline the story goes that conception replaces discovery, in fact neither entirely overwrites the other. On the contrary, for most of the long sixteenth century, both of these senses are at least immanent where the term *invention* appears.[11] The disinclination of many rhetoricians and poetic theorists to define *invention* in this period attests to the term's power as palimpsest, its access to complementary and perhaps contradictory meanings. Notice that what I call here the meaning of each term entails its objects, its construal of a degree of dependency on earlier models, and its temporal horizon. *Invention* as discovery posits a more or less inert object, a concessionary (if not a superstitious) approach to textual authority, and a temporal project that brings matter out of the past into the present. By contrast, *invention* as conception supposes a lively, sometimes ineffable object, a greater degree of independence from past authorities, and a project that creates fictions in the present destined to be encountered in the future. The mutual resistance of these two senses can be found embedded in many of the dichotomies and debates of the period: between the discoverer Christopher Columbus and the freehanded conceivers of American reality such as Amerigo Vespucci and Walter Ralegh; between the generations of Clément Marot and the Pléiade; between the Puritan literalist Stephen Gosson and the theorists of fiction Philip Sidney and George Puttenham; and between the poet and custodian of quantitative prosody Thomas Campion and the defender of vernacular rhythm and rhyme Samuel Daniel.

At the start of the early modern period, as the classical concept of invention is revived and reinterpreted, the principle of reality against which human capacity asserts itself is matter, or the raw things or facts of the world as organized by logic.[12] In the middle sixteenth century, the rhetorician Thomas Wilson draws on this sense of the concept when he notes the first of "five thynges to be considered in an Oratour" as "the findyng out of apte matter, called otherwise Invencion," defined in turn as "a searchyng out of thynges true, or thynges likely."[13] By the end of the early modern period, however, that principle has many names, of which *matter* and *things* are only two: others are *experience*, *fiction*, and the *world* itself. In between, in the era I am charting, the concept of *invention* indicates, in its various appearances, the state of early modern thinking on such questions as how to honor the past, how to reflect the present, how to balance nativist cultural interests against importations—in short, how to make a mark on the world. Further, the word *invention* maintains a wide range of corresponding terms in the several vernaculars—the French *invention*, the Italian *invenzione*, the Portuguese *invenção*, and the Spanish *invención*, not to mention partial synonyms such as the Spanish *ingenio*—and each of these finds its own balance among these questions. Of course, there is a great deal of cultural particularity that departs from this anecdote. The words themselves are more unstable than received literary history often allows, and often become more evocative in their instability. Many thinkers of the period enact the counterposition of *invention* to its reality principles in ways that are motivated by their own circumstances, and perhaps no one lives out the anecdote quite as neatly as I have described it.

Still, if *invention* often registers the confrontation between the singular rhetor or artist and a reality principle that changes character across the sixteenth century, from matter to a more abstract experience, the word itself is a kind of palimpsest, with some of its senses in the foreground and others barely visible but available. As the balance of these senses shifts away from discovery and toward creation, *invention* changes until it becomes the modern concept that in the seventeenth century will be indispensable to empirical science and technology. When we encounter it as a seemingly static feature in a particular setting, say in a treatise on rhetoric, *invention* often seems legible as a specimen of humanist triumphalism, the term that perhaps most vividly expresses the early modern interest in the human propensity for devising and creating. This is how literary history typically treats the concept. But in fact the term is never static. It carries multiple senses, shifts implications from one usage to another, is often strikingly different from one decade to the next, and always evokes an array of problems and attitudes about finding and making, the classical past and the open-ended present. Even its most ardent exponents, such as Rabelais, are often ambivalent about what they mean by it, exactly because the term contains the uncertainties of a period suspended between complementary but distinct notions of what it means to make customs, objects, or works of art. Moreover, *invention* is thought of as embedded always in material and political considerations. It is often an importation, a foreign fashion of working native matter, and thus cross-culturally coded; it is often gendered, usually male, so that female writers must contend with their relation to the term as a problem of authorship; and it is full of economic implications, since as the century goes on it becomes impossible not to see that *invention* is thoroughly based in not just the imaginative but the technological exploitation of things. In short, *invention* is a slate on which Renaissance writers reflect on their world but also their agency in it, their entanglement with things and works, and their historical situations.

It would be well to pause over what it means for the two senses of *invention* to occupy a semantic palimpsest. Such palimpsests occur where a single term of long standing and wide application covers concepts becoming situated against one another, exchanging priority, and taking on new senses. For instance, the Latin *historia* and its counterparts in the vernaculars make such a palimpsest. Between Guillaume Budé at the beginning of the sixteenth century and Justus Lipsius at the end, the term evokes starkly different assumptions about the unity and exemplarity of history as well as its strangeness to the present.[14] One might say there are several notions of history available in the period, some of them declining and others on the rise; but where one term covers all of them, it captures a type of conversation native to this moment in which differences are collated in and through a common vocabulary. The English *poesy* and *poetry* are likewise transformed over this period, becoming not so much metonymies for all kinds of imaginative writing as categories of literary production with their own powers and liabilities. The poets and theorists who argue over poetry's nature toward the end of the century sharpen their differences even as they accept shares of each other's arguments encoded in the word itself. The semantic palimpsest is the site of a probably irresolvable contradiction in early modern thought, and it belongs finally to the culture, not the actors who inscribe their particular understandings under a term such as *history* or *poesy*. In the case of *invention*, the senses exchange the conditions of being *in presentia* and *in absentia*, imply a range of different objects, and often seem to be present at once.

Cicero is foundational to this story because in the early modern period he was often regarded as the locus classicus of invention, not least for his *De Inventione* (84 BCE), which along with the undated *Rhetorica ad Herennium* is one of the most cited treatises on rhetoric of the time. Of course, Ciceronian rhetoric cannot be reduced to invention. Because it figures as preliminary in any process of rhetorical composition, invention is merely among the earliest chapters one would expect to find in such a treatise. But *De Inventione* is an unfinished work of Cicero's youth and was supplanted later by the *De Oratore* and *Orator* (55 and 46 BCE, respectively) of his mature career. It is unfinished precisely from the point where Cicero treats invention, before he reached the projected chapters on memory, delivery, and other elements. He might well have given the completed book a general title such as *Rhetorici Libri*, but the name of the section on invention became attached to the fragmentary volume. While Cicero disparaged *De Inventione* later in his life, its treatment of invention is perhaps a parable of how invention came to claim a central position in modernity as not simply one element of rhetoric among several but a figure for humanist preoccupations.[15]

In one sense, Cicero's rhetoric is fundamentally materialist. When he considers the conditions of reality from which the discipline proceeds, he begins at the relation between *materia* and *inventio*, the threshold from which an art of organizing thought and speech becomes necessary or conceivable. In his art there is, first, *materia* or matter, which is his principle of reality: *materia* may be literally material or it may not, but Cicero leaves no doubt that like other disciplines, rhetoric takes place in an ontological setting conditioned by an existing matter.

Materiam artis eam dicimus in qua omnis ars et ea facultas quae con-
ficitur ex arte versatur. Ut si medicinae materiam dicamus morbos ac
vulnera, quod in his omnis medicina versetur, item, quibus in rebus
versatur ars et facultas oratoria, eas res materiam artis rhetoricae
nominamus. Has autem res alii plures, alii pauciores existimarunt.
Nam Gorgias Leontinus, antiquissimus fere rhetor, omnibus de rebus
oratorem optime posse dicere existimavit. Hic infinitam et immensam
huic artificio materiam subicere videtur. Aristoteles autem, qui huic
arti plurima adiumenta atque ornamenta subministravit, tribus in
generibus rerum versari rhetoris officium putavit, demonstrativo,
deliberativo, iudiciali.

(The material of the art I call that with which the whole art, and the
faculty produced out of the art, are concerned. For example, we say
the material of medicine is diseases and wounds because medicine is
wholly concerned with these; in the same way we call the material
of the art of rhetoric those subjects with which the art and power of
oratory are concerned. However, some have thought that there are
more and some less of these subjects. Gorgias of Leontini, almost the
earliest teacher of oratory, held that the orator could speak better than
anyone else on all subjects. He assigned to rhetoric a vast—and in
fact infinite—material. Aristotle, on the other hand, who did a great
deal to improve and adorn this art, thought that the office of the orator was concerned with three kinds of topics: the demonstrative or
epideictic, the deliberative, and the judicial.)[16]

The *materia* of medicine is disease, while the *materia* of rhetoric is
"those subjects with which the art and power of oratory are concerned"—but of course rhetoric is not to any defined area of life as
medicine is to disease, but an art of speaking, as Aristotle noted, of
"any subject whatever."[17] While he accepts the Aristotelian position
about the organizing topics of rhetoric, Cicero continues to entertain
something like Gorgias's sophistic scope in its *materia* or principle of
reality. In practice more than in theory, this is where a strict disciplinary definition admits an opening to a more indistinct one, authorizing
rhetoric in effect to claim everything material as its matter. In *De
Oratore* this position will be refined to argue that rhetoric prevails over

philosophy and law because the orator must know these disciplines as well as eloquence; Quintilian, in turn, insists that oratorical skill, joined to knowledge, is the catalytic element in rhetoric (and he more or less accepts Ciceronian invention, treating it indirectly and then declaring that "enough, I imagine, has now been said about Invention").[18]

This compromise—a vast material, coextensive with reality itself, encountering the closely defined rhetorical process of which invention forms a preliminary but determining part—is a founding condition of rhetoric in the West making the discipline an art striving against its limits, a way of speaking always about to become a kind of knowledge. At the same time, this is the primordial relation between an enveloping materiality and a serving invention that Renaissance artists often revisit, continually adjust, and sometimes overthrow. Where Cicero goes on to enumerate the "parts" of rhetoric, he provides an array of possibilities from which early modern rhetors implicitly agree to isolate and develop one, as indispensable to their historical moment:

> Inventio est excogitatio rerum verarum aut veri similium quae causam probabilem reddant; dispositio est rerum inventarum in ordinem distributio; elocutio est idoneorum verborum ad inventionem accommodatio; memoria est firma animi rerum ac verborum perceptio; pronuntiatio est ex rerum et verborum dignitate vocis et corporis moderatio.

> (*Inventio* is the excogitation of true things or seemingly true things to render one's cause plausible; *dispositio* is the distribution of invented things in the proper order; *elocutio* is the fitting of the proper language to the invention; *memoria* is the firm mental perception of words and things; *pronuntiatio* is the control of voice and body in a manner suitable to the dignity of the subject matter and the style.)[19]

Invention for Cicero is not what it will become in the sixteenth century, a metonymy for human capacities, but merely a stage in the procedure called rhetoric. What is preliminary in Cicero's sequence becomes predominant in the early modern view. While the Ciceronian understanding holds, and matter, circumscribing invention, implicitly determines what invention may do with it, the latter term can retain the sense of a neutral, equal, and perhaps passive encounter with things and the world. In this sense, which persists through the Middle Ages, *inventio* is often translated as "discovery," the finding of what is already there instead of (or more emphatically than) the purposive act of conception or creation. This is the sense elaborated by Augustine and passed into the hermeneutic tradition he reinvigorates, where Holy Scripture is a divine matter to be plumbed by the enterprising Christian reader. The material counterpart to this interpretive process is the Invention of the Cross by Saint Helena in the fourth century, in which the wood on which Christ died was supposedly recovered as a relic.

Invention changes with the first phase of humanism in the later fifteenth and early sixteenth centuries, which was engrossed in the exploration of human capacities. Having named a multifarious relation between matter and thought, where the former is almost always infinite and the latter often accessory to it, *invention* becomes human centered rather than matter centered, a way of conceiving how human beings give meaning to the world of things instead of the other way around. *Invention* as discovery recedes by stages into obsolescence in most western European languages, to be replaced by what amounts to a new concept under the same term, the thrust of which is to install consciousness over materiality and often to mystify the conditions that enable materiality at all: where matter comes from, how it envelops consciousness, and how it might make consciousness possible are only three of the questions that *invention* in the emergent sense seems determined to render invisible. The rest of the chapter will be concerned with the implications of this decisive episode in the making of a modern outlook in which the material becomes a function of the intellectual and the spiritual, until by degrees we are estranged from the world of matter. The conceit of the palimpsest will be critical to this discussion, for it allows us to reassemble the concept of *invention* in its several senses and to remember that every statement about invention entails a corresponding statement, sometimes direct and sometimes implicit, about its objects such as matter. Following the fortunes of a term that is often set against itself, that encodes unacknowledged assumptions about human capacities to move things and the world, we ought to read every early modern instance of the word *invention* as written on the general palimpsest—a second context that often means more than the immediate, local settings in which we encounter invention as word and concept.

Through the play of its senses, *invention* often serves as a general trope that is disputed, modified, and passed around by writers of opposed positions. When a writer of antiquarian, nativist inclinations such as the English scholar Roger Ascham addresses invention, he sees an instrument of unquestioned power that is nonetheless exposed to the dangers of historical blindness, empty cleverness, and prolixity. In *The Scholemaster* (1570) Ascham praises the priest and historian Jerónimo Osório, known in their time as "the Portuguese Cicero," for a fertile inventiveness that sometimes "over reach[es]" the limits of decorum, "as though [he] had bene brought up in some schole in *Asia* . . . rather then in *Athens* with *Plato*, *Aristotle*, and *Demosthenes*."[20] Ascham was probably much concerned by Osório's *Epistola ad Serenissimam Elisabetham Angliae Reginam* (1563), which argues deftly for the return of Roman Catholicism in England, proposing to Queen Elizabeth that her realm's Reformation is to be attributed not to her "ingenium, litterae, [or] humanitas" but "to many men which being verbes active I knowe not of what mad moode, go about to pul insondre the fences and inclosures of all lawe and religion."[21] Osório's Latin original scarcely uses the terms *inventio* or *invenire*, but he depicts a Reformation in which the two senses of the term are manifest: an authentic religion that was once discovered by wise and holy men is now under dangerous reinvention by others of lower character and an unduly active disposition. For Osório and other Catholics, a more circumscribed invention, discovering what is hidden rather than feigning or counterfeiting religion (Osório's verb is *ementiri*), offers the promise of an authentic Christianity ("quid enim cogitari potest . . . melius[?]" (for what can be invented . . . better?).[22] His English translator, Richard Shacklock, in turn, brings out the two senses of *invention* by adducing the word in many of these contexts, and Ascham responds in kind.

When he considers the polemic to Elizabeth, who as a princess had been his student (he taught her to read Greek), Ascham casts about for a way not to change Osório's views but to trammel his inventiveness. For this theologian and polemicist, he supposes, creative invention is the process of a heresy, and Ascham strikes at the process, not the heresy itself. Accordingly, he recommends the procedure of "epitome" ("a way of studie, belonging, rather to matter, than to wordes; to memorie, than to utterance"), a practice of research into the cultural past that subjects invention to discretion and precedent. He recognizes, however, that epitome succeeds not by itself, but over and against invention, for without the latter it is "a silie poor kinde of studie, not unlike to the doing of those poore folke, which neyther till, nor sowe, nor reape themselves, but gleane by stelth, upon other mens growndes."[23] Ascham emphasizes epitome because in this era's contest of inventions, it pulls the term away from free conception and toward the discovery of an already existing matter; it would make an Osório into a scholar of discovery rather than conception "if [he] would leave of his lustines in striving against S. Austen, and his over rancke rayling against poore Luther, and the troth of Gods doctrine, and give his whole studie, not to write any thing of his owne for a while, but to translate Demosthenes."[24] These two figures, Osório and Ascham, are debating religious politics through the medium of *invention*, where that term entails the opposed values of their faiths as well as the shared assumptions of their humanist worldviews (the latter of which leads Ascham to remark the brief "distance betwixt London and Lysbon"[25]). When they invoke their senses of *invention*, then, are they speaking at cross purposes? Or do they share a private language of sorts, in which a single term can be both question and answer, problem and solution? These friendly opponents (and Osório's translator, Shacklock), I believe, are writing directly on the palimpsest that is the contemporaneous notion of invention. Doing so, they demonstrate the ethical and polemical force in the equivocality between the senses, which encourages many of their contemporaries to cultivate ambiguity and semantic equilibrium—discovery balanced by conception. For Ascham, Osório, and their contemporaries, the term is constructed in the tension between these alternatives.

If *invention* is a palimpsest where several other terms are written beneath the surface, we are able to see Renaissance writers treating the concept not as an ideal—that is our empty notion of how they saw it—but as many things: a rule, a procedure, a set of values, and always an occasion for thinking their way across some of the most durable problems of the age. Among these problems, invention is best attuned to certain questions that appear and reappear in sixteenth-century thinking. Against the background of a classical past endowed with immense authority and cultural prestige, and a foreground of quickly expanding knowledge about the world of the present, what sort of inventor ought one to be—custodian, creator, or something else? What is the object of invention: a mass of knowledge, often called matter, that confirms the invention in which it is suspended, or a dynamic event, called experience or world, that reacts upon that invention? The mobility of the standpoints from which such questions are addressed is visible in the debate between Osório and Ascham, each of whom condemns the transformative sort of invention while participating in it and urging his interlocutor to settle for a custodial approach. Each one desires but also fears what becomes increasingly imaginable in the late century, a sedulous invention that remakes the world in which it takes place.

With this account of the semantics of *invention* in view, I turn to consider how the early modern understanding of the term and concept revises the classical and how sixteenth-century figures other than Ascham and Osório negotiate with that understanding to clear imaginative room for their own projects. Moreover, what might we think of those writers for whom invention remains, like Pantagruelion, suspicious for its sheer ubiquity and adaptability? In some instances the palimpsest becomes the site of not a dialogue or a collective revision but an effacement; the hard-won Renaissance meanings of invention are challenged or subverted by materially inclined philosophers, marginal poets, and religious dissenters who wish (or find) themselves excluded from the social and cultural privilege the term conveys. All of these gestures of discussion and discord belong to a properly circumstantiated story of invention at the end of the century.

I consider briefly three very different writers who stand within what might be called the reinvention of invention. The reweighing of the concept occurs in an uneven rhythm across Europe, so the transitional figures in various cultures are not necessarily contemporaneous with each other. I will get a factitious dialogue going among three English poets, the prodigal experimentalist George Gascoigne and the Protestant fictioneer Philip Sidney, both poets of invention as conception, and the all but invisible Calvinist Anne Lock, a poet of invention as discovery who maintains a special interest in matter. Any number of European poets might fill the roles they do as exponents of different senses of *invention* and alternate understandings of matter. England comes late to the modern understanding of *invention* as it does to the Renaissance, but by the same token, Gascoigne's and Sidney's statements about it are unusually explicit, probably because they have the benefit of some decades of commentary in other languages.

Gascoigne's "Certayne Notes of Instruction" (1575) is the first essay in English on versification in the vernacular, and perhaps the first influential statement on poetics of the late-century moment that includes the younger Sidney and Spenser. The treatise begins thus:

> The first and most necessarie poynt that ever I founde meete to be considered in making of a delectable poeme is this, to grounde it upon some fine invention. For it is not inough to roll in pleasant woordes, nor yet to thunder in *Rym*, *Ram*, *Ruff*, by letter (quoth my master *Chaucer*) nor yet to abounde in apt vocables, or epythetes, unlesse the Invention have in it also *aliquid salis* [some salt]. By this *aliquid salis*, I meane some good and fine devise, shewing the quicke capacitie of a writer: and where I say some *good and fine invention*, I meane that I would have it both fine and good. For many inventions are so superfine, that they are *Vix* [hardly] *good*. And againe many Inventions are *good*, and yet not *finely* handled. And for a general forwarning: what Theame soever you do take in hande, if you do handle it but *tanquam in oratione perpetua* [as in continuous speech], and never studie for some depth of devise in the Invention, and some figures also in the handlying thereof: it will appeare to the skilfull Reader but a tale of a tubbe.[26]

As unremarkable as it may seem, Gascoigne's premise here marks a milestone in the early modern rethinking of invention. For the generation of Ascham, Gascoigne's elder by twenty years or so, invention is a tool for delicate handling, and every claim made toward its use entails a corresponding claim of human dominion over knowledge and matter. For Ascham as educator, the preponderance of culture exists in the classical and late medieval pasts that are accessible to his students as matter. His Cicero is the author of the *De Oratore*, "the best booke that [he] ever wrote," and, as Ascham sees it, "the whole booke consisteth in these two points onelie: In good matter, and good handling of the matter."[27] Invention makes its discoveries and devices from within that matter, but scarcely overgoes it or stakes out a position as a principle of reality itself. Ascham settles on imitation as the concept that arbitrates between an existing matter and an enterprising invention, for imitation "is a facultie to expresse livelie and perfitlie that example: which ye go about to folow. And of it selfe, it is large and wide: for all the workes of nature, in a maner be examples for arte to folow."[28] As he expresses in his cautions to Osório, Ascham's is a world of matter quickened by invention but renewed and consolidated by imitation, which binds one generation of thinkers to the next and tethers all of us to precedent, available knowledge, and one another.

But Gascoigne is no educator, and his sense of the past emphasizes how poets and dramatists can turn old matter into new works. Perhaps the leading English literary importer and adapter of his time, Gascoigne belongs to the front edge of a generation that is impatient with a poetics circumscribed by matter, and he insists on an invention that comes first not only in order of procedure but as "most necessarie" to establishing the poems and fictions that will distinguish his generation and himself. Addressed to a Master Eduardo Donati, who might be an invention himself, the first sentence of "Certayne Notes" makes Gascoigne's position immediately legible, as though he takes up the palimpsest of *invention* and writes over it in gaudy letters. In the rest of the essay, one notices, the questions become more complicated.

To deliver unto you generall examples it were almoste unpossible, sithence the occasions of Inventions are (as it were) infinite; neverthelesse take in worth mine opinion, and perceyve my furder meanyng in these few poynts. If I should undertake to wryte in prayse of a gentlewoman, I would neither praise hir christal eye, nor her cherrie lippe, etc. For these things are *trita et obvia*. But I would either finde some supernaturall cause wherby my penne might walke in the superlative degree, or els I would undertake to aunswere for any imperfection that shee hath, and thereupon rayse the prayse of hir commendacion. . . . Thus much I adventure to deliver unto you (my freend) upon the rule of Invention, which of all other rules is most to be marked, and hardest to be prescribed in certayne and infallible

Invention

31

rules, neuverthelesse to conclude therein, I would have you stand most upon the excellencie of your Invention, and sticke not to studie deeply for some fine devise. For, that beyng founde, pleasant woordes will follow well inough and fast inough.[29]

This is a superstitious celebration of invention as something that has "infinite" occasions but cannot be defined explicitly; that avoids subjection to what is common or obvious, but finds its own way across and over received examples ("some supernaturall cause," "walke in the superlative degree"); and that stands above both the matter that envelops it and the imitation that often controls their negotiations with each other. Where for other writers such as Ascham the line between matter and invention is often a threshold between past and present, ideas worth preserving and those yet to be proven, and even the ethnically assimilable material of ancient Greece and Rome versus the overripe inventiveness of "some schole in *Asia*," Gascoigne works to undo or reverse these values. For him, matter is a realm of the dead, while invention conveys life, bespeaks nature, and creates the possibility of Englishness even through diction ("the more monasyllables that you use, the truer Englishman you shall seeme"[30]). Gascoigne makes especially tangible what is at stake in crossing such a threshold. On the one side are poets and their conceptions, while on the other is matter, including old inventions that have become familiar, lost their *aliquid salis*, become inert. Many rhetorics and manuals of the period concern themselves with a benign view of the boundary between inventions past and present. In the *Introductio ad sapientiam* (1524), for instance, Juan Luis Vives urges his students to "make a book of blank leaves" and fill it with what amount to past inventions by other writers.[31] But Gascoigne, by neglecting matter and attending to the liminal character of invention itself, depicts speakers, writers, and poets as agents of process who distill invention out of its opposite. In his account the lines between these conditions are continually being redrawn, and poems are the alembics. When we follow matter in Gascoigne's "Certayne Notes," then, it is always being turned into an invention that controls it; infinite invention has replaced infinite material. This is a transitional statement in English of a view that can be found earlier in Erasmus's *Adagia* (1500–1536), Vives's *Introductio*, and many other exploratory projects. Gascoigne's sense of *invention* is taken up again at the end of the 1570s by George Puttenham, who argues that when the "phantasticall" capacity works properly "by it, as by a glass or mirror, are represented unto the soul all manner of beautiful visions, whereby the inventive part of the mind is so much helped, as without it no man could devise any new or rare thing. And where it is not excellent in his kind, there could be no politic captain, nor any witty enginer or cunning artificer, nor yet any lawmaker or counselor of deep discourse."[32] Together these treatises build up an aggressive invention that is no longer one element of a process but contains the process in itself. Instead of answering to a reality principle such as matter, invention is for this moment its own reality principle.

While in this climate of semantic development it is thoroughly examined in treatises of rhetoric and poetics, the word *invention* scarcely appears in the poems, plays, and fictions about which such treatises speculate. Invention is a problem that generates literature, not a word that easily shows up in literature. In this connection, the proem of Philip Sidney's *Astrophil and Stella*, one of the most famous English works of the time, attempts a striking demonstration of the process. For its duration it becomes the hypothetical palimpsest in which *invention* is inscribed. The word is written and rewritten there, three times altogether, as Sidney dramatizes the rethinking of his era.

> Loving in truth, and faine in verse my love to show,
> That the deare She might take some pleasure of my paine:
> Pleasure might cause her reade, reading might make her know,
> Knowledge might pitie winne, and pitie grace obtaine,
>   I sought fit words to paint the blackest face of woe,
> Studying inventions fine, her wits to entertaine:
> Oft turning others' leaves, to see if thence would flow
> Some fresh and fruitfull showers upon my sunne-burn'd braine.
>   But words came halting forth, wanting Invention's stay,
> Invention, Nature's child, fled step-dame Studie's blowes,
> And others' feete still seem'd but strangers in my way.
> Thus great with child to speake, and helpless in my throwes,
>   Biting my trewand pen, beating my self for spite,
>   "Foole," said my Muse to me, "looke in thy heart and write."[33]

Invention

33

Despite the poem's renown, the fate of matter or materiality in it has scarcely been considered. On the other hand, much has been said about Sidney's play with *invention* here, but that discussion shows the limits of treating the term without its complementary principles.

As the conventional argument goes, Astrophil gets the protocol I quoted earlier from Cicero—where *inventio* leads to *dispositio* and then to *elocutio*—precisely backward, seeking "fit words" before he has organized his thoughts or settled on an invention.[34] Invention is an imperative here, reiterated insistently, but Astrophil seems estranged from it in inverse proportion to Sidney's display of mastery over it. That is, one of several things that are stirring about the poem is that it debates invention in terms that are recognizably obtuse for the 1580s, while at the same time it carries off invention of the modern sort. At first, invention is implicitly opposed to Astrophil's condition in that he can have feelings "in truth," but he is not poet enough to find the invention with which to express those feelings. At the same time, matter fails him in the form of the stock approaches in "others' leaves." The first appearance of the word *invention* in line 6 comes where one might expect *matter*, indicating how he is unable to draw the line between one and the other that is indispensable to a humanist self-articulation. Until this point, it is an implicit article of faith for everyone from Petrarch to Gascoigne that matter is invention's object. Invention stands at the liminal position between a world of things and ourselves as constructed through rhetoric or poetics, and whatever remains unconverted by invention remains other to us. But for most of the poem, Astrophil estranges invention by drawing the line between invention and matter in an unconventional place: not between his own invention and a world of material, but between the inventions of others ("others' leaves," "others' feete," "strangers in my way") and his own—and now it is time to use this word, as it was not yet time for Gascoigne a mere ten years earlier—*experience*. While it does not appear here or elsewhere in *Astrophil and Stella*, *experience* has a powerful stake in this poem, which tells the story of its emergence as a concept. We might even say that the poem embodies the historical emergence of experience as a category for events that were previously named otherwise and narrates an opening through which other concepts in the same categorical relation to a comparatively static *matter* (such as *world*, *truth*, and *reality*) will establish their own relations to *invention*. Something like this takes place as well in the *Apology for Poetry*, where, observing the moral effects of drama on its audience, Sidney reaches for a term that takes his argument past the moral: "With hearing it we get as it were an experience, what is to be looked for of a nigardly *Demea*, of a crafty *Davus*, of a flattering *Gnato*, of a vaine glorious *Thraso*, and not onely to know what effects are to be expected, but to know who be such."[35]

For the first thirteen lines of the poem, then, Astrophil looks at the entire complex of *invention* in relation to *matter* without participating in it, with all the requisite feelings but on the outside of poetry, looking in. He cannot get to invention through matter. Against the precepts of all the rhetorical and poetic treatises of the age, the passage between them is blocked. Only with the ending, a deus ex machina, does it happen that he gets to invention through experience—an opening that, in the worldview of this poem, did not exist before, as it did not exist for Gascoigne, Wilson, or Ascham. Now the line between invention and the material is redrawn to put Astrophil on the inside looking out; the estranging of invention is decisively undone; and Sidney renders matter obsolete and invention heroic, as the triumph of the rhetorical and poetic self. Moreover, the poem accomplishes in little what is happening semantically to *invention* throughout this era. In any number of poems, plays, and other writings, and especially where one or another of these key terms (as here) is present in its absence, a reinvestment from matter to experience is taking place. For some of Sidney's contemporaries, the displacement of one by the other is not so implicit. "What we derive from foreign examples will hardly be much use for our education," Montaigne writes in 1587, "if we make little profit from the experience we have of ourselves, which is more familiar to us, and certainly sufficient to inform us of what we need."[36] A year later he adds that "I would rather be an authority on myself than on Plato," and in a further revision, he changes "Plato" to "Cicero"—likely a direct acknowledgment of this argument's implications, where experience replaces matter through an "invention" that is "easy and salutary."[37] When John Florio translates Montaigne's preface in 1603, he renders "Ainsi, lecteur, je suis moy-mesmes la matiere de

Invention

35

mon livre" as "Thus gentle Reader my selfe am the groundworke of my booke."[38]

What has become of matter? Together with the earlier rescriptings of invention to detach one of Cicero's rhetorical elements from the rest and to marginalize the sense of invention as discovery, this transfer from matter to experience is one of the decisive turns in the making of modern invention. But in the manner of the palimpsest, a term such as *matter* is hardly erased, but only overwritten. Even in *Astrophil and Stella*, it will reappear after the first sonnet in other guises—as what "words say" (35.1) or "lovers speak" (6.1)—only to be put in its place again by a speaker who prizes experience above all. Throughout the Renaissance, the concept of a primordial body of fact, knowledge, and literary precedent remains tacitly associated with invention until it reappears in the seventeenth century under several rubrics, such as evidence, nature, and the material world. One of the appeals of Sidney's arch-canonical lyric is that it embraces a terminology that is very much in flux, recording the reinvestments and projecting toward their outcomes in the next generation or two. It tells a story of its moment, neither finally nor reductively but with the urgency that his contemporaries bring to the reconception of invention as an accomplishment of humanist, worldly, and (in his case) imperialist man.[39]

Of course one of the undertows of the preceding account is that the concept of *invention* is gendered and racialized in this period. Who fails to notice that when Astrophil is unable to muster invention, when he belongs to either matter or experience (depending on which vocabulary one chooses), he has a black face and a sunburned brain and is pregnant? Invention is what brings him out of that condition, making him a subject rather than an object. But the same struggle between invention and otherness occurs widely in Sidney's time, and as a final instance I would like to consider a poet who treats the entire complex of ideas very differently than he does. The Calvinist poet Anne Lock is older than Sidney by a generation; her son, the poet Henry Lock, is his contemporary. In 1560 she produced the first sonnet sequence in English, the *Meditation of a Penitent Sinner*, which expands on the text of Psalm 51, turning it into twenty-six sonnets in an extraordinary feat of enlargement. Of course Lock sees herself chiefly as contributing to the Calvinist cause through poetry, but she recognizes her sex as a factor in the enterprise too. As she explains her work, "Every one in his calling is bound to doe somewhat to the furtherance of the holy building; but because great things by reason of my sex, I may not do, I have according to my dutie, brought my poore basket of stones to the strengthening of the walls of that Jerusalem, whereof (by Grace) we are all both citizens and members." This is not entirely the standard disclaimer it seems, nor merely a straightforward allusion to the reformed reading of Psalm 51, where building the walls of Jerusalem implied working for the Protestant cause. Lock is a poetic craftswoman to whom bricklaying is a better analogy for poetry than architecture, and who demonstrates a poetic practice that relies on a very different sense of the genre than is found in the treatises. At the time of this statement, toward the end of her life, she had thought a good deal about how a poetry doggedly devoid of invention may nonetheless contribute its own peculiar sort of weight to the Calvinist project. In some ways, Lock's project recalls the Augustinian transfiguration of *inventio*, where a rhetorical art concerned with an undifferentiated matter became, in the Middle Ages, a hermeneutic procedure trained on the closed books of Holy Scripture, and every Christian reader became, in potential, an inventor of meanings.[40] But Lock's poetry actually avoids invention in both senses, not only her own conceits but Augustine's "quae intellegenda sunt," those things that are to be understood out of Scripture. Her periphrasis steers between these alternatives, opening an undiscovered third space, neither humanist nor Augustinian, neither fictional nor allegorical. When we look at the *Meditation of a Penitent Sinner*, then, we see something that is recognizable in terms of the proem of *Astrophil and Stella* and other poems that render invention sexually, socially, and finally heroically, but exactly opposed to them: a series of poems that refuse invention, where the poet emphatically chooses to remain on the side of the rapidly obsolescing category called matter.

How does one write sonnets that expand their original twelvefold while struggling to say nothing new? The fourth of Lock's psalm sonnets offers a model. Lock starts from a single line of the original psalm—"For I knowledge my wickednes, and my sinne is ever before me"—and turns it into the following fourteen lines:

Have mercie, Lord, have mercie: for I know
How muche I nede thy mercie in this case.
The horror of my gilt doth dayly growe,
And growing weares my feble hope of grace.
I fele and suffer in my thralled brest
Secret remorse and gnawing of my hart.
I fele my sinne, my sinne that hath opprest
My soule with sorrow and surmounting smart.
Drawe me to mercie: for so oft as I
Presume to mercy to direct my sight,
My Chaos and my heape of sinne doth lie,
Betwene me and thy mercies shining light.
What ever way I gaze about for grace,
My filth and fault are ever in my face.[41]

Of course, there is invention here. It would be impossible to translate, dilate, or circumlocute without committing invention, and in fact periphrasis or circumlocution (sometimes conflated with paraphrasis or speaking in other words) is commonly treated in this period as a species of invention. Ascham addresses it cautiously because, while he sees its pedagogical value, he also acknowledges its risks, namely, "to choose worse wordes, to place them out of order."[42] But there is no better or worse for Lock, and her interventions are not coded as inventions. Instead, she goes out of her way to choose sheer matter. Sometimes she imports vocabulary or figures of speech from other verses of the same psalm or others of similar themes; sometimes she draws on the rhetoric of contemporaneous love poems and other courtly lyrics, which are her antithesis but provide matter from what has ceased to be invention, in the manner of Astrophil's "others' leaves." In some measure this is a response to the emerging doctrine of Protestant poetics, according to which devotional poetry must be God's work as well as the poet's, and to a certain tradition of religious poetry in Europe, stretching from England to Italy and across all sects, that has a consistently ambivalent relation to invention, even if that only means that the poets aver, like George Herbert, that their elaborate inventions belong to God.[43]

Lock takes this problem a considerable step further not only because of the Calvinist emphasis of her writing but because she responds to the sundering of invention from discovery, the estranging of matter and materiality, the making of invention inseparable from experience and subjecthood that are taking place in her time. In her own way Lock wants to speak against all of these events, foregrounding matter and adopting that as her vantage. Her son Henry elects the same poetics and begins his paraphrase of Ecclesiastes with this statement of purpose: "And that you might truly consider the cariage of the matter, according to the scope of the text, I have caused the same to be quoted in the margent, reducing for memorie sake into two abstract lines of verse set in the top of everie leafe: the substance of every page's content, which afterwards as thou seest, is paraphrastically dilated page by page, in the plainest form I can devise."[44] He continues his work against invention in his *Sundry Christian Passions* (1597): "In the cause of my writing [Christian themes] in verse ... I was induced, for that I find many oftentimes (speciallie such as had most neede to praie and meditate) to reade books rather for the affection of words then liking of matter, and perhaps more to control the compiling, then commend the contents."[45] In the son's avowal that in spite of his extended paraphrasis he does not invent anything, we hear the mother's stand on principle toward what he calls here "matter." One also hears an inverted echo of Ascham's protest: "Ye knowe not, what hurt ye do to learning, that care not for wordes, but for matter, and so make a devorse betwixt the tong and the hart."[46] Ascham sees in a robust matter "ill deedes" and "strange maners," including the corruption of religion, while the Locks imagine matter as a refuge from the self-assertion and Protestant practice that celebrate invention in the setting of prayer and praise. And remembering Gascoigne's warning against writing *tanquam in oratione perpetua*, we notice that writing as though in perpetual speech, without the topography of invention, is exactly the design of these sixteenth-century poets of matter.

Earlier I mentioned that Montaigne's *Essais* enact the movement from matter to experience that is, I argue, definitive of the sixteenth century rethinking of invention. Montaigne himself addresses poets such as the Locks, poets of Scripture and matter, in his final essay, fittingly titled "Of Experience": "Those people must be jesting who think they can diminish and stop our disputes by recalling us to the express words of the Bible. For our mind finds the field no less spacious in registering the meaning of others than in presenting its own. As if there were less animosity and bitterness in commenting than in inventing!"[47] This early modern episode, then, traces the reorientation of *invention* as well as the resistances to it. There is obviously much more to say about how the concept gathers meanings. In the broad view, this rethinking in the prime epoch of humanism is prologue to the renewed emphasis on invention that comes with the rise of experimental science and to the eventual joining of invention and technology as mutually dependent concepts. The Renaissance sees a number of thinkers writing the first chapter of what will become the human domination of the world of things. Not everyone can exercise invention, we might observe, but the term obfuscates its own politics by insisting on its face (through the contingency coded into *venire*, "to come" or "to happen") that it names not a socially maintained but a somehow spontaneous capacity. Accordingly, *invention* is one of the key terms in which early modern relations of authority—the movements of power across divisions of society and culture—are enclosed in a seemingly neutral, classical marker. As the term hardens, the sense of *invention* as conception becomes firmly entrenched, and the alternative sense of *invention* as discovery gradually recedes into an ancillary position. In the sixteenth century, the priority of these senses is moving from matter toward experience and other concepts, but is still open to dispute, with self-proclaimed winners such as Sidney, self-designated resisters such as the Locks, and those who watch the entire business unfolding from a vantage of ambivalence, such as Montaigne. They write together on a single palimpsest called *invention*.

LANGUAGE

In 1654, on the fifth Sunday of Lent, the Jesuit priest António Vieira addressed his congregation in the city of São Luiz, in the territory of Maranhão in northeastern Brazil, about truth and lies, virtues and vices. The pressing issue of the moment was the plight of the Indians. While their forced servitude to the Portuguese settlers maintained the colonial economy, the crown and the church had come to see slavery as a moral danger to be abolished, and Vieira, as the newly arrived superior of the Society of Jesus in Maranhão, found himself in a bitter struggle over the nature of the entire enterprise of Brazil. Perhaps the greatest prose writer of the transatlantic world in his time, a Baroque stylist of staggering ingenuity and productivity, Vieira had begun to minister to Maranhão a year earlier with sermons considering the conflicts between Christian values and economic gain, but he soon turned to homilies that must have seemed highly indirect, if not diffuse. The sermon of the fifth Sunday begins with an account of the unreliability of communication between "the truth of the preacher and the lies of the hearers."[1] Vieira proceeds to search out the origins of the moral catastrophe he sees slowly unfolding in the colony, including words that have no purchase on deeds and the lies that the settlers tell to God and to themselves:

Dizem que quando o diabo caiu do céu, que no ar se fêz em pedaços, e que êstes pedaços se espalharam em diversas províncias da Europa, onde ficaram os vícios que nelas reinam. Dizem que a cabeça do diabo caiu em Espanha, e que por isso somos furiosos, altivos, e com arrogância graves. Dizem que o peito caiu em Itália, e que daqui lhes veio serem fabricadores de máquinas, não se darem a entender, e trazerem o coração sempre coberto. Dizem que o ventre caiu em Alemanha, e que esta é a causa de serem inclinados à gula, e gastarem mais que os outros com a mesa e com a taça. Dizem que os pés caíram em França, e que daqui nasce serem pouco sossegados, apressados no andar, e amigos de bailes. Dizem que os braços com as mãos e unhas crescidas, um caiu na Holanda, outro em Argel, e que daí lhes veio—ou nos veio—o serem corsários. Esta é a substância do apólogo, nem mal formado, nem mal repartido, porque, ainda que a aplicação dos vícios totalmente não seja verdadeira, tem contudo a semelhança de verdade, que basta para dar sal à sátira. E, suposto que à Espanha lhe coube a cabeça, cuido eu que a parte dela que nos toca ao nosso Portugal é a língua, ao menos assim o entendem as nações estrangeiras que de mais perto nos tratam. Os vícios da língua são tantos, que fêz Drexélio um abecedário inteiro e muito copioso dêles. E se as letras dêste abecedário se repartissem pelos estados de Portugal, que letra tocaria ao nosso Maranhão? Não há dúvida, que o M. *M*—Maranhão, *M*—murmurar, *M*—motejar, *M*—maldizer, *M*—malsinar, *M*—mexericar, e, sobretudo, *M*—mentir: mentir com as palavras, mentir com as obras, mentir com os pensamentos, que de todos e por todos os modos aqui se mente.[2]

(They say that when the devil fell from heaven, he came to pieces in the air, and that these pieces were scattered in diverse parts of Europe, where remained the vices that ruled those parts. They say that the devil's head fell in Spain, and for this reason we are furious, haughty, and arrogantly serious. They say that the breast fell in Italy, and thence they came to be makers of machines, they have trouble making themselves understood, and they keep their hearts covered. They say the belly fell in Germany, and thus they are inclined to gluttony, and spend more than the rest on the table and the cup. They say that the feet fell in France, and therefore it came to be that they are restless, in a hurry, and love dancing. They say that of the arms, along with the hands and long fingernails, one fell in Holland, another in Algiers, and from that it fell to them—or to us—to be pirates. This is the substance of the argument, not badly formed or poorly arranged, because even though the application of the vices may not be accurate in total, it has overall a likeness to truth, enough to give bite to the satire. And, supposing that the head fell in Spain, I take care to note that the part touching us in Portugal is the tongue, or so say the foreign nations that see us up close. The vices of the tongue are so many that [Jeremias] Drexel made an entire, very copious abecedarius of them. And if the letters of this ABC were distributed among the states of Portugal, which letter would be our Maranhão? No doubt, it would be M. *M* Maranhão, *M* to murmur, *M* to criticize, *M* to speak ill, *M* to slander, *M* to gossip, and above all *M* to lie: lie with words, lie with deeds, lie with thoughts, for in and through all ways, here is lying.)

Vieira goes on to consider the vicious collaborations of the tongue and the imagination, pauses over the fourth line of Psalm 52 as an indictment of the tongue ("tota die iniustitiam cogitavit lingua tua" [all day long thy tongue conceived injustice]), reaching this conclusion:

Os falsos testemunhos formam-se na língua; os juízos temerários formam-se na imaginação; e como da imaginação à língua há tão pouca distância, para que não haja falsos testemunhos na língua, proíbe que não haja juízos temerários na imaginação. Não se contentou Deus com meter o inferno entre a imaginação e a língua, com um preceito de pecado mortal, mas meteu outra vez o inferno entre o entendimento e a imaginação, para que com êstes dois muros de fogo tivesse defendida a nossa honra das nossas línguas. E, contudo, isto não basta. Por que? Porque em se passando a primeira muralha, está vencida a segunda; em chegando à imaginação, já está na língua.[3]

(False testimonies are formed in the tongue; reckless judgments are formed in the imagination; and since between the imagination and the tongue there is such little distance, if there were to be no false testimonies by the tongue, it would prohibit rash judgments by the imagination. God was not content to thrust the inferno between the

imagination and the tongue, with an injunction against mortal sin, but
thrust the inferno again between the understanding and the imagination, so that with these two walls of fire he might have defended our
honor from our tongues. And for all that, it does not suffice. Why not?
Because in crossing the first wall, the second is breached; in reaching
the imagination, one is already at the tongue.)

In this striking sermon, Vieira comes late to a conversation about
the tongue—its nature as both an organ and a conceit for language
itself—that preoccupied early modern writers and scholars. Over the
sixteenth century it became possible to think speculatively about the
relation between two concepts, *tongue* and *language*, that are sometimes synonyms but often alternatives, counterparts, or foils to one
another. The uninflected version of this dichotomy represented the
tongue as primordial, natural, and irreducibly human, while *language*
was imagined as self-conscious, artificial, and potentially inhuman.
Having inherited these terms from the beginning of the early modern
era, Vieira, near the end of that era, conflates them again for effect: for
him the *tongue* will absorb all the properties associated with *language*,
becoming not quintessentially human but alien or animal: "Saint James
the Apostle says that there is no wild beast more difficult to bridle than
the tongue."[4] That kind of statement is a Renaissance commonplace,
but it means something else in Vieira's work and depends on the preceding conversation to give it body. This chapter reconstructs what
amounts to a symposium of more than one hundred years, carried on
across languages and societies, that makes the relation between the
two terms a scene for thinking. Without recalling that virtual conversation, we can scarcely understand Vieira's (or any early modern
writer's) attraction to these terms.
　　We might enter the symposium through a book that taught many
Renaissance readers to think seriously about the phenomenon of language as an intellectual problem. Early in his *Déffence et Illustration
de la Langue Française* (1549), one of the most influential vindications
of a European vernacular against those who held for the primacy of
ancient Greek and Latin, Joachim Du Bellay pitches his argument
against the conventional view of language as organic. And where the
argument challenges this notion, his terms do the same. "Les langues"

or tongues, Du Bellay proposes, are not like "herbs, roots, and trees," among which some are vigorous and others weak, nor do they have different capacities for carrying out the work of the imagination.

Mais tout leur vertu est née au monde du vouloir, & arbitre des mortelz. Cela (ce me semble) est une grande rayson, pourquoy on ne doit ainsi louer une Langue, & blamer l'autre: veu qu'elles viennent toutes d'une mesme source, & origine: c'est la fantasie des hommes: & ont eté formees d'un mesme jugement, à une mesme fin: c'est pour signifier entre nous les conceptions, & intelligences de l'esprit.⁵

(For all their virtue is born in the world of desire and will of mortals. That [it seems to me] is a great reason that one should not praise one tongue and blame another: for they all come from the same source and origin, which is the conceit of men; and are formed from the same judgment for the same end, that is to signify among us the conceptions and intelligences of the spirit.)

Neither autochthonous nor spontaneous, Du Bellay insists, tongues such as Latin or French find cause and purpose in the cultural productions of human beings.⁶ And taking this position, uncommon for his time, Du Bellay remarks that he

ne puis assez blamer la sotte arrogance, & temerité d'aucuns de notre nation, qui n'etans riens moins que Grecz, ou Latins, deprisent, & rejetent d'un sourcil plus que Stoïque, toutes choses ecrites en Francois: & ne me puys assez emerveiller de l'etrange opinion d'aucuns scavans, qui pensent que nostre vulgaire soit incapable de toutes bonnes lettres, & erudition: comme si une invention pour le Languaige seulement devoit estre jugée bonne, ou mauvaise.⁷

(cannot blame too much the foolish arrogance and temerity of some in our nation who, being neither Greek nor Latin, misprize and reject, with a more than stoic disdain, all those things written in French; and I cannot marvel enough at the strange opinion of certain learned men who think our vernacular incapable of good letters and erudition: as if an invention should be judged good or ill solely for Language.)

With the appearance of the term "Languaige" or language in the latter sentence—as something to be distinguished from *langue* or tongue— Du Bellay explores a fluid way of thinking about the phenomenon of language that will become irresistible to his contemporaries. The idea here is modest: if *langue* as tongue is a metonymic displacement from the physical organ, *langage* or language is a further metonymy, the French tongue not as an undifferentiated fact but as the epitome of its productions ("toutes choses ecrites" [all those things written]). While he is not the first to consider such a distinction and does not maintain it to consistent purpose in the *Déffence*, Du Bellay here models a suggestive turn of thought—neither an identity nor a contradiction between the terms *tongue* and *language*, but a proximity and a pendency, and the sense that to think seriously about the nature of language requires the mutual perspective of two related terms, whatever their precise usages. For the rest of the sixteenth century and well into the seventeenth, a great deal of linguistic speculation is constituted in the small distance between these semantic pendents, *tongue* and *language*. The culmination of this era of heightened awareness of language is the first universal grammar, the *Grammaire générale et raisonée* of 1660, known as the Port-Royal Grammar, contemporaneous with Vieira's reflections on the Baroque tongue.[8]

The English *tongue*, the French *langue*, the Spanish *lengua*, and the Italian and Portuguese *lingua* are the general terms with which natural languages were conceived in the Middle Ages and after, especially in a tradition of linguistic reflection that runs from Petrarch to Lorenzo Valla. In many cultures, it remains so today. Not only does the fact of the human tongue locate speech in the body, but the word *tongue*, out of the Indo-European *dinghu*, imagines the organ at the root of all sorts of communication, spoken and otherwise.[9] In his treatise *Lingua* (1525), Erasmus speaks to a humanist commonplace when he names the tongue as a living metonymy of human capacities for good and ill: "So Nature made the tongue [to show that] no part of the body was more destructive if abused, and no part more salubrious under diligence and moderation."[10] At its most constructive, the tongue occupies a liminal office as "interpreter of the heart and mind."[11] Nearly every early modern commentator remarks its power to hurt, out of proportion to its size but in keeping with its direct channel to thought and feeling: "But a little peece of flesh," John Calvin observes, "and yet it kindleth such a fire, as is able to burne vp the greatest woods in the worlde."[12] The tongue's varied capacities were often noticed in its character as a kind of musical instrument, a plectrum that can make not only the letters, syllables, and words but all the "pauses, clashes, and hisses" peculiar to natural languages.[13] Ambiguous but indisputably natural, the tongue is sometimes a medium, sometimes a protagonist in a lively early modern literature about the limits and possibilities of speech.[14] As Erasmus wonders, self-consciously quoting the rhetorician Zenobius, "O my tongue, where are you going? Are you about to destroy a city, and raise it up again?"[15]

And yet despite the dominion of the tongue in the word *langue* and its counterparts, nearly always there is a supplementary term that represents the phenomenon of language encountered from outside the speaking subject—the tongue abstracted, estranged. This is the perspective that gives us the English word *language* and all the equivalents that come into prominence in the sixteenth century, notably the French *langage*, the Spanish *lenguaje*, the Italian *linguaggio*, and the Portuguese *linguagem*. Many of these terms have a long history as alternatives to *tongue*, such as usages of *langage* to mean a discourse or manner of speaking as distinct from a natural language such as French. Such is the fourteenth-century polymath Nicole Oresme's account of Aristotle's mention of a plural divinity as determined by "le comun langage qui estoit lors" (the common way of speaking that existed then).[16] Only during the sixteenth century, one notices, does the relation between these terms, and the semantically charged space between them, become manifest across the humanist cultures of Europe and America. In a sense, the emergence of *language* in the sixteenth century represents an elaboration of this relation until it becomes a semantic object in its own right, an occasion for renewed reflection on the phenomenon of language.

That relational thinking has little to say about natural languages such as French or English, which tend to remain tongues. Rather, the supplementary term and the relation it opens are reserved for something, language itself, that does not require a name and a conceptual space until the era of several things at once: the programmatic cultivation of ancient Greek and Latin, the rise of learned vernaculars, the encounters with indigenous languages occasioned by empire, and humanist self-consciousness. *Language, langage,* and other such terms make thinkable the issue of the tongue as disembodied and make possible a vantage from which tongues, and the conventions of human communication, can be reflected on. The grammarians of the vernaculars, such as Antonio de Nebrija and Richard Mulcaster, count among the first who prepare this vantage. Mulcaster observes that the knowledge of grammar provides "the entrie to language," which allows us to see the concrete as abstract and the foreign as natural; in his view we cultivate the artifice and foreignness of language only to return to our "tungs" as though to a native place.[17] Unlike the semantic history of *blood*, in which a largely figurative concept becomes adjusted to its literal reality, the emergence of *language* and related terms tells of a bodily member, the tongue, that must accommodate a more abstract counter to itself.[18] As my argument will follow this semantic process through linguistic writings of Spain, Portugal, France, England, New England, Peru, and Brazil, all of which are locally important but participate in a common project, *tongue* is naturalized while *language* is negotiated; *tongue* remains connected to an essential self and a scriptural understanding of discourse, while *language* is adapted to an often impersonal, unpredictable world. Out of this rethinking emerges the early modern concept of language itself.

Readers of medieval literature will be reminded of a distinction that precedes and informs this one, Dante's contrast between *prima locutio* and *locutio secundaria*, primary and secondary speech, the mother tongue and the grammatical language. As developed in the *Convivio* and *De Vulgari Eloquentia*, these are alternative experiences of language, the one "primordial and immediate" in its vernacularity, the other "unalterable and perpetual" in its grammaticality.[19] In one sense, the early modern theorists and practitioners who concern themselves with *tongue* and *language* reinhabit this dichotomy between mother tongue and grammatical language. But there is something new here as well, because unlike the medieval distinction, the emergent terminology of the sixteenth century is maintained only inconsistently and promiscuously. *Tongue* and *language* are often used interchangeably, except when, like Du Bellay or Mulcaster, someone stops to insist strikingly on the power of the distinction as he employs it ad hoc.

Further, it never happens that the emergent sense, carried in *language* and its counterparts in the other vernaculars, cancels or overcomes the older *langue* or tongue. As a pattern of thinking, pendency replaces the rigidity of the medieval dichotomy with a fluidity, making the two principal terms not the codification of established ideas but an instigation to new relations.

As it happens, the various terms for tongue are enlivened by the contrast and perspective afforded by the supplementary term and take on a fresh relevance through the sixteenth century, as in Du Bellay's *Déffence*. In fact, *langue* is his principal term. The early chapters of the treatise develop the idea of *langue* as a natural resource that must be improved through culture. The tongue is enriched, he argues, by imitation of classical authors, not slavishly or in a spirit of inferiority but by careful cultivation of what most deserves praise in them. Since the praiseworthy elements are often the "hidden and innermost" parts of an author's example, the challenge is for one tongue to learn from another only what is appropriate.[20] Moreover, these chapters involve an indefinite friction between *langue* and *langage*, putting the two terms into a suggestive counterpoint and distancing the reader of the *Déffence* from them. Entering a debate about the vernacular that had been started by Rabelais and Dolet and would be continued by Maigret and Peletier, for instance, Du Bellay writes that he does not consider "our vernacular, as it is now maintained, to be so vile and abject as these ambitious admirers of the Greek and Latin tongues suppose. . . . [They would not think] they could speak anything good if it were not in a foreign language, not understood by the vulgar."[21] While there is nothing definitive here to the contrast between the classical "tongues" and a foreign "language"—Du Bellay's argument, after all, is that natural languages are intrinsically the same—the passage encourages us to think of language itself as not natural but made, not singular but multiform, not easily grasped but open to standpoints.

If *tongue* and *language* make for Du Bellay a dichotomy without fixed substance, the effect is to convince us that the phenomenon called by these words has an inside and an outside that we inhabit at different times. In Du Bellay's view, we experience tongues from the inside, but it takes as little as a striking figure of speech to render them into languages. Likewise, this passage's notion of "foreign languages"—

seen from the outside, and about to be seen again as the tongues of others—is vital in an early modern world that treats cross-cultural exchange as a quotidian fact. In the same chapter, for instance, Du Bellay goes on to extol the late king Francis I for bringing elegance and exactitude into French, "nostre Langaige," and making it a "faithful interpreter of all the others."[22] A few sentences later, in the first lines of chapter 5, French and the others become tongues again, struggling to communicate across the barrier of translation.[23] Where "others" are concerned, where self-awareness appears, *tongue* and *language* begin to change places restlessly, and neither term will fully express all the senses of the concept. The developing commutability of these pendents is more important than anything said through them—a habit of linguistic thinking that is typical of the threshold of 1549.

In the same spirit of estrangement that maintains *tongue* and *language* at an indefinite distance from each other, Du Bellay's *Déffence* touches now and then on the conceit of natural languages as landscapes or polities into which strangers come. When it comes to seeing virtues in the peculiar felicities of classical tongues, Du Bellay observes, "we always favor strangers," while the particular Greek terms that pertain to science and mathematics "will be in our tongue like strangers in a city: for whom, however, paraphrases serve as intermediaries."[24] To the example of strangers, one might infer, we owe the perspective that makes it possible to keep *tongue* and *language* uncollapsed. Strangers stand for the productive estrangement that provokes us to hear our own tongue as foreign and to hear foreign tongues as someone's own. At the same time, this awareness of strangers is bound up into a fundamental value of Du Bellay's treatise, namely, the perfect equality and adaptability of all tongues. No tongue is better suited to science or poetry than any other, but our estate is to live in a world in which differences of meaning are continually mistaken for differences of value. In the space between tongues of equal virtue, Du Bellay implies, language itself comes into existence.

This is one of the most moving passages of the *Déffence*, in which Du Bellay seems to struggle for a vocabulary that will speak to the perfection and inviolability of each natural tongue, and yet the ethical necessity of something of greater scope, something that might be called *language*:

Et si on veut dire, que diverses Langues sont aptes à signifier diverses conceptions: aucunes les conceptions des Doctes, autres celles des Indoctes & que la Grecque principalement convient si bien avecques les Doctrines, que pour les exprimer il semble, qu'elle ait eté formée de la mesme Nature, non de l'humaine Providence. Je dy, qu'icelle Nature, qui en tout Aage, en toute Province, en toute Habitude est tousjours une mesme chose, ainsi comme voluntiers elle s'exerce son Art par tout le Monde, non moins en la Terre, qu'au Ciel, & pour estre ententive à la production des Creatures raisonnables, n'oublie pourtant les iraisonnables: mais avecques un egal Artifice engendre cetes cy, & celles la: aussi est elle digne d'estre congneue, & louée de toutes personnes, & en toutes Langues. Les Oyzeaux, les Poissons, & les Bestes terrestres de quelquonque maniere, ores avecques un son, ores avecques l'autre, sans distinction de paroles signifient leurs Affections. Beaucoup plus tost nous Hommes devrions faire le semblable, chacun avecques sa Langue: sans avoir recours aux autres. Les Ecritures, & Langaiges ont été trouvez non pour la conservation de la Nature, la quelle (comme divine qu'elle est) n'a mestier de nostre ayde: mais seulement à nostre bien, & utilité: affin que presens, absens, vyfz, & mors manifestans l'un à l'autre le secret de notz cœurs, plus facilement parvenions à notre propre felicité, qui gist en l'intelligence des Sciences, non point au son des Paroles: & par consequent celles Langues, & celles Ecritures devroint plus estre en usaige, les queles on apprendroit plus facilement. Las & combien seroit meilleur, qu'il y eust au Monde un seul Langaige Naturel, que d'employer tant d'Années pour apprendre des Motz.[25]

(And if someone were to say that diverse tongues are prepared to signify diverse conceptions, some the conceptions of the learned, others those of the ignorant; and that the Greek principally is so well engaged with learning that it seems to have been formed by Nature, not by human Providence, to express it: I say this Nature, which is the same thing in every age, every province, and every habitude, thus by will exercises its art through the entire world, no less on earth than in the heavens, and while it applies to the productions of reasonable creatures, yet for that it does not forget the unreasonable; but with an equal artifice engenders now this, now that; so it deserves to be known and praised of all persons in all tongues. The birds, the fishes, and the beasts of the earth in their own ways, now with one sound and now with another, signify their affections without the distinction of words. We men should do something similar more quickly, each with his own tongue, without recourse to others. Writings and languages have been invented, not to conserve Nature, which (being divine) needs not our help; but solely for our good, our use, so that the present and the absent, the living and the dead may manifest to each other the secret of our hearts and arrive at our happiness, which belongs to the intelligence of the sciences and not to the sound of words. Accordingly, those tongues and writings should be most used that are most readily learned. Alas, it would be better if there were in the world a sole natural language, rather than to employ so many years in learning words.)

Tongues are treated here as inescapably natural, belonging to the bodily reality that connects birds and beasts (with their sounds of unmistakable feeling) to human beings. No one, and no society, can do without the tongue's access to what is irrational and indeliberate as well as what is orderly and reasonable in human thought. And still, the profusion of tongues promises to leave us in the condition of birds, each speaking of and to his own without addressing other societies, the hidden and esoteric, the past and the future. Some measure of estrangement brings us out of that condition. If paraphrase acts as interpreter among mutually foreign words, then *language* is a tongue under the pressure of paraphrasis, the organ partly estranged from itself, continuing its reach beyond the speakers and societies in which it grew. For this account, tongues are manifest while languages are partly ideal; tongues are made of sounds while languages trade in knowledges. Tongues, we might say, are always inside languages, and in mind and custom the two terms are often exchangeable: hence Du Bellay's assertion that in order to cultivate languages we should learn tongues, because the former enable, though they do not circumscribe, the latter. All human beings have tongues, as do animals in their ways, but everyone who aspires to be more than merely human should aspire to have language. "Un seul Langaige Naturel," a sole natural language, is the oxymoron toward which the passage moves—a vehicle of speaking and writing that feels like a tongue but works like a language. Du Bellay's treatise shows the possibility of intriguing relations between these pendent terms, as I call them, and establishes a precedent that they will seldom remain apart from one another during the sixteenth and seventeenth centuries.

The space between *tongue* and *language*, as pendents, becomes one of the early modern semantic zones in which knowledge is configured, meanings are parceled out, and disciplines are imagined. What is a semantic pendent? In the era beginning about 1500 that has been described as "the discovery of language in early modern Europe," *tongue*, a term of bodily reference, is no longer able to hold the reflections on linguistic possibilities that preoccupy late fifteenth- and early sixteenth-century humanists, travelers, and writers of fiction.[26] Another term, *language*, which has in effect always been present, gains visibility as a site, and eventually a medium, for that reflection.[27] But the original bodily reference remains not merely latent but present in the word *language* and its counterparts in the several vernaculars; it is not cancelled even as further terms—*locutio, sermo, discourse*—become available or are rediscovered in this semantic field. Accordingly, the various terms are neither dependent on nor independent of one another. Rather, they are pendent. In such a set of semantic pendents, what matters is that the elements are entirely present and that they provide distance and perspective on each other. Unlike the semantic palimpsest of *invention*, where the formative relation is between alternative senses of the same term and the objects they imply, the terms *tongue* and *language* stand apart as entirely present and available, like keys on a ring or pearls on a string. Their nonidentity with one another only highlights their reciprocal investment in descrying a field of knowledge, the domain of language itself. Other examples of such mutually invested terms in the early modern vernaculars include *troth* and *truth*, which together delineate an ethical domain, and *experience* and *experiment*, which evoke philosophy and science.

Tongue and *language* are distinctive as concepts, however, in that disciplinary thinking—in this case, about the emergent sciences of language—takes place between and among them. The conceptual space that allows Du Bellay and his contemporaries to theorize these terms against one another comes to be implicated in any number of early modern enterprises: humanist educational reform, the rise of translation as a literary mode, the theory and practice of empire. For instance, the project of recovering and theorizing indigenous languages as carried out in Bernardino de Sahagún's *Florentine Codex* (circa 1540–85) would scarcely have been possible without pendency, which gives Sahagún and his four indigenous translators—moving among Latin, Spanish, and Nahuatl—the license to conceive the latter two languages as literally adjacent to each other in the manuscript. Moreover, because the bodily reference to tongues is always adjacent to any other pendent, the somatic and concrete experience of tongues, a kind of predisciplinary thought, is always available as well. There is a semantic richness in this pendency that makes it feasible to say simple things and complex things at the same time, that allows fresh or advanced thinking on the nature of tongues and languages not to break with older, more conventional thought but to remain adjacent to it.

If the middle sixteenth century begins a long moment of pendency between *tongue* and *language*, Du Bellay shows his contemporaries how to think pendently, which is to say productively, about these concepts in relation to each other. The provision of pendency involves a conceit or story about the terms, and it ought to be possible to make an approximate anatomy of their relation, however inexact or easily contradicted. Until the seventeenth century, *tongue* remains the general term for natural languages such as English or Spanish as well as for acts of speaking and writing represented as uncontested, even Adamic within their immediate cultural circles. *Language*, by contrast, is often the term for such acts as heard by a stranger's ears, or with uncertain meanings, or equivocally. William Wood, an early visitor to New England, depicts a single fact—Indians of Massachusetts speaking English—from two sides, exposing the often subjective character of this pendency: English is a "tongue" spoken "as much as their own" when they encounter English settlers, but "an unheard language" when they meet Indians with no knowledge of English.[28] In Wood's treatise the possibility of treating the same natural language, depending on who hears it, under the two alternative terms is more than a matter of vocabulary, for it shows in a single contrast the exhilaration many sixteenth- and seventeenth-century people felt at discovering that their English or Dutch or Spanish, not to mention their world, had an outside and therefore an inside—that there were others to whom it was not merely unlearned but utterly strange, a sensation made vivid by pendency. In this moment of its semantic impressibility, *language* also maintains a sense as discourse that improves on the capacities of tongues. *Tongue* and its counterparts convey socially and culturally legible information, while *language* can give us what is more *and* less comprehensible, more and less urgent, more and less true.

Du Bellay conceived his *Déffence* on the cusp of a decisive change in the cultural semantics around *language*, in which the pendent relation between the relevant pair in each vernacular invited a rethinking of linguistic possibilities. Only fifteen years earlier, the Castilian humanist and theologian Juan de Valdés had written his influential *Diálogo de la lengua* (Dialogue of the tongue), in which four friends consider the origins, uses, and merits of their common tongue:

> *Valdés.* He aprendido la lengua latina por arte y libros, y la castellana por uso, de manera que de la latina podría dar cuenta por el arte y por los libros en que la aprendí, y de la castellana no, sino por el uso común de hablar.[29]

> (I have learned the Latin tongue through art and books, and the Castilian through use, in such a manner that I would be able to give an account of Latin through the art and books in which I learned it, and not of Castilian, only of how it is used in common speech.)

Since Dante, of course, the early modern habit of reflection on tongues or natural languages was an emphatically comparative exercise, and in Valdés's case Spanish is measured against not only Latin but the other tongues of the Iberian peninsula:

> Y porque la lengua que oy se habla en Castilla, de la qual vosotros queréis ser informados, tiene parte de la lengua que se usava en España antes que los romanos la enseñorreassen, y tiene también alguna parte de la de los godos, que suciedieron a los romanos, y mucha de la de los moros, que reinaron muchos años, aunque la principal parte es de la lengua que introduxeron los romanos, que es la lengua latina,

será bien que primero esaminemos qué lengua era aquella antigua que se usava en España antes que los romanos viniessen a ella. Lo que por la mayor parte los que son curiosos destas cosas tienen y creen, es que la lengua que oy usan los vizcaínos es aquella antigua española. Esta opinión confirman con dos razones harto aparentes. La una es que, assí como las armas de los romanos quando conquistaron la España no pudieron passar en aquella parte que llamamos Vizcaya, assí tampoco pudo passar la lengua al tiempo que, después de averse hecho señores de Spaña, quisieron que en toda ella se hablasse la lengua romana. La otra razón es la disconformidad que tiene la lengua vizcaína con qualquiera de todas las otras lenguas que el día de oy es España se usan. Por donde se tiene casi por cierto que aquella nación conservó juntamente con la libertad su primera lengua.[30]

(And because the tongue that today is spoken in Castile, of which you wish to be informed, has part of the tongue that was being used in Spain before the Romans took possession of it, and also has some part of the tongue of the Goths, who succeeded the Romans, and much of the tongue of the Moors, who reigned for many years, although the principal part is from the tongue that the Romans introduced, which is the Latin tongue, it will be well that we first examine which tongue was that antique one that was used in Spain before the Romans came. What the majority of those who are curious about such things believe is that the tongue that the Biscayans use today is that old Spanish. They confirm this opinion with two reasons, both quite apparent. One reason is that, since Roman arms did not reach Biscay during their conquest of Spain, neither did their tongue at the time that, having made themselves lords of Spain, they wished that all of it would speak the Roman tongue. The other reason is the disconformity the Biscayan tongue has with any and all the other tongues that are used today in Spain. Thus it is held almost to a certainty that the Biscayan nation conserved, along with its liberty, its first tongue.)

Apart from this speculation about the Biscayan dialect, Valdés subscribes to the humanist position that tongues are necessarily hybrid and complex. His Spanish gathers up elements of several other tongues, and those tongues in turn, Latin and Greek among them, are "mixed" and "corrupted."[31] For him, Spanish is one of the most synthetic modern tongues, like Latin in its structure and sound but damaged in its diction—and much of its character is found in the corruption.

Unlike several of his contemporaries who consider their vernaculars, however, Valdés accounts for the differences among and within tongues while maintaining a single term throughout. His *Diálogo de la lengua* recognizes everything in its ambit as *lengua* or tongue, knowing nothing of *lenguaje* or language, even when contrasting one with another, marking disconformities, or observing a tongue such as the Biscayan to be "so alien to all the others of Spain."[32] In contrast to what will become, with Du Bellay and his successors, a play of two terms thrown against one another to many effects, Valdés in his moment insists on the primordial, unitary *lengua*. While he sees the fact, he overwrites the force of difference, differentiation, and alienness as elements of linguistic communication, preferring to maintain an idealist investment in the bodily term.

Valdés's counterpart in the early sixteenth century is his exact contemporary, the Portuguese colonial historian and administrator João de Barros, whose *Diálogo em Louvor da Nossa Linguagem* (Dialogue in praise of our language) appeared in 1540. Valdés and Barros share certain humanist assumptions about the early modern project of theorizing language, but where Valdés hypostatizes a single tongue that gathers up the differences that everyone recognizes in contemporaneous languages, Barros presents a more relational account that probably owes much to his experience in India, Africa, and Brazil during the preceding years. Valdés was an Erasmian of evangelical inclinations who wished languages, especially Spanish, to reflect the unity in diversity that characterizes the divine *sermo* and the reason that should characterize human affairs. Barros, by contrast, was a Vivesian of an empirical bent who recognized that diversity between and within languages was a territory worth exploring for itself. Humanist dialogues written within a few years of one another, these two treatises nonetheless occupy adjacent spaces that open toward Du Bellay's *Déffence*.

In his dialogue between father and son, Barros reaches back to Genesis and the Tower of Babel to explain the present state of language itself.

Pay. Os Hebreos, por serem os primeiros a quem Deos quis communicar a criaçam do mundo, afirmam que a língua do nosso primeiro padre Adam foy hebrea: aquella em que Mouses escreveo os livros da ley. Os gregos querem que seja a caldea porque nesta linguagem confessou Habram a Deos: e dizem que a língua hebrea nam é mais que caldeu corrumpido. Qual destas seja a verdade em contenda de tam graves barões, a nós nam é líçito afirmar.[33]

(The Hebrews, being the first people to whom God wished to communicate the creation of the world, affirm that the tongue of our first father Adam was Hebrew: that tongue in which Moses wrote the books of the Law. The Greeks wished it to be Chaldean because this was the language in which Abraham confessed to God: and they said that the Hebrew tongue was nothing more than Chaldean corrupted. Which of these may be true, in the contention of such grave men, it is not licit for us to judge.)

Puzzled, the son asks how tongues multiplied, how Adamic language lost its hold on humankind, and how the episode of Babel came to happen. Even before Babel, the father observes, men had created things ("cousas") for which Adam had no names:

Porque mal poeria Adam nome à nao pois nunca navegara, nem à bombarda se nam avia de quem se defender, nem ao libello se nam tinha quem demandar. . . . Ao tempo da edificaçam de Babilónia, em que a linguagem era toda hũa, averia muitas cousas inventadas pera o uso daquelle edifíçio e doutras neçesidades, às quaes poseram elles [os inventores] nome, e às naturaes pôs Adam.[34]

(for Adam could hardly put a name to a boat, never having sailed, nor to a bombing, not having defended against anyone, nor to a lawsuit, never having had anyone to sue. . . . At the time they built the Tower of Babel, when all language was one, many things would be invented for the use of that edifice and other necessities, to which the inventors put names, while Adam named natural things.)

In this setting, God's strike against the tower does not alter the number or character of human tongues so much as it estranges them from their speakers and hearers:

Quando Deos naquella soberba obra confundio a linguagem, nam foy inventarem-se em hum instante setenta e hum vocábulos diferentes em voz, que todos sinificassem esta cousa: "pedra"; mais confundio o intendimento a todas pera, por este nome: homem, hũus entenderem "pedra," outros as diferentes cousas que se naquella edificaçam tratavam. E este termo: confusam, nenhũa outra cousa quer dizer, senam tomar hũa cousa por outra. . . . E a este modo trastrocou Deos o intendimento de tantas nações como foram presentes ao sermam de Pedro no dia de Pentecoste, que em hum vocábulo hebreu, que era sua natural linguagem, os ouvintes de diversas nacões entendessem hum si(g)nificado, e estas eram as desvairadas línguas de que se elles espantavam.[35]

(When in that proud work God confused language, it was not that seventy-one words different in sound were at once invented, all signifying this same thing "stone"; rather, he confused the understanding of all tongues, so that for this word "man," some understood "stone," others the different things that were discussed in that edifice. And this term—confusion—means nothing else but to take one thing for another. . . . And in this way God switched the understanding of as many nations as were present for Peter's sermon at Pentecost, when in one Hebrew word, his natural language, the hearers of diverse nations understood one meaning, and these were the hallucinated tongues that frightened them.)

With this account, Barros narrates a transvaluation that is especially relevant to the period, the making of *linguagem* out of *língua*. The episode of Babel, as he sees it, merely marked God's aggravation of a condition already under way, tongues growing apart from themselves through human invention. It emphasizes not the absolute difference between a primordial tongue and multifarious languages but the fact that these are not fixed categories, that a *tongue* can become a *language* and vice versa, and that the two terms may change places according to experience—for instance, of travel, war, and the courts. The typological relation between Babel and Pentecost is undermined when we are brought to realize that we make our own Babels and Pentecosts all the time, that a *tongue* is a *language* that has not been inflected by ingenuity, movement, and experience, while a *language* is a "desvairada língua," a hallucinated *tongue*. Babel becomes less remarkable because the capacity for misunderstanding that it unleashes is already at large in everyday tongues that contain languages within them; Pentecost is likewise less about the power of faith to induce understanding and more about the fact that such understanding is an illusion. This argument is more complex than that of Valdés, for whom *lengua* names a human capacity and a cultural orbit that he theorizes and celebrates, and *lenguaje* does not figure at all. Barros is more interested, as Du Bellay will be, in the space between these concepts, especially their interchangeability in particular cultural circumstances. As though to signal that he will not subscribe to a distinction between *nossa língua* (our tongue) and *sua linguagem* (their language), even his title, *Nossa Linguagem*, points to an adjustment that takes place between the pronoun and the noun. As I have suggested, it is natural to suppose that these contrasting views of language owe something to the orientations of Valdés and Barros, the one mostly a theologian, the other mostly a colonial administrator. When they meet on an intellectual ground that unfailingly interests early modern humanists, namely, the nature of language itself, they test the semantic limits of the available terms, comment implicitly on one another, and map an emerging relation. While Barros's position better anticipates the influential approach that appears in Du Bellay's *Déffence* less than a decade after the *Diálogo em Louvor da Nossa Linguagem*, the object here is not the arguments or the outcomes in linguistic thought, but the semantic proximity and pendency they enact again and again.

That pendency will find an answer in a number of episodes that define this moment in linguistic thinking through fiction. One recalls the two dogs, Cipión and Berganza, in Cervantes's *Coloquio de los perros* (Colloquy of the dogs). Like the Valdésian interlocutors they parody, they are concerned with *lengua* rather than *lenguaje*, despite the fact that talking dogs must embody the difference expressed through un-natural discourse that often characterizes *lenguaje* in the period. The two dogs refer rather grandly to the works of their tongues, speaking in both Spanish ("Vete a la lengua, que en ella consisten los mayores daños de la humana vida" [Watch your tongue, for the greatest harms of human life come from it]) and Latin ("Habit bovem in lingua" [He has an ox on his tongue]), while the reader must think of what they speak as *lenguaje* (and of the natural work of their tongues as licking, not speaking).[36] And Shakespeare's Caliban in *The Tempest* famously rails against Prospero: "You taught me language, and my profit on't is, I know how to curse. The red-plague rid you for learning me your language!"[37] The semantic conceit of pendency prompts us to ask why Caliban does not learn a tongue. Though he is taught Prospero's Ital-ian, he learns it as a language he enters from the outside rather than a tongue he can inhabit from within. Not only for Caliban but for every-one, Prospero's island turns tongues into languages. Ferdinand hears Miranda speak for the first time in Italian and exclaims: "My language! heavens! / I am the best of them that speak this speech, / Were I but where 'tis spoken."[38] In both of these usages, we register not only the semantic space between the pendents but the unfulfilled desires that they activate together. In these cases it is a longing to turn (or to return) a language to a tongue, but elsewhere it might be a humanist's urge to step away from his usual circumstances and hear his own tongue as a language. Where the semantic space between pendent terms opens, the affects that animate early modern thought—philological curiosity, exploratory hubris, humanist pathos—stream in.

This condition of pendency is especially relevant in a colonial set-ting. Much has been made of Antonio de Nebrija's notorious declara-tion in the dedicatory epistle of his *Gramática de la lengua castellana* (1492), the first European vernacular grammar: "Siempre la lengua fue compañera del imperio" (the tongue was always the compan-ion of empire).[39] Would Nebrija mean something very different if he had written "Siempre el lenguaje fue compañero del imperio" (language was always the companion of empire)? It is seldom noted that Nebrija offers his opening remark with a note of retrospective regret, looking back at "the antiquity of all the things that remain written for our recollection and memory": the tongue is no longer the companion of empire, Nebrija believes, because in his present day, "los ombres de mi lengua" (the men of my tongue) squander their common inheritance reading chivalric romances and other inferior literature.[40] The aim of the *Gramática* is "reduzir en artificio nuestro lenguaje castellano" (to convert our Castilian language into art), with the unmistakable implication that such a reduction will subdue an unruly outgrowth of the tongue. This proposed relation between *tongue* and *language*—wielding one term to locate the other and employing both of them to think about the phenomenon of language—anticipates the condition of pendency that will emerge over the next century. Nebrija's position will quickly be overtaken by the unfolding reality of empire, in which the potential of pendency becomes increasingly urgent for Barros, Du Bellay, and many other administrators, theorists, and observers.

Through the first decades of the European colonial enterprise in the Americas, the semantic pendents afforded a vocabulary for the languages encountered there, where the question of correspondence to Greek, Latin, and the vernaculars was always in view. Sometimes the indigenous language is represented as a damaged or incomplete tongue. Thus the Portuguese chronicler Pero de Magalhães Gandavo, in the *Tratado da Terra do Brasil* (Treatise on the land of Brazil), written about 1570, observes that "the tongue of all the people of the coast is one: it lacks three letters: there is neither *F*, nor *L*, nor *R*, a thing of wonder because likewise there is neither *Faith*, nor *Law,* nor *King*; and in this manner they live without justice, in disorder."[41] One thinks of Barros's construction "nossa linguagem," of which this is the obverse: their tongue. Many colonial writers and apologists adopt an explicitly contrastive vocabulary. In *A View of the Present State of Ireland* (written 1596), Edmund Spenser has one of his dialogists, Eudoxus, observe that "it semethe straunge to me that the Englishe [in Ireland] shoulde take more delight to speake that language then theire owne wheareas they shoulde (me thinkes) rather take scorne to acquainte theire Tounges thereto for it hathe bene ever the vse of the Conquerour to despise the Language of the Conquered and to force him by all meanes to learne his."[42] This is a late restatement of a notion of *tongue* and *language* in a colonial context that would not have been strange to Nebrija: that the conqueror speaks a tongue while the conquered has a language and that the movement between these formations—*tongue* invoked here more or less literally as the organ that should not be compelled to adapt to mere *language*—reflects the proposed colonial policy toward Ireland. Will the "Conquerour" insist on his tongue or accommodate the "Language of the Conquered"?

If Spenser stands for an especially uncompromising position, his antitheses are Jean de Léry and Roger Williams. The French Huguenot Léry recounts a voyage more than twenty years earlier in his *Histoire d'un voyage fait en la Terre du Brésil* (1578). Trying to introduce himself in the "langage" of the Tupinambá Indians he encounters, Léry notices that his name sounds the same as their word for oyster. To everyone's mirth, Léry presents himself to the Tupi as *"Lery-oussou* or large oyster," and he remarks that "never did Circe metamorphose a man into such a fine oyster, nor into one who could discourse so well with Ulysses, as since then I have been able to do with our savages."[43] The uncommon comparison of himself not to Ulysses but to a talking oyster must be an effect of Léry's seeing himself through an alien *langage* rather than a domesticated *langue*, a condition that he embraces with acute tact and curiosity.[44] To embrace the scope of difference found in a complex world, Léry wants to live not in a tongue but in a language. Going further, Williams, the Baptist theologian who once taught Dutch to John Milton in exchange for lessons in Hebrew, published in 1643 his landmark grammar of indigenous Rhode Island, titled *A Key into the Language of America*.[45] Williams's *Key* largely omits the word and concept of *tongue* except as a relic of a distant, self-enclosed past ("I have found a greater *Affinity* of their Language with the *Greek* Tongue") and in the chapter naming parts of the human body in the Narragansett vocabulary, where it appears among the eyes, the nostrils, the ears, and the teeth; Léry does the same with the Tupinambá word for tongue.[46] Unlike Spenser, Valdés, and others, Léry and Williams seem to regard the idealist conception of *tongue* as a vestige of a humanism for which cross-cultural contact was more an abstract fantasy than a lived reality. Williams tends to see responsiveness to *language*, the emergent alternative to *tongue*, as a cornerstone of an empirically oriented colonial project, better oriented to "use" and "exchange" than to coercion or indoctrination:

For my selfe I have uprightly laboured to suite my endeavours to their pretences: and of later times (out of desire to attaine their Language) I have run through varieties of *Intercourses* with them Day and Night, Summer and Winter, by Land and Sea, particular passages tending to this, I have related divers, in the Chapter of their Religion. . . .

. . . [After a list of greetings]: From these courteous *Salutations* Observe in generall: There is a savour of *civility* and *courtesie* even amongst these wild *Americans,* both amongst *themselves* and towards *strangers.* . . .

. . . I have knowne them contentedly [to sleep outdoors], by a fire under a tree, when sometimes some *English* have (for want of familiaritie and language with them) been fearefull to entertaine them. In Summer-time I have knowne them lye abroad often themselves, to make room for strangers, *English*, or others.[47]

Williams gives us one of the most memorable conceits for pendency in this period: "A little *Key* may open a *Box*, where lies a *bunch* of *Keyes.*"[48] A language is a bunch of keys, but terms such as *tongue* and *language* are themselves keys or pendents that we use with discrimination. From Du Bellay's "strangers" to the visual form of Sahagún's codex, one is continually reminded how often serious thinking about language in this period is shown through these graphic instances of pendency.

The most intriguing early colonial writers on language are those who move between these terms and reimagine their relation in a specifically colonial setting.[49] For such figures, pendency is not an abstract matter but a salient fact that recapitulates the difficult relations between Old and New Worlds, between received knowledge and empirical discovery, between a here and a there that can exchange positions and priorities in many fashions. Seeing one's *langue* as a *langage*, for instance, or apprehending another's *langage* as a *langue*: these perceptions are often inseparable from the expanded worldviews of explorers and colonizers. One colonial historian I would like to consider for his movement between pendents is the mixed-race chronicler of Peru known as the Inca Garcilaso de la Vega.

In the first volume of his *Comentarios reales de los Incas* (1609), after the dedicatory epistle and a note to the reader but before the history proper, the Inca Garcilaso introduces an exposition titled "Notes on the General Tongue of the Indians of Peru." If Williams's project entails treating the Narragansett language in a fashion apart from the conventions of the humanist inquiry into familiar and exotic tongues (and he explicitly announces his decision to write neither a dictionary nor a dialogue), the Inca Garcilaso de la Vega's *Comentarios reales* and *Historia general del Perú*, the latter part of which appeared in 1617, share that purpose with respect to the Inca language but accept a further dimension of complexity—to show the Castilian and Inca languages in relation to each other, to explain how one society appears to the other through the medium of language. Perhaps it is not enough to observe that projects like those of Léry, Williams, and the Inca Garcilaso de la Vega require the capacity for distance and reflection that comes with the emergence of a second term such as *language* and *lenguaje*; perhaps we should entertain the notion that such projects become possible only through these terms, which enable historians, poets, and linguists to depict not merely *tongues* or *languages* but language itself. To Léry, Williams, and the Inca Garcilaso, the cultural import of language is a matter of the different degrees of proximity, understanding, and identification we feel among the natural languages we know, know in part, learn, or hear. To find oneself at a distance and in some measure estranged from one's tongue is the common factor in their works. Still, the Inca Garcilaso's *Comentarios reales* deploys a more complicated recognition of the pendency of concepts for language.[50]

In the introductory note, the Inca Garcilaso's first venture is to establish the common tongue of the Indians in Peru as a "lengua general," against which the misunderstandings of it by the Spaniards appear to be barbarisms:

> Para acentuar las dicciones se advierta que tienen sus acentos casi siempre en la sílaba penúltima y pocas veces en la antepenúltima y nunca jamás en la última; esto es no contradiciendo a los que dicen que las dicciones bárbaras se han de acentuar en la última, que lo dicen por no saber el lenguaje.[51]

> (To accentuate the words it must be noticed that the stress almost always falls on the penultimate syllable, rarely on the antepenultimate,

and never at all on the last syllable. This does not contradict those who say that barbarous words should be stressed on the last syllable: they say this because they do not know the language.)[52]

También es de advertir que en aquella lengua general del Cuzco (de quien es mi intención hablar, y no de las particulares de cada provincia, que son innumerables) faltan las letras siguientes: *b*, *d*, *f*, *g*, *j jota*; *l* sencilla no la hay, sino *ll* duplicada, y al contrario no hay pronunciación de *rr* duplicada en principio de parte ni en medio de la dicción, sino que siempre se ha de pronunciar sencilla. Tampoco hay *x*, de manera que del todo faltan seis letras del a.b.c. español o castellano y podremos decir que faltan ocho con la *l* sencilla y con la *rr* duplicada. Los españoles añaden estas letras en perjuicio y corrupción del lenguaje, y, como los indios no las tienen, comúnmente pronuncian mal las dicciones españolas que las tienen.[53]

(It is also to be noted that in the general tongue of Cuzco [of which it is my purpose to speak, rather than of the local pronunciations of each province, which are innumerable], the following letters are lacking: *b*, *d*, *f*, *g*, *jota*. There is no single *l*, only double *ll*; on the other hand, there is no double *rr* at the beginning of words or in the middle: it is always pronounced single. There is no *x*; so that in all six letters of the Spanish ABC's are missing, and we might say eight if we include single *l* and double *rr*. The Spaniards add these letters to the detriment and corruption of the language; and as the Indians do not have them, they usually mispronounce Spanish words where they occur.)[54]

Otras muchas cosas tiene aquella lengua diferentísimas de la castellana, italiana y latina; las cuales notarán los mestizos y criollos curiosos, pues son de su lenguaje, que yo harto hago en señalarles con el dedo desde España los principios de su lengua para que la sustenten en su pureza, que cierto es lástima que se pierda o corrompa, siendo una lengua tan galana, en la cual han trabajado mucho los Padres de la Santa Compañía de Jesús (como las demás religiones) para saberla bien hablar, y con su buen ejemplo (que es lo que más importa) han aprovechado mucho en la doctrina de los indios.[55]

(In many other respects the tongue differs from Castilian, Italian, and Latin. These points will be noted by inquisitive mestizos and creoles, since the language is their own. For my part, it is sufficient that I point out for them from Spain the principles of their tongue, so that they may maintain its purity, for it is certainly a great pity that so elegant a tongue should be lost or spoilt, especially as the fathers of the Holy Society of Jesus, as well as those of other orders, have worked a great deal at it so as to speak it well, and have greatly benefited the instruction of the Indians by their good example, which is what matters most.)[56]

Over the two pages of this note, the Inca Garcilaso develops some of the possibilities of two pendent terms for language itself—moving Quechua, the natural language at issue, near to and away from his reader, making it seem now familiar, now an object of study. In describing the Indian language he moves between *lengua* and *lenguaje* in a more or less regular semantic alternation. Sometimes he insists on the differences of Quechua from Spanish and other European languages while designating it, like them, a tongue with the connotations of ethnic and national import that term carries; sometimes he observes that even native speakers, such as creoles and mestizos inquisitive enough to be reading this history, will come to see the features of what is "their own" as *lenguaje*, and a body of "principles" as belonging to "their tongue." This feat of estrangement, which puts every reader of the *Comentarios reales* both inside and outside a *lengua general* that becomes a *lenguaje* of particularity and distinction, is a decisive moment in the colonial phase of the pendency that characterizes these terms since the sixteenth century. Here pendency finds its expression, its motivation, in a historical and cultural situation for which it is not a vagary or an accident but a form of thought.

Every reader of the *Comentarios reales* knows that, where this history is concerned to render indigenous language a deeply textured concept, a twist of plot will appear early in the seventh book of part 1. This is the Inca Garcilaso's revelation that what he calls the *lengua general* is such because the Inca elite maintained "otra lengua particular" (another, particular tongue), which they spoke among themselves even as the kings ordered the general language to be learned by the population of their many provinces, especially those united with the kingdom by conquest.[57] On first naming this courtly tongue, the Inca Garcilaso immediately shows it according to both terms: it is both a "lengua particular" and a "lenguaje divino."[58] Articulated in a single sentence, these epithets carry out an open-ended exchange of terms and connotations among all the *tongues* and *languages* that have been broached in this history. The Inca Garcilaso's disclosure of this tongue provides in precolonial Peru a second language counterposed to the *lengua general* of Quechua, much as Quechua was itself counterposed to Spanish, as Spanish was counterposed to Latin. It is not that any of these has an intrinsic character that makes it a *tongue* or a *language*, general or particular, secular or divine. Rather, it is that where a relation between counterposed tongues is found, we also find language itself, the concept that enables reflection on the linguistic capacities of human beings. By introducing the *lengua particular*, the Inca Garcilaso neither augments nor diminishes the *lengua general* of Peru, but reframes Peru and the colonial world altogether as a site of language in the most expansive sense, part of the continuous symposium begun by Nebrija, Valdés, and Barros and to be continued by Williams.

And by Vieira, with whom this chapter began. The colonial episode represented in the *Comentarios reales* finds its sequel where so many humanist notions get inflected by American reality, in the mode of the Baroque. Vieira was born in Lisbon and spent many years there, in Rome, and elsewhere, but his greatest achievements were as preacher and founder of missions in the region of Maranhão.[59] For the present argument, he is important as one of the first Europeans to return to the concept of *tongue* not in the closed sense of the early humanists, but with the attributes and complexity of a *linguagem* built out of contact and exchange. That is, Vieira reconceives the dimensions and capacities of the *tongue*, rendering it a pendent to the earlier sense as well as to *language*. It is a new key, alongside the others:

TONGUE (1)	LANGUAGE	TONGUE (2)
Valdés	Barros	Vieira
	DuBellay	

Language

For linguistic thought, this imagining of a new pendent brings a Baroque sensibility to this discussion, adapting and conflating these alternative terms into something unexpected, neither one or the other, but what amounts to a stroke that breaks open the pattern, a third alternative. Vieira's tongue is not always natural but sometimes a kind of machine, sometimes a supernatural force; it is often the bodily organ, but in a fashion that deliberately confuses the Neoplatonic conventions about the tongue's correspondences with other parts of the ideal body such as the mind or the heart; and it is emphatically social and ethnic, so it needs no demotically inflected *linguagem* to counter itself.

Vieira's denaturalizing of the tongue appears in many contexts throughout the sermons. In the penitential mode, for instance, he encourages his audience to reflect on their material tongues as alien objects implicated in a process of sin. A sermon on the tears of Saint Peter, which departs from the narrative of the passion in Luke 22, articulates a relation between the tongue and the eye that casts the former as purely instrumental, the latter as essential to salvation. This sermon is entirely Baroque in its attentions to the body according to a protocol that draws on both Catholic theology and Neoplatonism for a new fusion hardly limited by their doctrines. Vieira severs the conventional tie between the *verbum dei* and the tongue of the preacher, only to reconstruct it again: for this sermon, the eye of Christ, like the Neoplatonic eye in the search for beauty, conveys what is necessary for salvation, and the tongue in turn—even Vieira's own preaching—is merely a secondary instrument. Commenting on the episode in which Peter denies Jesus for the third time, a cock crows, and Jesus looks at Peter, provoking his withdrawal and bitter weeping, Vieira observes:

> Notável caso! De maneira que faz Cristo sete pregações a Judas, e não se converte Judas; canta o galo uma vez, e converte-se Pedro? Sim: porque tanto vai de olhar Cristo, ou não olhar. . . . Se Cristo põe os olhos, basta a voz irracional de um galo para converter pecadores; se Cristo não põe os olhos, não basta a voz, nem bastam sete vozes do mesmo Cristo para converter. *Non est satis concionatoris vox, nisi simul adsit Christi in peccatorem respectus*—disse gravemente neste caso S. Gregório Papa. Do pregador são so as vozes; dos olhos de Cristo é

tôda a eficácia. E quando temos hoje os olhos de Cristo tão propícios, que pregador haverá tão tíbio, e que ouvinte tão duro, que não espere grandes efeitos ao brado de suas vozes? Senhor, os vossos olhos são os que hão de dar as lágrimas aos nossos.[60]

(A notable case! In the way that Christ made six exhortations to Judas and did not convert Judas; a cock sings once, and Peter is converted? Yes: because so much depends on Christ's looking or not looking. . . . If Christ casts his eyes, the irrational voice of a cock is enough to convert sinners; if Christ does not cast his eyes, the voice is not enough, seven voices of Christ himself are not enough to convert. *The voice of the preacher is not enough, if there is not together the look of Christ at the sinner*—said Pope Gregory gravely in this case. From the preacher there are only voices; from the eyes of Christ comes all efficacy. And when today we have the propitious eyes of Christ, what preacher will be so tepid, and what listener so hard, as not to expect grand effects from the roar of their voices? Lord, your eyes are the ones that must give tears to ours.)

"From the preacher there are only voices": does this pronounce-ment affirm or subdue his power? At first glance it seems to deny Vieira's own office, but if the preacher's tongue expresses not one voice but many, this is a *língua* that has absorbed the capacities of *linguagem*. Even its subjection to the eye is a kind of power to the degree that, as a multivocal instrument, the tongue escapes respon-sibility to emerge again. Whatever it loses as a formerly natural and integral piece of the body, it reaps a greater force as something factitious and adaptable. Peter's denials of Jesus were the tongue's work, Vieira concedes:

As negações de S. Pedro, tôdas foram pecado de língua. A língua foi a que na primeira negação disse: *Non sum*. A língua foi a que na segunda tentação disse: *Non novi hominem*. A língua foi a que na terceira negação disse: *Homo, nescio quid dicis*. Pois se a língua foi a que pecou, por que foram os olhos os que pagaram o pecado? Por que não condenou S. Pedro a língua a perpétuo silêncio, senão os olhos a perpétuas lágrimas? Porque ainda que a língua foi a que pronunciou as palavras, os olhos foram os primeiros culpados nas negações; a língua foi o instrumento, os olhos deram a causa.[61]

(The denials of Saint Peter, all were the fault of the tongue. It was the tongue that in the first denial said: *Non sum*. It was the tongue that in the second temptation said: *Non novi hominem*. It was the tongue that in the third denial said: *Homo, nescio quid dicis*. Then if it was the tongue that sinned, why was it the eyes that paid for the sin? Why did Saint Peter not condemn the tongue to perpetual silence, instead of the eyes to perpetual tears? Because while it was the tongue that pronounced the words, the eyes were the principal culprits in the denials; the tongue was the instrument, the eyes gave the cause.)

This conception of a purely instrumental but signally, even strangely mobile tongue in the body where the natural and national tongues of Valdés and other humanists once resided—this amounts to an exposition of the human faculties that might serve as a manifesto for the Baroque idea of language itself. It is as though, recapitulating the semantic and conceptual changes we have witnessed, Vieira imagines the humanist *tongue* removed from the body, conflated with the properties of the emergent *language*, and restored to its original place.

Through many of his central sermons, Vieira remains deeply interested in the tongue. Addressing the Jesuits of the College of Bahia on the eve of Pentecost in 1688, he sermonizes on Acts 2:3, where the apostles, who had been of a single mind, are confronted with cloven tongues of fire. As Vieira notes, this episode is the counterpart of the Tower of Babel in Genesis 11. The difference, he preaches, is that

as línguas dos edificadores da tôrre eram línguas que os homens ignoravam e não entendiam, e essas mesmas línguas no Cenáculo de Jerusalém eram línguas que os apóstolos entendiam, e de que tiveram inteira e perfeita ciência, e essa é a grande diferença que há em obrar com ciência das línguas ou com ignorância delas.[62]

(the tongues of the builders of the tower were tongues of which these men lacked knowledge and understanding, while those of the

Apostles in Jerusalem were tongues they understood, of which they had perfect and entire knowledge, and that is the great difference between working with a science of tongues or with an ignorance of them.)

Where the apostles carried out their evangelism with tongues of fire, the Jesuits, their antitypes, experience an effect of knowledge and passion particular to their sixteenth- and seventeenth-century moment: the fire of tongues. This notion gives Vieira the occasion to explicitly describe a sense of *tongue* as constructed out of encounters and exchanges. The fire of tongues, he argues, "is the ardent zeal and fervor that the heirs of the apostolic spirit have, always will have for knowing, studying, and learning the tongues of strangers, so as to preach the gospel, spread the faith, and amplify the Church with them." Where tongues of fire represented a radiation outward from a single source, the fire of tongues comes to exist against a changed horizon, where in the sixteenth century "two new worlds in the one world" had been discovered, and "new men and new nations had appeared, as different in their tongues as in their colors."[63] If not for the constant application to the gospel, one might conclude that the tongues in "the fire of tongues" are essentially different from those in "tongues of fire," the source rather than the medium of the fire. And where the conception of *tongue* is concerned, they are utterly different, as Vieira recognizes. For him the early modern conception is no mere inversion of the other, but absorbs the ferment around the idea of *linguagem*, the "science of language," and renames that complex of ideas by the older name: a reconstituted *tongue* that is pendent to both *language* and the original *tongue*.[64]

Where pendents appear, they witness a semantic operation distinct from that of the palimpsest of *invention*. Both the palimpsest and the pendent are figures of relation, but with the manifest difference that one involves relations within a single word, the other relations among discrete words. If a semantic palimpsest is about multiple senses past and present inhabiting one term, the pendent shows related senses as uncontainable within a single word and thus the provision of two or more terms that exist alongside each other. The palimpsest often involves a contrast between one sense held *in presentia* and others that remain *in absentia*, perhaps to change places abruptly as when Sidney inscribes *invention* three times in the same poem; but pendents are present together, throwing off sparks as they meet again and again, accidentally as well as purposely, in many pieces of writing. Early modern thinkers looked to both figures to imagine how a quickening intellectual culture was mapped onto a vocabulary both old and new.

RESISTANCE

In Fernando de Rojas's *La Celestina* (1499), the first work of early modern Spanish literature and a prose drama that voices many of the confusions of the transition to modernity, the protagonist Celestina interrogates Pármeno, one of the two servants of the lovesick nobleman Calisto, near the conclusion of act 1, scene 5. A procuress and practitioner of sundry arts of simulation and counterfeit such as the making of perfumes and the mending of maidenheads, Celestina has been brought into the play by the other servant, Sempronio, to devise a charm with which Calisto might win the love of the chaste Melibea; and because Celestina accomplishes her illusions in part by exploiting rents in the fabric of the social order, the differences between Sempronio and Pármeno are germane to her purpose. Sempronio is a pícaro, adept in double talk, and already a steady client of Celestina's brothel when the drama opens; Pármeno is better schooled in books than experience, despite the fact that his mother was a fellow prostitute of Celestina's and is invested in the kinds of idealist beliefs that Celestina openly mocks. When Calisto and Sempronio withdraw inside the former's house to get the money with which to pay Celestina, she moves in to neutralize Pármeno as an obstacle, urging him to put a friendship with the treacherous Sempronio and a vague money-making scheme ahead of his loyalty to his master Calisto. Pármeno replies in these words:

PÁRMENO.   Celestina, todo tremo de oýrte. No sé qué haga. Per-
plexo estó. Por una parte, téngote por madre. Por
otra a Calisto por amo. Riqueza desseo, pero quien
torpemente sube a lo alto, más aýna caye que subió.
No querría bienes mal ganados.

CELESTINA.   Yo sí. A tuerto o a derecho, nuestra casa hasta el techo.

PÁRMENO.   Pues yo con ellos no viviría contento, y tengo por on-
esta cosa la pobreza alegre. Y aun más te digo: que no
los que poco tienen son pobres, mas los que mucho
dessean. Y por esto, aunque más digas, no te creo
en esta parte. Querría pasar la vida sin embidia, los
yermos y aspereza sin temor, el sueño sin sobresalto,
las iniurias sin respuesta, las fuerças sin denuesto, las
premias con resistencia.[1]

(PÁRMENO.   Celestina, I tremble all over to hear you. I do not know
what to do. I'm perplexed. On the one hand, I take
you for a mother; on the other, Calisto is my master. I
desire riches, but he who rises viciously to the heights
falls even faster. I would not want ill-gotten goods.

CELESTINA.   Me, I want them! I'm for my own, by fair means or
foul!

PÁRMENO.   In fact, I would not be happy with them; I take happy
poverty to be an honest thing. And what is more, it is
not those who have little that are poor, but those who
desire much. Whatever you say, I do not believe you
in this part. I would like to pass my life without envy,
deserts and wildernesses without fear, sleep without
disquiet, injuries without answering them, violence
without dishonor, oppression with resistance.)

Resistance, it seems, is one of Pármeno's idealist values: the skein of
affirmations that carries him from his ethical perplexity to his perora-
tion here—"I would like to pass my life without envy . . ."—leads by
intuitive association to the final pairing of "premias" or oppression
with "resistencia" or resistance. Moreover, Pármeno's stock characterization, as a credulous young man on whom the pieties of late medieval

Resistance

society still have a claim, marks him as the only person in the fiction who still believes these things.

Pármeno identifies six conditions, six challenges to the human spirit, and proposes to meet each of them "without" some action or outlook that undercuts a Christian or courtly system of values— "without" envy, fear, disquiet, injuries, dishonor. But the pattern is broken at the sixth challenge, as Pármeno's self-affirmation demands that he act not without a vice or a weakness, but "with" something else—and both the change in preposition and the unexpected noun seem to indicate that this is something new, or askew. A conventional portrait of Christian forbearance would entail a system of values such as the following, where each virtue in the *with* column expresses a dimension of ideal conduct:

WITHOUT	WITH
Envy	Generosity
Fear	Bravery
Disquiet	Equanimity
Injuries	Forgiveness
Dishonor	Honor
Resistance	Forbearance

But when the last item comes, Pármeno and Rojas interrupt the developing pattern to present something very different, another template for moral action. The sudden shift from a set of *withouts* to a single *with* calls our attention to a corresponding shift in values:

WITHOUT	WITH
Oppression	Resistance

What has changed? In shifting from *without* to *with*, Pármeno does not complete the pattern of Christian action, but elevates a mere practice, resistance, to the position of a virtue. Endorsed by a distinctive voice, the departure from a set of received medieval values is emphatic. This modern Pármeno, like everyone else in *La Celestina* the spokesman for an outlook that responds to the stresses and contradictions of the age, will resist where his forerunners might have patiently acquiesced. In this original disposition of Christian selfhood, *La Celestina* registers the emergence of values that are not entirely conventional but inflected by a new consciousness of individualism and agency.

A passage such as this one might be treated as though it reveals a concept, resistance in the face of oppression, and a discourse, that of the resister; it is tempting to think of the crack opened in the conversation as revealing a world of thoughts and feelings, and perhaps it does. Rebellions against authority, whether traditions of resistance in Trastámaran Spain, the Peasants' War of 1525 condemned by Martin Luther, or the *motínes* or rebellions of mestizos and others forty years later in Peru, were hardly uncommon in the medieval and early modern world. Modern observers have often been concerned with how such events are represented in art: how the violence with which rebellions were put down is transmuted into images and tropes, how artists work across the interests of rebels and the upper classes, how art both foments and attenuates the tensions of such encounters.[2] I am interested in a more circumscribed and perhaps more inchoate topic, namely, how the term *resistance* comes into the European vernaculars at about this time—as a semantic sketch, a nearly blank term to be filled in by action and reflection—and how it changes over the period.[3]

Rebellion is everywhere, but *resistance* has a particular semantic and conceptual history. Over the decades following its ambiguous appearance in *La Celestina*, the concept exchanges opacity for vividness because it enables a taking stock that is both demanded by early modern humanism and openly critical of it; in the atmospheres of absolutism and imperialism, the term itself becomes ever more visible and necessary, indicating the state of early modern thinking about action against tyranny and oppression. If it begins as the vague, metaphorical application of a word for a physical phenomenon, by the middle of the sixteenth century resistance to absolute authority is a more than respectable idea, and social critics such as the English clergyman John Ponet, the Spanish Jesuit Francisco Suárez, John Calvin's aide Theodore Beza, and the author of the anonymous *Vindiciae, Contra Tyrannos* speculate on the conceivable terms of resistance against an absolute monarch.[4] Meanwhile, in the overseas colonies of Spain, Portugal, and England, the accumulation of semantic force behind *resistance* as first a mere word and then a concept—the application of the term to a range of conditions that extend the boundaries of the struggle against absolutism—foreshadows what is becoming thinkable in the strictly European setting. That force behind the word *resistance* in turn regenerates the practice of resistance by emplacing it in a worldview or ethical system, as in *La Celestina*, and converting it in effect into an idea. This chapter concerns the exchange of the semantic cartoon across languages, societies, and oceans, where it gathers the dimensions and colors that become visible in its literary manifestations. At the end of the seventeenth century, *resistance* as word and concept is recognizable as modern. Like *revolution*, it becomes part of a vocabulary that imagines and emplots the political developments of the Enlightenment and the late colonial period.

The early modern notion of resistance began to emerge in the fourteenth century, when critics of papal absolutism such as the political theologian Marsilius of Padua and the philosopher William of Ockham revisited in an inquisitive spirit the scriptural and patristic injunctions against ecclesiastical and temporal disorder, such as Paul's lesson to the Romans: "He that resisteth [higher] power, resisteth the ordinance of God."[5] But while Marsilius in the second discourse of his *Defensor Pacis* (1324) explored the boundaries of papal authority and Ockham in the *Breviloquium de Principatu Tyrannico* (circa 1340) proposed that "it is sometimes permissible, indeed sometimes necessary, to resist, not with obdurate pride but moderately, those which go beyond the bounds of apostolic power or go beyond due measure," neither these figures nor their contemporaries imagined a place for the resister in society or anything like an ethical program called *resistance*.[6] A mere sketch of unspecified action, the word alone appears often at the edges of the discourses concerned with absolutism from the end of the Middle Ages to well into the later phases of humanism. Accordingly, apart from the circumscribed topic of the theory of resistance that appears in the sixteenth century, little has been said about *resistance* as a historical and imaginative concept of the early modern period. Whether idealist or materialist in its assumptions, the study of humanism has tended to stress the intellectual dimensions of the movement over the political, and for much of this period resistance was largely a political effect, almost without an intellectual program of its own apart from the theory of governance, though it had a complicated dependency on certain early modern theories of individual agency, justice, and good government as well as observations of courtly politics and the behavior of crowds. As we have reconstructed it, humanism has emphasized ideas—and resistance was at first a practice, not an idea. By the middle of the sixteenth century, however, the word was finding more contexts across a range of writing and assembling a new semantic force.

Resistance comes to exist only in the presence of, or at a close remove from, absolute power; it is the catchall name given to the struggle against power by the absolutely or comparatively disempowered. As Marsilius and Ockham speculated and their early modern successors saw, absolutism and resistance hold each other in a mutual embrace. How the powerful and the disempowered not only speak to but construct each other; how the latter measure out their resistance in degrees of defiance and acquiescence; and how resistance feels from the inside, in the person of the resister—these questions become available for imaginative exploration in this period. Moreover, in an absolutist society, the standpoints of powerful and powerless can shift with blinding speed—think of the fates of those who crossed Henry VIII or defied the Spanish viceroys in the New World—or they can change places in the fall of one absolutism before another, as in the conquest of the Inca empire by that of Spain. These facts and attitudes are addressed by the poetry, drama, and emergent prose fiction of the sixteenth century with rich attention.

Not surprisingly, the normative outlook on resistance by those in power was entirely absolutist. They tended to believe that they created resistance by their own omissions and miscalculations, discrediting the possibility of its independent existence or its drawing on a well of general sentiment. Machiavelli's obdurate ruler of Florence, the Duke of Athens Walter of Brienne, is the canonical instance of this problem. As Machiavelli tells it in his *Istorie fiorentine* (Histories of Florence [1532]), there is an improvisational quality to the duke's rule until he is challenged by the aristocracy over his plan to compel the appearance of every Florentine, nobles as well as commoners, in the Piazza of Santa Croce. Once they hear of his plans to make "all the people" appear before him, the aristocrats appeal to the duke's respect for their historic freedom, and an inexorable process begins: they challenge him, he remains obdurate, and the standoff between the two positions damages the polity and eventually brings the duke's rule to an end. Absolutism, it seems, contains the seed of resistance even in its most arbitrary and improvised acts. At the same time, a fantasy haunts the period, one that supposes a perfect exercise of absolute power that would engender no resistance. Edmund Spenser, who almost invariably speaks for and to the powerful, represents this view of resistance in his dialogue on English rule in Ireland:

> By this act of parlament wherof we speake, nothing was given to King Henry, which he had not before from his auncestors, but onelie the bare name of a King: [f]or all other absolute power of principallity he had in him selfe before derived from many former Kings, his famous progenitours and worthy conquerors of that land, the which since they first conquered and by force subdued vnto them, what neede he afterward to enter into any such idle tearmes with them to be called ther King, when as it is in the power of the Conqueror to take upon him self what title he will over his dominions conquered: for all is the conqueror's, as Tully to Brutus saith: and therfore me semes in stead of so great and meritorious a service, as they boast they performed to the King, in bringing all the Irish to acknowledge him for ther liege, they did great hurt to his title, and have left a perpetuall gall in the mind of that people, who before being absolutely bound to his obedience, are now tyed but with tearmes whereas both ther lives, ther lands, and their liberties were in his fre power to appoynt, what tenures, what lawes, what condicions he would over them, which were all his: against which ther could be no rightful [re]sistance, or if there were, he might, when he would, establish them with a stronger hand.[7]

The passage goes on to observe that in fact there is considerable resistance to the Tudor regime in Ireland, the result of the fissure in Henry VIII's claim to absolute power by which he asked to be acknowledged as king. In other words, true conquest allows no resistance, while imperfect or incomplete conquest ensures continual resistance. This is the absolutist platform; its opposite would be the view that all conquest provokes resistance in the nature of the process.

If the latter view belongs to many of his contemporaries, and more so as the turn of the seventeenth century approaches, Spenser perhaps acknowledges it in the last sentence here. There could be no rightful resistance to Henry's rule properly applied; "or if there were," the king could make himself stronger by suppressing it.

The correspondence of resistance to shifts in fortune, its fugitive and situational quality, is a commonplace in this era. Moreover, the openness of the concept, its following from practice, and the fact that it is always relational make it easier to chart the appearances of the term than to follow, and to theorize, its emergence into intellectual and literary history. An authentic resistance literature in this period is either lost to suppression and censorship or—what seems the opposite, but witnesses the mutual involvement of resistance with power—found in archives, where the authorities consigned suspect testimonies and subversive writings and where we can read the histories of those who paid for their resistance, often with their lives.[8] Examples such as these are not part of my argument here. I would like to consider, instead, how to think about the term and concept of *resistance* when it appears as a sketch or cartoon in canonical literature and to look at a cluster of works for their participation in both an ethics and an affect of resistance. My concern is with defining a concept that in some measure resists definition and recovering its early history through uses.

Resistance, however, is one of the most elusive terms in our accounts of the remote past: always in danger of being imposed anachronistically on the past by the present, often merely thematic in its applications, and usually poorly defined and theorized. In its earliest appearances of the early modern period, as in *La Celestina*, *resistance* enters as a semantic cartoon, like the *cartoni* on which the painters of frescoes captured physical attitudes and motions for later elaboration, with paint on plaster. A semantic cartoon eludes definition because it depicts only motion, the pull of one body against another, and defers the ideas and feelings that make such motion necessary. Like other such cartoons of this period, including *subversion*, *overthrow*, and *revolution*, *resistance* renders a stock of attitudes in a crude black on white. It gathers under one vivid word the motives for the bodily act, not only passive repugnance but friction and active counteraction, as well as shadings of emotional coloration such as degrees of accommodation and ambivalence. Often, it effaces cause and change. As Giorgio Vasari writes of the procedure that turns a cartoon into a fresco, a semantic cartoon is "working in the dark, or with spectacles of colors different from the truth."[9] In the passages where *resistance* appears, it often stands out as a nominalization of something more inchoate and abstract, as in this striking translation from Ecclesiastes in Miles Coverdale's Bible of 1535:

> Therfore two are better than one, for they maye well enioye the profit of their laboure. If one of them fall, his companyon helpeth him vp againe: But wo is him that is alone, for yf he fall, he hath not another to helpe him vp. Agayne, when two slepe together, they are warme: but how can a body be warme alone: One maye be ouercome, but two maye make resistance: A thre folde cable is not lightly broken.[10]

For contrast, observe the versions in the Geneva Bible (1560) and the King James Bible (1611):

> Two are better then one: for they have better wages for their labour. For if they fall, the one will left up his fellowe: but wo unto him that is alone: for he falleth, and there is not a second to lift him up. Also if two slepe together, then shal they have heat: but to one how shulde there be heat? And if one overcome him, two shal stande against him: and a threfolde coard is not easely broken.[11]

> Two are better than one; because they have a good reward for their labour. For if they fall, the one will lift up his fellow: but woe to him that is alone when he falleth; for he hath not another to help him up. Again, if two lie together, then they have heat: but how can one be warm alone? And if one prevail against him, two shall withstand him; and a threefold cord is not quickly broken.[12]

In Coverdale's version, the noun *resistance* contributes something that scarcely appears in the other passages, a physical event that implies political and emotional motives. As in the passage of *La Celestina*, the unexpected word exerts a pressure: it is a noun in search of a context, a history. In many instances the cartoon remains a sketch, its implications latent. For some poets and playwrights such as Spenser and Shakespeare, the term was not worth developing. It was a verb or perhaps a noun, but never an idea. In *The Faerie Queene* Spenser depicts grotesque and foolish characters involved in what might be considered resistance to the established order of society, but he avoids using the term in this setting; he will scarcely grant it a subjective position.[13] His dialogue on Ireland was obliged to take the term more seriously. But in many cases, resistance came to be filled out semantically and conceptually in fiction, even while churchmen, jurists, and philosophers explored the nature and limits of the concept in political and imperial settings. I will consider here the inflections of the word and the concept together in three works of the later sixteenth and earlier seventeenth centuries, all of which might be understood as chains of significant usages, namely, the *Lusiads* of Luis de Camões, the *Arcadia* of Philip Sidney, and the aforementioned *Comentarios reales* of the Inca Garcilaso de la Vega. We can thread our way through these works by attributing to each its distinctive approach to the term. Where Camões explores the concept in action, Sidney gives it an interior, and the Inca Garcilaso treats it as if it were conquest seen from a different perspective. The works are very different from one another, but by stages they color the *cartone* of resistance until we can recognize the modern sense of the term.[14]

The epic of early modern Portugal, the *Lusiads* might be seen as a study in the fortunes of *resistance*. Camões imbues his plot, based on Vasco da Gama's voyage to India between 1497 and 1499, with an intermittent but careful attention to the term that reflects its shifts over the sixteenth century, from merely semantic to cultural applications. In his earliest iterations of *resistance*, Camões employs the cartoon in its most literal sense, meaning martial struggle against a foe in battle. When in canto 1 the Portuguese mariners are anchored in the harbor of Mozambique Island on their northward way along the eastern coast of Africa, they repel with artillery a population of threatening Muslims and afterward gather their fleet

> Co despojo da guerra e rica presa,
> E vão a seu prazer fazer aguada,
> Sem achar resistência nem defesa.[15]

Resistance

83

(With spoils of battle and rich plunder,
And went to take on water at their pleasure,
Encountering no resistance or defense.)[16]

Likewise in canto 2, Gama and his fleet find two ships between Mombasa and Malindi and, to gain information, capture one with a few Muslim sailors who "had no resistance, and if they had shown any, would have received more harm by resisting."[17] This schematic picture of resistance, however, grows more complicated in canto 3 where Gama relates the history of Portugal to the sultan of Malindi. In the early twelfth century, when Portugal was still a client state of the Iberian kingdom of Castile and León, the young Count of Portugal Afonso Henriques fought for independence near the northwestern city of Guimarães. When the battle seemed lost, Afonso's tutor, Egas Moniz, approached the Castilians to secure mercy for his prince in return for a promise of submission:

Mas o leal vassalo, conhecendo
Que seu senhor não tinha resistência,
Se vai ao Castelhano, prometendo
Que ele faria dar-lhe obediência.
Leventa o inimigo o cerco horrendo,
Fiado na promessa e consciência
De Egas Moniz; mas não consente o peito
Do moço ilustre a outrem ser sujeito.[18]

(But the loyal vassal, knowing
That his lord was unable to resist,
Went to the Castilian, promising
That Afonso would give that king his obedience.
The enemy lifted the horrendous siege,
Trusting the promise and conscience
Of Egas Moniz; but the breast of that illustrious
Young man consented to be subject to none.)

This episode is the pivot of a historical narrative that eventually delivers both Afonso's victory over Alfonso VII of Castile and León and the establishment of Portugal as kingdom and nation. "Resistência" is invoked here indistinctly, in two conceivable senses: Afonso, so Egas Moniz believes, is unable to resist either the superior numbers of the Castilians or the wise expedient of his councilor. Moniz is wrong in both ways, and Afonso's resistance becomes a founding condition of Portugal. Turning then to the Muslim realms south of the Tagus, Afonso won the battles of Ourique (1139) and Lisbon (1147) to fashion a unified Christian Portugal, of which he was proclaimed king after Ourique. As Camões narrates the siege of Lisbon, Afonso's army, augmented by crusaders from England and elsewhere, further develops its relation to resistance by becoming an irresistible force:

> Que cidade tão forte porventura
> Haverá que resista, se Lisboa
> Não pôde resistir à força dura
> Da gente cuja fama tanto voa?[19]

> (What city peradventure will be strong enough
> To resist, if Lisbon cannot resist
> The hard forces of those
> Whose fame soars so high?)

From this moment, resistance in the *Lusiads* gains two aspects that were only latent before. First, as a property of encounters it becomes reflexive, so that in any particular context, any and all sides may exhibit resistance, as in the invasion of Portugal by the Almohads in canto 3: "All of them showed with spirit and prudence / That in all parts there were determination and resistance."[20] When in canto 10 the nymph Tethys favors Gama with a prophecy of Portugal's enterprises in India, she foretells the battle of Chaul (1508), "where in blood and resistance / All the sea with fire and iron boils."[21] While a national perspective dominates such an account—Chaul saw the death of the valiant Lourenço de Almeida, the viceroy's son, in the struggle against Egypt and Gujarat—this semantic cartoon tends to defer and complicate that perspective. Moreover, resistance comes to be a feature not merely of battle but of conquest. It persists, absorbing a political dimension to accompany its physical sense. When, in canto 7, Gama converses with the emperor's factotum in the Indian kingdom of Malabar and is shown tableaux representing past empires, a pointed prophecy is offered:

"Tempo cedo virá que outras vitórias
Estas, que agora olhais, abaterão.
Aqui se escreverão novas histórias
Por gentes estrangeiras que virão;
Que os nossos sábios magos o alcançaram,
Quando o tempo futuro especularam.

"E diz-lhe mais a mágica ciência
Que, pera se evitar força tamanha,
Não valerá dos homens resistência,
Que contra o Céu não val da gente manha;
Mas também diz que a bélica excelência,
Nas armas e na paz, da gente estranha
Será tal, que será no mundo ouvido
O vencedor, por glória do vencido."[22]

("Other conquests are fast approaching
To eclipse these you are looking on;
Fresh legends will be carved here
By strange peoples yet to appear,
For so the pattern of the coming years
Has been deciphered by our wisest seers.

"And their magical science declares
Further, that no human resistance
Can prevail against such forces,
For man is powerless before destiny;
But the newcomers' sheer excellence
In war and peace will be such, they say,
Even the vanquished will feel no disgrace,
Having been overcome by such a race.")[23]

While this ambiguous forecast will be construed by the Portuguese as referring to their maritime empire, its equivocality—who conquers? who resists?—allows Gama as well as the epic's readership to consider both standpoints, their imperatives and challenges.[24] When resistance can belong to "all parts" in a struggle, and when it is represented as the countertendency to conquest, a semantic cartoon that was merely a study of raw movement becomes something colored and circumstantiated. Thrown into motion and inhabiting a context, the term names not a reaction only but a phenomenon in its own right.

These revisions of resistance are integral to the last canto, where Camões concludes the epic with a panorama of Portuguese colonies in Asia, Africa, and Brazil. Tethys's prophetic account prepares for that display by narrating the colonization of India by a series of viceroys, including Martim Afonso de Sousa, who established in 1530–33 the first settlement in Brazil before taking office in India:

> "Tendo assi limpa a Índia dos immigos,
> Virá despois com ceptro a governá-la,
> Sem que ache resistência nem perigos,
> Que todos tremem dele e nenhum fala.
> Só quis provar os ásperos castigos
> Baticalá, que vira já Beadala:
> De sangue e corpos mortos ficou cheia
> E de fogo e trovões desfeita e feia."[25]

> ("Having cleaned India of enemies
> He will take up the viceroy's sceptre
> Without finding resistance, or any danger,
> For all fear him and none complains,
> Except Bhatkal, which brings on itself
> The pains Beadala already suffered;
> Corpses will strew the streets, and shells burst
> As fire and thundering cannon do their worst.")[26]

As the foregoing episodes have shown, there is no conquest without resistance, an observation that this stanza corroborates in a self-correcting gesture that makes the final four lines very different from what precedes them. The succeeding two stanzas offer more evidence of what the project of empire entails:

> "Este será Martinho, que de Marte
> O nome tem co as obras diriuado;
> Tanto em armas ilustre em toda parte,
> Quanto, em conselho, sábio e bem cuidado.
> Suceder-lhe-á ali Castro, que o estandarte
> Português terá sempre levantado,
> Conforme sucessor ao sucedido,
> Que um ergue Dio, outro o defende erguido.

> "Persas feroces, Abassis e Rumes,
> Que trazido de Roma o nome tem,
> Vários de gestos, vários de custumes
> (Que mil nações ao cerco feras vem),
> Farão dos Céus ao mundo vãos queixumes,
> Porque uns poucos a terra lhe detem.
> Em sangue Português juram, descridos,
> De banhar os bigodes retorcidos."[27]

> ("So Martinho, his mighty name deriving
> From deeds themselves derived from Mars,
> As famed, throughout the empire, for arms
> As for wise and thoughtful counsel.
> João de Castro will follow him
> Hoisting Portugal's banner high;
> The inheritor will match the inherited;
> One building Diu, the other saving it.

> "Ferocious Persians, Abyssinians, and Turks
> [*Rumes,* they are called, after ancient Rome],
> Varied in faces, varied in dress
> [A thousand nations will join the siege],
> Will curse the heavens that a mere handful
> Down on earth withstands them,

Vowing in Portuguese blood and ashes
To baptize their scimitar moustaches.")[28]

Far from encountering no resistance, the Portuguese in all their out-posts confront an osmotic condition familiar throughout the colonial world, in which a few settlers ("uns poucos") maintain power against opposing forces both within the country and without. The conclud-ing stanzas of the canto and the epic portray a world of Lusitanian achievement in which resistance is martial, political, and cultural at once—an unavoidable condition of power. The resisters are gathered just over the margin, and the colonists will have to take that prospect into account, their actions becoming reactions. Rendering resistance in this fashion, Camões redefines conquest as not merely physical but political in the purest sense, and imagines resistance as part of its force and logic. Looming over the horizon is the intuition that in the life of a polity, resistance must also be psychic. In the setting of a martial epic, that understanding might count as incidental, but nonetheless it reflects what was in process for this generation and this world, an adaptation of the concept to present realities. Over the next generation and in an expanded world, the *cartone* will be revised again.

I turn now to perhaps the most far-sighted European prose fiction of the two decades before *Don Quijote*, Philip Sidney's *Arcadia*, because in its two versions (especially the second), the *Arcadia* fulfills the process of turning a semantic cartoon into a fully circumstantiated concept. Drawing resistance toward the foreground of the fiction, Sidney's ro-mance nonetheless does not fully endorse it. In the early 1580s Sidney wrote a prose romance, known today as the *Old Arcadia*, that tells how two exiled princes, Pyrocles of Macedon and Musidorus of Thessalia, undergo various trials such as battles, disguises, and seeming deaths until they can be joined in marriage to the two Arcadian princesses, Philoclea and Pamela. Having completed this fiction, Sidney imme-diately began refashioning it into a version now known as the *New Arcadia*, a project that was halted by his death in 1586. Scholars of early English prose fiction debate a deathless question: why did Sidney see the *Old Arcadia* as inadequate, and what was he trying to do in pro-ducing the *New Arcadia*?[29] My view is that he was moved to revision by a sense of change, both literary and political, encroaching on the completed work. In this moment of innovation for the literary technology of prose fiction, Sidney came to recognize that the kind of fairly conventional romance represented by the *Old Arcadia* was quickly becoming obsolete, while at the same time the attenuated absolutism of the Elizabethan regime was becoming increasingly legible as a play of contending forces rather than a projection of the monarch's authority. I believe he reached the conclusion of the *Old* and took measure of several factors: the stratification of power around the English court, changing attitudes about chivalry and kingship, the rise of genres such as the picaresque, a new understanding of the possibilities of prose as medium, and his own developing political sophistication. Sidney saw that the fictional modes that had been viable a generation earlier, such as Jorge de Montemayor's pastoral romance *Diana*, were under pressure from these new standpoints and that a generically conservative work such as the *Old Arcadia* was only a rough approximation of something more shaded and complex—in its way, a fictional *cartone*. Even in its incomplete form, the *New Arcadia* is vastly more nuanced and reflective than the *Old*. There are many more characters to represent gradations of morality and ethics, more social classes to show in ways both conventional and surprising, more societies to discover. In short, the *New Arcadia* gives us a vastly more complex world.

Itself a semantic cartoon, *resistance* represents this process of revision metonymically. During the 1570s Sidney had cultivated a correspondence with a group of European intellectuals who, concerned over Spanish and papal authority, were exploring the nature of tyranny and oppression as well as the claims of resistance. While this conversation was charged with risk in Elizabeth's England, it drew Sidney into the international circle of forward Protestants who watched the expansion of Catholicism and especially Spanish power on several fronts, from France and Portugal to the Netherlands and the Americas. The Frenchmen Hubert Languet and Philippe Duplessis-Mornay and the Scotsman George Buchanan were centrally involved in this project; the former two may have been the authors of the influential *Vindiciae, Contra Tyrannos*, which appeared in 1579, the same year as Buchanan's *De Iure Regni apud Scotos*.[30] Buchanan's argument is the more radical, with greater indulgence for private persons who would resist an overbearing monarch, but these treatises alike address resistance as a proper response to absolutist oppression and—at the same time—a portentous event to be undertaken for only the most urgent reasons. In these legal and philosophical discussions across Europe, Sidney was an observer more than a framer. He fulfilled a special office, however, in giving these terms a body and an emotional life in his fictions, such as *Astrophil and Stella* and especially the *New Arcadia*.

In the eclogues after book 3 of the *Old Arcadia*, the shepherd Philisides, who has been seen as Sidney's persona in the romance, is invited to reveal "his estate" to the other pastoral characters.[31] He answers with a song that names "old Languet" as his inspiration, a fable of how men came to rule over beasts.[32] When it was absorbed into the composite version published after Sidney's death, the song offered one of the famous cruxes in the *New Arcadia*, the couplet at the end of a stanza that enjoins rulers against oppression:

> But yet, O man, rage not beyond thy need;
> Deem it no gloire to swell in tyranny.
> Thou art of blood; joy not to make things bleed.
> Thou fearest death; think they are loath to die.
> A plaint of guiltless hurt doth pierce the sky.
> > And you, poor beasts, in patience bide your hell,
> > Or know your strengths, and then you shall do well.[33]

If the advice to the "poor beasts" who are humankind's subjects is equivocal, urging both "patience" and a counting of strengths that may extend to struggle against oppression, the couplet seems nonetheless to evoke *resistance* without using the word. While Philisides stops well short of acknowledging the fraying of received values in favor of a new creed of rights against tyranny, his fable raises the question of how the subjects of an oppressive monarch ought to think and act, and even the shepherds who demanded the song then wonder "what he should mean by it."[34] Much as the last term in Pármeno's idealist system replaces the established relation between resistance and patience with a sketch of something new, a striking link between oppression and resistance, Philisides speaks two of these terms, *tyranny* and *patience*, and leaves us to imagine the third as the outcome of knowing one's strengths. This remarkable passage enacts a semantic *cartone* in one sense, where a few strokes of context summon a missing term, rendering it visible *in absentia*. In the following treatment of Sidney's two *Arcadias*, I will consider *resistance* as a cartoon in another sense, in which the term is filled out with a coloration more fulgid than what the European resistance theorists imagined. For Sidney, who was taught the concept of resistance in geopolitical and religious contexts by Languet and the others, the *New Arcadia* is an opportunity to return the teaching with a new force and to show what literature can give back to law, theology, and philosophy.

Resistance appears as a term from time to time in the *Old Arcadia*, but rarely as more than a stock attitude.[35] Near the end of the fiction, the four lovers are under guard for their roles in disrupting the kingdom of Arcadia and the supposed death of the king, Basilius. (The two princes will be sentenced to death, only to be reprieved when Basilius awakens.) Pamela reflects on her imprisonment:

> Although endued with a virtuous mildness, yet the knowledge of herself, and what was due unto her, made her heart full of a stronger disdain against her adversity; so that she joined the vexation for her friend with the spite to see herself, as she thought, rebelliously detained, and mixed desirous thoughts to help with revengeful thoughts if she could not help. And as in pangs of death the stronger heart feels the greater torment, because it doth the more resist to his oppressor, so her mind, the nobler it was set (and had already embraced the higher thoughts), so much more it did repine; and the more it repined, the more helpless wounds it gave unto itself.[36]

With resistance merely a conventional stance that directly responds to oppression and a recognition of "what was due," this sort of formulation, native to the *Old Arcadia,* is a sketch of what will be developed in the *New*. In the more populous and complex world of the later fiction, there are varieties of resistance, psychological and moral as well as martial; characters resist one another in several ways at the same time; and resistance has an interior. More than a stance, it is a feeling that may be exchanged across different standpoints around a single event. Most important, resistance is distinguished from mere rebellion, and the subjective position of the resister often lands in unexpected quarters. In a notorious episode in book 2, the lovers Philoclea and Pyrocles (the latter still disguised as the Amazon Zelmane but now known to the princess as himself) are about to reveal their feelings to Basilius when they are interrupted by a mob of "clowns and other rebels, which like a violent flood were carried, they themselves knew not whither." Directed at their absentee ruler Basilius but extending to ladies and Amazons, the mob's anger is answered by deadly blows that strike off heads, noses, and hands. The nobles having taken refuge in their lodge, the rebels "then, though no more furious, yet more courageous when they saw no resister, went about with pickax to the wall and fire to the gate to get themselves entrance."[37] Zelmane brings a pause to the battle by stepping out among the rebels and, in a masterly speech, warns them against mistaking "the right nature of valure [for that] which . . . leaves no violence unattempted while the choler is nourished with resistance."[38] Speaking on behalf of the feckless Basilius, Zelmane both shames and appeases the rebels, and their rebellion comes apart from its own confusions.

While a version of the episode appears in the *Old Arcadia*, something notable happens in this revision for the *New*. Sidney brings out a political dimension that was barely imaginable before, the distinction between a rebel and that rebel's resister, and the emerging sense that Arcadia's heroes as well as Sidney's readers, all invested in the social order of Elizabethan England, want to see themselves as enacting resistance over and against mere popular rebellion. In the revision, the nobles' refuge in the lodge is depicted as a stay not only in the hostilities but in their resistance; moreover, the characterization of the battle as resistance against the peasants' choler is moved from the narrator's voice to Zelmane's speech, as though to confirm that the word itself penetrates the fiction down to the level of the heroes' self-description. In book 1, when Pyrocles first accounts for his passion for Philoclea, he wonders "what resistance was there when ere long my very reason was—you will say corrupted—I must needs confess, conquered."[39] Resistance has become not only the effect of conquest and tyranny but as the readers of *La Celestina* might have supposed, the name of a process by which early modern people of action and reflection identify themselves and define their stance toward the forces that beset them as subjects, lovers, and thinkers. As equipment for humanist reflection, resistance must be broadly available, even at the cost of obscuring its conventional relation to oppression and absolutism; and as a semantic *cartone*, the term gets filled out with the desires of many—perhaps too many—standpoints, at the risk of becoming for readers and observers a concept more emotional than strictly political.

In this spirit, the core of the fiction, book 3, is organized as a stand-off of resistances. Basilius's rule of Arcadia is resisted by Amphialus, the son of Cecropia, in military rebellion; Basilius recruits the famous knight Argalus to confront Amphialus in single combat; and Argalus in turn is opposed by his wife, Parthenia, who implores him not to fight:

> "My Argalus! My Argalus!" said she. "Do not thus forsake me! Remember, alas! remember that I have interest in you, which I will never yield shall be thus adventured. Your valour is already sufficiently known. Sufficiently have you already done for your country. Enow, enow there are besides you to lose less worthy lives. Woe is me! What shall become of me if you thus abandon me? Then was it time for you to follow these adventures when you adventured nobody but your self, and were nobody's but your own—but now (pardon me, that now or never I claim mine own!) mine you are, and without me you can undertake no danger. And will you endanger Parthenia?"[40]

Part of the appeal of this passage is that it offers without qualification an authentic voice of resistance disposed in terms of mutual interest, albeit in romantic and familial as well as political terms. Argalus replies that "this is the first time that ever you resisted my will. I thank you for it—but persevere not in it, and let not the tears of those most beloved eyes be a presage unto me of that which you would not should happen." In the climactic fight, "the cruelest combat that any present eye had seen," Amphialus and Argalus, the latter in white armor covered with knots of women's hair, are interrupted by Parthenia, who throws herself into the joust and beseeches them to "leave off" fighting. The two knights desist lest they strike Parthenia, who "would not make resistance" (but of course she is making another, more powerful kind of resistance), and then resist their own urges to continue the combat. The outcome has it that Argalus, caught up in a web of resistances that prevent him from acting and finally "labouring against his own power," suffers a sort of stroke and dies.[41] Sidney often depicts his heroes immobilized by the competing claims of defiance and authority—no doubt the tendency reflects his own situation before Elizabeth, even the enforced rustication during which he conceived the *Arcadia*—but this is to join his suspicion of heroism to the gathering interest in political and other resistances.[42] In a fictional society that treats resistance as not an expedient for confronting dire conditions but an effect generated as much by the abrasions of individual action as by tyranny, the concept will be naturalized, as Sidney probably wants, and attenuated, as he probably fears.

Can resistance be explored without being exploded? Still, as the *Arcadia* stages this compromise, and Sidney realizes his idea of fiction as putting moral and political philosophy into personal terms, the concept of resistance gains what it scarcely had a generation earlier: a body and a reach into the awareness of ordinary people. In effect, resistance becomes domesticated. Every reader is invited to think about the implications. The most accomplished knight in the *Arcadia* is defeated not by a physical force but by the emotional and ethical resistances (including self-resistance) that are produced through relation, through love as much as war. If resistance follows power, Sidney shows his contemporaries that martial and political entanglements take place along a continuum that includes the personal as well.

In what remains of this chapter, I will consider a colonial history that represents the renewal of a politically charged notion of resistance, but now against the setting of absolutism in large, the expansion of empires across cultures. My object again is the *Comentarios reales de los Incas* (Royal commentaries of the Incas) of the Inca Garcilaso de la Vega, the mixed-race chronicler whose work retells the conquest of Peru by Spain in the light of the centuries-long series of conquests, of neighboring societies by the imperialist Incas, that preceded it. Begun toward the end of the sixteenth century and, as I mentioned in the last chapter, published in two installments in 1609 and 1617, the Inca Garcilaso's history foregrounds the problems of differentiating the humanist variety of resistance—more intellectual than practical—from a kind that is cultivated in colonial conditions, anticipating what in the middle twentieth century comes to be called a postcolonial consciousness. He writes as a citizen of a conquered society who has been acculturated by the conditions of conquest itself. He tells preconquest history from secondhand knowledge, relates postconquest history from direct experience, and plays the two historical dimensions against one another for contrasts. Moreover, the Inca Garcilaso is one of the first chroniclers of the Peruvian conquest to recapitulate the views of earlier (and invariably Spanish) observers and historians while counterposing them to his own. A typical gesture is his disquisition on the origins of the name "Peru," where he observes that the spelling of the name varies among generations and outlooks (*Peru* or *Piru*), sometimes pedantically, but in every case it conflates the name of a single Indian encountered at random with the name of a river, and hence is built on misunderstanding.[43] If the name itself is subjective, how much more so the events? The instability of the name becomes an opening through which he justifies his dimensional approach to history. When he relates a stratiform history of conquest, then—in which one empire, the Tahuantinsuyu (four united regions) of the Incas, supplants another Indian society and is in turn overthrown by the Spanish empire—and collates multiple sources representing different generations and perspectives for each stratum of the history, the Inca Garcilaso applies to colonial history a measure of retrospection, critical distance, and self-consciousness that will become the principal elements of this renewed sense of resistance.[44] The doubling of colonial histories ensures a mutual criticism: almost everything the Incas did to conquer the societies they absorbed into their empire reflects on the corresponding actions of the Spaniards, casting a critical light on Spanish colonial practice through narrative via abstraction and evaluation.[45] The value of the Inca Garcilaso's history in this context is that it invites us to see the continuities between the political, martial, and psychic resistances of his humanist precursors and a version native to transatlantic empire. How the recoil from imperialism even by its agents repeats the early semantic history of resistance but also revives its political import in a new world is the final episode of my argument.

Resistance, as anticipated by Rojas's Pármeno and developed into a concept during the sixteenth century, figures intensely in the *Comentarios reales*, where the Inca Garcilaso tells of the pattern of conquest that established the Inca empire, no small part of which was the struggle to quell the resistance of Indian tribes.[46] Many of the colonial procedures of the Incas seem to have been elaborated in view of resistance, real and expected, resulting in a depiction of conquest and resistance as correlative, inevitable elements of imperialism. This account of the custom called *mítmac* is typical:

> Trasplantábanlos por otro respecto, y era cuando habían conquistado alguna provincia belicosa, de quien se temía que, por estar lejos del Cuzco y por ser de gente feroz y brava, no había de ser leal ni había de querer servir en buena paz. Entonces sacaban parte de la gente de aquella tal provincia, y muchas veces la sacaban toda, y la pasaban a otra provincia de las domésticas, donde, viéndose por todas partes rodeados de vasallos leales y pacíficos, procurasen ellos también ser leales, bajando la cerviz al yugo que ya no podían desechar. Y en estas maneras de mudar indios siempre llevaban Incas de los que lo eran por privilegio del primer Rey Manco Cápac, y enviábanlos para que gobernasen y doctrinasen a los demás. Con el nombre de estos Incas honraban a todos los demás que con ellos iban, porque fuesen más respetados de los comarcanos. A todos estos indios, trocados de esta manera, llamaban *mítmac,* así a los que llevaban como a los que traían: quiere decir: trasplantados o advenedizos, que todo es uno.[47]

(Whenever some warlike province had been conquered which was distant from Cuzco and peopled with fierce and restless inhabitants and might therefore prove disloyal or unwilling to serve the Inca peacefully, part of the population was moved away from the area—and often the whole of it—and sent to some more docile region, where the newcomers would find themselves surrounded by loyal and peaceable vassals and thus learn to be loyal themselves, bowing their necks under the yoke they could no longer throw off. In making these exchanges of Indians, they always used the Incas by privilege of the first king, Manco Cápac, sending them forth to govern and teach the rest. All others who went with these Incas were honored with the same title, so as to be the more respected by their neighbors, and all such Indians thus transplanted were called *mítmac*, whether immigrants or emigrants: the word means equally "settlers" or "emigrants.")[48]

Even the prospect of resistance incites this movement of conquered peoples to new settlements where they become colonists, enacting the office of colonialism within imperialism. Real or anticipated, resistance is important enough as a factor to motivate what the Inca Garcilaso depicts here as the cycle of imperialism:

conquest → [resistance] → colonialism

His narrative finds process and motive in events that might otherwise seem opaque, such as the origins of the custom of *mítmac* and the displacement of some numbers of Indians from one role to another, conquered to colonist. For the society of the Incas as he describes it, this cycle establishes empire as a manifestation of sheer power that, scarcely threatened by displays of resistance, accommodates them to its own unfolding. There are two vantages here that bring complexity to this colonial version of resistance, namely, that of the Indians in the Inca Garcilaso's account who change positions and become contented settlers and that of the Spaniards and Europeans who read his account and see narrated there a colonial practice that offers a critical sight into their own. The narrative implicitly addresses two types that will become something like stock characters in postcolonial analysis—the acquiescent colonial factor and the complacent metropolitan observer—and puts them into relation with one another through the fabric of history. As they enrich his account of resistance, they add annexes to the absolutist concept, as though Europeans must recognize their exercise of power from a transatlantic perspective to see all the varieties of resistance that accompany it.

The effects of resistance occasion some of the climactic events of the first part, which concludes with the civil war between the rival kings, Huascar and Atahuallpa, that fatally weakened the empire shortly before the arrival of the Spanish conquerors. Chapter 11 of book 9 finally makes explicit what the Inca Garcilaso believes to be the proleptic significance of the theme of resistance. Huaina Cápac, the reigning king and the twelfth in succession to the founder of the realm, Manco Cápac, hears that the conquered province of Carangue, at the edge of the kingdom of Quito, has risen up against the Inca empire out of a desire to maintain its barbarism. The Carangues, no pudiendo llevar el yugo del Inca, particularmente la ley que les prohibía el comer carne humana, se alzaron con otras provincias de su comarca, que eran de las mismas costumbres y temían el Imperio del Inca, que lo tenían ya a sus puertas, que les había de prohibir lo mismo que a sus vecinos, que era lo que ellos más estimaban para su regalo y vida bestial; por estas causas se conjuraron con facilidad, y en mucho secreto apercibieron gran número de gente para matar los gobernadores y ministros del Inca y la gente de guarnición que consigo tenían; y entretanto que llegaba el tiempo señalado para ejecutar su traición, les servían con la mayor sumisión y ostentación de amor que fingir podían, para cogerlos más descuidados y degollarlos más a su salvo. Llegado el día, los mataron con grandísima crueldad, y ofrecieron las cabezas, corazones y la sangre a sus dioses, en servicio y agradecimiento de que les hubiesen libertado del dominio de los Incas y restituídoles sus antiguas costumbres; comieron la carne de ellos con much gusto y gran voracidad, tragándosela sin mascar, en venganza de que se la hubiesen prohibido tanto tiempo había y castigado a los que habían delinquido en comerla; hicieron todas las desvergüenzas y desacatos que pudieron.[49]

(no longer able to bear the Inca's yoke, especially in regard to the law that forbade them to eat human flesh, had risen in revolt together with other provinces which shared their customs and also feared the empire of the Incas. The latter indeed now extended to their very gates and threatened to impose the same prohibitions on them as on their neighbors, particularly in regard to the things they cherished most for their beastly practices and pleasures. For this reason they were easily drawn into the plot and with great secrecy prepared a large force to slay the Inca's governors and officials and the garrison forces residing among them. Until the time they had fixed for the execution of their treacherous attack they served the Incas with the greatest submission and every possible display of feigned affection, so as to be able to take them unawares and kill them without risk to themselves. The day arrived, and the natives butchered them with the greatest cruelty, offering their heads, hearts, and blood to their own gods in gratitude for having freed them from the Inca's sway and restored their ancient customs. They ate the flesh of all their victims with great voracity and relish, swallowing it unchewed as a result of having been forbidden to touch it for so long under pain of punishment if they did so. They committed every possible kind of outrage and insult.)[50]

When the Inca Huaina Cápac characteristically proposes to bring the Caranques under his power again "if they [will] beg for mercy and bow to the will of their king," the rebels refuse and threaten the messengers from Cuzco. Finally the Inca resolves to win at any cost:

Mandó que la hiciesen [la guerra] a fuego y sangre, en la cual murieron muchos millares de hombres de ambas partes, porque los enemigos, como gente rebelada, peleaban obstinadamente. . . . y como a la potencia del Inca no hubiese resistencia, enflaquecieron los enemigos en breve tiempo; dieron en pelear, no en batallas descubiertas, sino en rebatos y asechanzas, defendiendo los malos pasos, sierras y lugares fuertes.[51]

(He ordered his followers to make war with blood and fire, and many thousands were killed on both sides, for the enemy fought stubbornly like rebels. . . . But as there was no possible resistance to the Inca's power, the enemy shortly weakened. They no longer gave open battle, but made sudden attacks in prepared ambushes, defending the difficult passes, the mountaintops and strong places.)[52]

The disposition of the conflict is swift: to the rebels and their allies who had not yet been conquered

se hizo un castigo riguroso y memorable; mandó que los degollasen dentro de una gran laguna que está entre los términos de los unos y de los otros; para que el nombre que entonces le pusieron guardase la memoria del delito y del castigo, llamáronla Yahuarcocha: quiere decir: lago o mar de sangre, porque la laguna quedó hecha sangre, con tanta como en ella se derramó.[53]

(was meted out an exemplary and rigorous punishment: they were to be beheaded in a great lake that lies on the borders of the districts of

Resistance

the Caranques and the rest, and so that its name should preserve the memory of their guilt and chastisement it was called Yahuarcocha, "lake or sea of blood," for the lake was turned into blood on account of the quantity that was spilt.)[54]

Converse to the institution of *mítmac*, this approach to resistance both denies it ("there was no possible resistance to the Inca's power" is the narrator's seemingly counterfactual observation) and memorializes it in the landscape. Yahuarcocha is one of many monuments mentioned by the Inca Garcilaso and other chroniclers as tokens of past rebellions; in this perhaps fabulous telling, the Incaic landscape is a record of conquests that often proves, on reflection, to be a record of attempts to wrest power from the conquering Incas. This is resistance as a motivating force in establishing the terms on which conquest remembers itself:

conquest → [resistance] → colonial landscape

In both *mítmac* and this kind of fable, resistance becomes an ideal that must be either anticipated or attempted for conquest to declare itself in full. Accordingly, the investments of the Inca Garcilaso's narrative discreetly shift over the run of the first volume—from conquest, and how it was realized, to resistance, and whether, when, and how it was attempted. This swing toward resistance is the natural extension of how the concept figured in the *New Arcadia* but in a transatlantic outlook, which turns to a colonialism past to weigh the forces that both established and vitiated it. In this valuation, written in the Inca Garcilaso's case from both inside and outside the Inca regime, it is resistance that is never fully realized but always deferred, thwarted, and finally monumentalized. In its failure that is also a success, the term acquires a luminosity that rivals that of conquest—an elaboration of the mutual entanglement already visible in the *Lusiads*. In fact, one notices in retrospect that in the *Comentarios reales* the Inca Garcilaso reserves the term "resistencia" for the exact opposite of conquest, namely, its complete overthrow—an anticonquest that never takes place. He uses terms such as *rebeldía* and *rebelión* for the local, contingent acts that would lead to an achieved resistance. In this telling, resistance has a hierarchy of effects that corresponds to that of conquest, and the narrative approach is not triumphalist in the manner of the chroniclers Francisco López de Gómara and Bernabé Cobo but analytical in the fashion of twentieth-century postcolonial observers such as Frantz Fanon, Aimé Césaire, and Albert Memmi.

The valuation of resistance against conquest produces a history that puts its contemporaneous readers in a stance that many modern readers have remarked—of looking at conquest from the outside—and therefore invites his Spanish readers to see their conquest of Peru the same way. To put it otherwise, the Inca Garcilaso writes what a Spanish readership considers a preconquest history and what an Incaic audience, if one existed for this book, would consider a postconquest account. For the emerging class of mestizos like himself and perhaps other readers, the narrative maintains two eras of conquest, the Incas over their neighboring Indians and the Spanish over the Incas, as its points of reference, both of which are at least implicit at every turn. Thus the *Comentarios reales*, while nominally complicit with the Spanish conquest, invokes a critical outlook on the material of Incaic history and in doing so makes it impossible not to see the Spanish conquest in similar terms, as a conversation between power and resistance whose outcome will become certain only in a distant future.

Several episodes in the history, like that of the Carangues, foreground how to discriminate resistance among the effects of conquest. It might even be said that the impetus for the Inca Garcilaso's emphatic rewriting of López de Gómara, Fernández de Oviedo, and the other established historians of the conquest is to install such an outlook in the narrative, rendering it polyvalent instead of monologic, anachronistic rather than presentist. Strategic anachronism—as a catalyst for this new model of resistance—might be the Inca Garcilaso's characteristic mode in the *Comentarios reales*, corresponding to the irony and multiple perspectives that emerge across colonial situations throughout this period.

I will conclude by concentrating on one such episode of strategic anachronism. In book 9, chapter 15, the Inca Garcilaso retells the passing of the reign of Huaina Cápac. It seems the Inca king felt a chill after bathing in a lake and saw in his illness the fulfillment of a prophecy about the end of not only his reign but the state itself. As the

Inca Garcilaso tells it, Huaina Cápac announces his imminent death to the elite of Inca society and puts his son Atahuallpa in his place as king. Then the historian goes on:

Hecha esta plática a sus hijos y parientes, mandó llamar los demás capitanes y curacas que no eran de la sangre real, y les encomendó la fidelidad y buen servicio que debían hacer a su Rey, y a lo último les dijo:

"Muchos años ha que por revelación de Nuestro Padre el Sol tenemos que, *pasados doce Reyes de sus hijos*, vendrá gente nueva y no conocida en estas partes, y ganará y sujetará a su imperio todos nuestros reinos y otros muchos; yo me sospecho que serán de los que sabemos que han andado por la costa de nuestro mar; será gente valerosa, que en todo os hará ventaja. También sabemos que se cumple en mí el número de los doce Incas. Certifícoos que pocos años después que yo me haya ido de vosotros, vendrá aquella gente nueva y cumplirá lo que Nuestro Padre el Sol nos ha dicho y ganará nuestro Imperio y seran señores de él. Yo os mando que les obedezcáis y sirváis como a hombres que en todo os harán ventaja; que su ley será major que la nuestra y sus armas poderosas e invencibles más que las vuestras. Quedaos en paz, que yo me voy a descansar con mi Padre el Sol, que me llama."[55]

(After making this speech to his sons and relatives, he bade the other captains and curacas who were not of the royal blood to be called, and urged on them loyalty and good service to their king, concluding:

"Many years ago it was revealed to us by our father the Sun that after twelve of his sons had reigned, a new race would come, unknown in these parts, and would gain and subdue all our kingdoms and many others to their empire. I suspect that these must be those we have heard of off our coasts. They will be a brave people who will overcome us in everything. We also know that in my reign the number of twelve Incas is completed. I assure you that a few years after I have gone away from you, these new people will come and fulfil what our father the Sun has foretold, and will gain our empire and become masters of it. I bid you obey them and serve them as men who will be completely victorious, for their law will be better

Resistance

than ours and their arms more powerful and invincible than ours. Remain in peace, for I am going to rest with my father the Sun, who is calling me.")[56]

The Inca Garcilaso then collates the accounts of several Spanish historians who provide versions of the same anecdote, which has resistance (or the lack of it) as its subtext. How did an empire that had exercised absolute power over others, and thwarted resistance to itself, exhibit so little force against the conquering Spanish? In this polyvalent outlook the question must be asked from two sides. What made the Spanish conquest possible? What made the Inca resistance impossible? The Inca Garcilaso's narrative to this point is careful to give the Incaic perspective via Huaina Cápac's prophecy and then the Spanish point of view (or better—several Spanish points of view in the competing historians of the conquest period, such as Cieza de León and López de Gómara) of the same matter. Finally, the chapter offers this moving, illuminating supplement:

> Acuérdome que un día, hablando aquel Inca viejo en presencia de mi madre, dando cuenta de estas cosas y de la entrada de los españoles y de cómo ganaron la tierra, le dije: "Inca, ¿cómo siendo esta tierra de suyo tan áspera y fragosa, y siendo vosotros tantos y tan belicosos y poderosos para ganar y conquistar tantas provincias y reinos ajenos, dejásteis perder tan presto vuestro Imperio y os rendísteis a tan pocos españoles?" Para responderme volvió a repetir el pronóstico acerca de los españoles, que días antes lo había contado, y dijo cómo su Inca les había mandado que los obedeciesen y sirviesen, porque en todo se les aventajarían.
>
> Habiendo dicho esto, se volvió a mí con algún enojo de que les hubiese motejado de cobardes y pusilánimos, y respondió a mi pregunta diciendo: "Estas palabras que nuestro Inca nos dijo, que fueron las últimas que nos habló, fueron más poderosas para nos sujetar y quitar nuestro Imperio que no las armas que tu padre y sus compañeros trajeron a esta tierra." Dijo esto aquel Inca por dar a entender cuánto estimaban lo que sus Reyes les mandaban, cuánto más lo que Huaina Cápac les mandó a lo último de su vida, que fue más querido de todos ellos.[57]

(I remember how one day, when the old Inca was speaking in the presence of my mother and relating these things and the arrival of the Spaniards and how they won Peru, I said to him: "Inca, how is it that as this land is naturally so rough and rocky, and you were so numerous and warlike, and powerful enough to gain and conquer so many other provinces and kingdoms, you should so quickly have lost your empire and surrendered to so few Spaniards?" In order to answer this he repeated the prophecy about the Spaniards which he had told us some days before, and explained how their Inca had bidden them obey and serve the Spaniards since they would prove superior to them in everything.

Having said this, he turned to me with some display of anger that I should have criticized them as mean-spirited and cowardly, and answered my question by saying: "These words, which were the last our Inca uttered, were more effective in overcoming us and depriving us of our empire than the arms your father and his companions brought to this country." The Incas said this so as to show how much they honored whatever their kings bade them do, and in especial the dying words of Huaina Cápac, the most beloved of their rulers.)[58]

If the Inca Garcilaso embodies something like a resistant outlook, he also casts himself, as the wise child, in the role of the one who speaks the subtext of much of the *Comentarios reales*: namely, that conquest and resistance are correlative to and dependent on one another in that one can succeed only where the other fails, or else they become fixed in a stalemate where imperial destinies will remain unresolved. In narrating a history of conquest, both anticipated and achieved, one also tells a history of resistance, both successful and failed; resistance is a sketch within the larger depiction of conquest.

This is an insight of a different quality than what appears in most of the colonial writings about Peru and the Spanish empire in the Americas before the *Comentarios reales*, even those histories that devote substantial attention to Indian resistance. For one thing, in relation to the Spanish enterprise, with its strong narrative and subjective purchase for a continental readership, the Inca Garcilaso treats resistance not as obstacle or effect but as a countervailing enterprise itself, having its own subjective purposes, a kind of history, and a hierarchy of results from mutiny and rebellion to a fully realized resistance—the latter strictly hypothetical in this history. The interdependence of the concepts of conquest and resistance—not to mention the sheer attention concentrated on resistance throughout the history—compels some questions. Is conquest ever more than hypothetical in this history? How might we understand a conquest that in its narrative details continually takes on the aspect of resistance? What is the nature of a conquest made from resistance? Moreover, like any postcolonial account, the *Comentarios reales* makes it feasible to observe in stratiform fashion what the agents of empire and resistance themselves, caught up in their purposes, are unable to see: that they are enacting a historical process larger than those purposes, in which the nature of power, more than any particular application of it, is at issue and on display. Telling of colonial practices that are fully assimilated only through irony and anachronism, counterposing empires against one another, and treating conquest as made from resistance and vice versa, the *Comentarios reales* is an anatomy of colonial Peru that anticipates many of the properties of a postcolonial analysis. The Inca Garcilaso becomes the Pármeno of this work, the inquisitor of a resistance to absolute power that exists less perfectly in fact than in discourse, but has become thinkable, and sayable, in the interval since the start of the colonial period. It is the nature of a semantic *cartone* to go from blank to colored, from conceptually impoverished to circumstantially rich, over the course of a work or an era, as literature both writes and responds to events.

BLOOD

A figure called Tragedy enters, carrying a bowl of blood. In a play concerning adulterous murder, where the murderer will dip his handkerchief in his victim's blood and send it ("a kalender of bloody letters") to the widow he would seduce, there is something oppressively obvious about such a foreshowing. With the word *blood* repeated insistently throughout the play, the audience hardly depends on a visual portent. And yet the bowl of blood means more—or perhaps less—than it seems. An allegorical figure offers us the blood as though handing it across from his world to ours, from allegory to literalness, a striking gesture that is allegorical and literal together. Here and throughout the play, the sheer excess of blood overruns all concepts of the substance, all attempts to read it as letters toward a text, "an ensign of despaire," or anything else.[1] In its abundance, it becomes simply, literally itself.

Or: a young boy conceived in the rape of a virtuous girl by an unknown assailant—the rapist actually the wastrel son of a noble family—is injured in an accident, and his spilt blood attracts the attention of an elderly gentleman of great authority. Once the gentleman brings him home for care, the boy's mother and grandparents come to realize that the absent son of this Samaritan must be the rapist, even as the gentleman's family sees in the child the face of their dissolute son. Of course the rapist and his victim are finally married and the families joined by what the narrator calls the power of the blood that the grandfather saw spilt on the ground.[2] On its face the story belongs to the convention called the *cri du sang*, in which members of a family who have been separated by fate are drawn together by the pull of consanguinity. But this is a peculiarly literal *cri du sang*, in which a pool of liquid blood stands in the middle of a story rendered otherwise in almost abstract fashion, with symmetrical episodes and motifs—the bed on which the girl is raped is the same one her son recovers in— and little moral or psychological complication. What is the power of this blood? It can be seen according to received symbolism, but it is chiefly a power derived from the unforeseeable outcomes and sheer presence of the liquid itself. In the end a blood that might have kept the girl and the rapist on distinct social planes becomes the impetus for making, however implausibly, a new family.[3]

These accounts of the anonymous domestic tragedy *A Warning for Fair Women*, which was likely performed by William Shakespeare's company, the Lord Chamberlain's Men, during the 1590s, and Miguel de Cervantes's novella *La fuerza de la sangre* (The power of blood), find these works in company with many others of the later sixteenth century. Where blood appears in this era, it threatens too much meaning—too many competing allegories in different degrees of revision— or the reduction of meaning to sheer spectacle, such as a bowl of blood. The literature of this moment recognizes the semantic shift under way, as older genres such as picaresque fiction become bloodier and new genres such as revenge tragedy make the display of blood essential to their projects. Conventions such as the bloody banquet, letters written in blood, and bloody maimings and killings are absorbed into works of all sorts.[4] The fate of blood in the period belongs to a concept under revision and a word that exchanges allegorical for literal meanings, even as literalness itself gains a fresh cultural authority across a range of disciplines from mathematics to natural philosophy to art.

At the turn of the sixteenth century in Europe and the colonial Americas, blood tends to be imagined allegorically, as a substance that represents ideas such as nobility, sacrifice, and heroism as well as emotions such as love and passion. It is implicated in a parcel of interlocking observations and speculations that both explains and is explained by the substance's material reality: I call this a conceptual envelope, the coherence of which depends on the continued validity of its complementary allegories.[5] Near the end of the century, however, most of the received allegories around blood have been compromised, and the envelope is frayed. While they retain latent or partial authority, there will no longer be unquestioned power in such allegories as Galen's doctrine of the humors, the authority of royal blood, or the sacrifice of blood in the Roman Catholic Mass.[6] The intervening era witnesses these changes and compromises under many offices—including the decline of feudalism, the Reformation of Christianity, and the rise of experimental science—and the fracture of these allegories occurs unevenly and in stages. For a time near the turn of the seventeenth century, while the conceptual envelope assembled in the Middle Ages is under revision, several bloods are imaginatively available at once; words such as *blood*, *sang*, and *sangre* draw alike on alternative or opposed understandings, making the words for blood rich, self-refuting, and polytropic. And while the received conceptual envelope is being remade, early modern readers become intrigued at seeing, between its contiguous but distinct planes, blood as simply itself—a substance, a liquid that has a reality apart from the allegories of religion, history, and medicine. Throughout the later sixteenth century, many of the central figures in blood's revision share this attention to the liquid: they observe its motions and speculate over its invisible life; they notice its appearances in the phases of bodily life and history; they comment on its abundance, its vividness, its symbolic complexity.[7] These observers often attribute to blood a kind of eloquence that stills the long-established allegorical conventions and clamors for new ways of situating the substance in all its settings.

The generation of Shakespeare and Cervantes sees this problem acutely, and some of the seeming modernity of its plays and prose fictions can be found in the consciousness of blood as a marker under revision—the power of which draws from its materiality as well as its figurative associations. *The Merchant of Venice*, the Henriad, *Hamlet*, the *Novelas ejemplares*, and *Don Quijote* are among the products of this consciousness, bringing renewed imagination and hard questions to the discussion of the preceding century. Materialism in itself means nothing outside a system of values, and where blood is concerned, the imperative to idealize allows that a material perspective tends to be corrective or contingent, not final.[8] I think of the later sixteenth century as an interval between conceptions of blood, in which the medieval horizons of nobility, divinity, and the cosmos come to be largely replaced by the modern notions such as family, class, and race. The medieval terms are ruled by a concern for ipseity (from the Latin adjective *ipse*, "self"), or the nature of a person or thing in the system of nature. While the modern horizons are no less allegorical than the medieval, they seem less abstract, they accord with the new science, and they make sense to societies that find their centers in emerging populations and standpoints below the aristocracy. They are ruled not by ipseity but by identity (from the adjective *idem*, "same"), the modern preoccupation according to which we inquire into a person's nature by reference not to an encompassing system but to other persons of the same nature. The reconception of blood in social rather than cosmic terms, as evidence of relations more than of a fixed reality, belongs to the replacement of ipseity by identity that gains momentum during the century. Moreover, the attraction to blood as substance, as a speaking liquid, bridges the space between one conceptual regime and the next. When new allegories connect blood to race, for instance, it will be with a renewed sense of material blood and the modern conviction that the blood of quotidian experience is continuous with that of the allegories.

My concern here is with the interval. How does the concept of blood get reinvented in the late sixteenth century to take fresh account of the material, the liquid itself? If the concept comes to include an account of the sheer bodily experience of the substance—an experience often and strangely put aside in the allegories of late medieval medicine, theology, and myth—how does it accommodate this aspect of the everyday? Many of us bear in mind a conventional account of how some aspect of the physical body comes to have figurative associations: we suppose that "language develops by metaphorical extension, in borrowing words from the realm of the corporeal, visible, tangible and applying them by analogy to the realm of the incorporeal, invisible, intangible; then in the course of time the original corporeal reference is forgotten, and only the incorporeal, metaphorical extension survives." In time, writes one of the most searching literary critics of the past century, poets rediscover the corporeal, grounding the now intangible concept in a tangible conceit.[9] Early modern blood offers a striking

Blood

110

revision of this account. The materiality of blood is never forgotten, of course, but during the interval between conceptual regimes, poets and others return obsessively to its corporeality and tangibility, as though finding their way home from a journey or awakening from a dream. They rediscover not "the realm of the corporeal" but blood itself—with what consequences? When the old allegories are uncertain and the new ones not yet in place, how many bloods are there? And how do mere words such as *blood*, *sang*, and *sangre* exhibit and contain the dynamic story of these changes?

This semantic history commences at about the turn of the sixteenth century, when blood is a largely figurative concept out of correspondence with its material reality, a heavily loaded symbolic principle that does not quite account for the physical fact.[10] There is the blood of legend, of Christian sacrifice, and of Galenism, all of which are made coherent by an elaborate conceptual envelope received from the Middle Ages; and then there is another blood, of the quotidian body, known to every human being from direct experience. The transformation of this term after 1500 has to do with its gaining a material story, an account of what it does as matter—toward the end of the century this story will become the theory of circulation—to put against its symbolic power, a becoming physical or material. When we turn to the fictions of the era, then, we see them engaged in a project that can seem unexpected. Instead of taking a physical reality and making it figurative, the poets and playwrights of the European and transatlantic Renaissance often take an idealized blood and render it quotidian, or at least imagine ways that the symbolic and literal dimensions of blood can exist in a single idiom. To put it another way, over the sixteenth century blood gains a conceptual relation to the everyday that is not entirely dependent on either the theory of the humors or the other abstractions—Christian, chivalric, and heraldic among them—that drive its representation until well into this period.

What is a conceptual envelope? I use the term to mean a phenomenon of a sort that preoccupied the Renaissance, namely, a reality understood through allegory or an allegory founded on reality. The object of such an envelope—human complexions, the moon, weather—is something that early modern people saw with their own eyes, and yet necessarily saw through the eyes of allegory. The envelope is closed:

that is, it tells a coherent story about its object (for instance, blood) that agrees with received thought. In such an envelope, available knowledge is disposed according to convention, and within some degree of difference, these parcels largely make sense of one another, much as Avicenna revises but generally endorses Galen, who does the same with Hippocrates. But the envelope is also open: it must explain the physical reality we see with unlettered eyes, making received knowledge seem as fresh as unmediated experience. Conceptual envelopes should be understood alongside large-scale scientific paradigms, as comparatively small-gauge beliefs that attach to natural phenomena, particularly when one paradigm is in the process of giving way to another. While an influential historian of science calls the kind of investigation that extends and develops a paradigm "normal science," we might suppose these beliefs to be "normal allegories," occupying not the "preformed and relatively inflexible box" of paradigm but the looser envelope of quotidian experience.[11] It is part of the nature of a conceptual envelope to seem, from within, identical to reality itself. Of course such an envelope is always provisional. Its unfinished character and its opening to empirical reality provide that it must be refashioned to accommodate new knowledge.

According to the conceptual envelope that passes from the Middle Ages into the sixteenth century, blood appeared in symbolic fashion at dynamic, climactic, and transitional (and for women, cyclical) moments, when wars were being won or lost, dynasties established or overthrown, fertility and continuance enacted. Where this multivalent concept of blood intersects history, "the father of the humors" becomes a marker of nobility and heroism. The flowing of such men's blood marks events that are worth recording, while the blood of exceptional women evokes the birthing and healing that makes history feasible.[12] Where this concept meets religion, it evokes the covenant of Genesis 9, the divine injunctions of Leviticus 17, and the statutes of Deuteronomy 12, where general blood is a metonym for life—humankind is forbidden to eat the flesh of animals in which blood flows—and where the "blood of man" is explicitly linked to the "image of God."[13] No less it includes the Christian economy of salvation, in which Christ's sacrifice on the cross "in a bloody manner" is represented in the "unbloody" sacrifice of the Mass.[14] In the middle of the fifteenth century, the city of Toledo, making civil war against King John II of Castile, articulated the first statute of *limpieza de sangre* (purity of blood) that enforced distinctions among long-established and recently converted Christians according to criteria of lineage that went by the name of blood.[15] Such laws, which came to be accepted by Iberian institutions of church and government, explicitly transposed blood from the domains of genealogy and religion into politics and social policy, revising "the potential meanings" of *judío*, *converso*, and *cristiano* — and, we should insist, of *sangre* as well.[16] And where it intersects natural philosophy, blood stands for the correspondence between the system of the body and the larger systems, of the earth, the elements, and the cosmos, in which it is embedded.[17] At this latter crossing barbers, butchers, and midwives opened veins as a way of curing or purifying or sometimes merely changing their patients, whether ritually, perhaps to mark the end of the season, or therapeutically.[18] Even the mundane blood of injuries and accidents tends to be recognized as heavy with meaning. The fabric of the conceptual envelope is made of these complementary bloods out of distinct but adjacent areas of knowledge and belief, while the dynamic principle that holds them together is allegory, a conviction written across the fabric that blood always stands for something other than itself. The Christian, heroic, and humoral concepts do not coincide with but complement one another—each explains blood in one area of human experience—and all alike they are generated from the interpretive model of allegoresis.

The semantics of blood in this period are connected to the fate of an intellectual program that has been much interpellated in recent years and has delivered a bounty to literary studies, namely, Galenism. For several generations, scholars of early modernity have agreed that the period's general theory of the constitution of the human body was established in a set of principles conceived in Hippocrates's treatise *Nature of Man* and refined in several works of Galen.[19] The explanatory power of Galenism, however, underwent a striking change of terms during the sixteenth century: under pressure from forces within natural philosophy such as the anatomical movement and Paracelsian thought, Galenism became less a satisfactory account of how the body works and more an allegory concerned with the mind and its passions.[20] For a tantalizing moment, until a new envelope was assembled around it, the blood of the physical body got free as a concept—became legible outside Galenism and susceptible to inductive observation. Certainly it remained possible to assimilate material blood to the system of the humors and Galen's theory of health well into the seventeenth century.[21]

But where blood is concerned, the most searching investigations of the later sixteenth century were already post-Galenic in character and complexity. Starting from the translator John Jones's version of *Galens Bookes of Elements* (1574), many of the treatises of this period that endorsed a Galenist ontology and physiology accounted for blood in terms that were becoming obsolete to medicine, while explainers such as Thomas Wright (*The Passions of the Mind in General*, 1604) and Thomas Walkington (*The Optick Glasse of Humours*, 1607) worked to make this system as relevant to the mind as it had once been to the body. The measure of their success was that a Galenic self survived in fiction even as the Galenic body struggled against the loss of its primacy in science.[22] Meanwhile, literary works, closely responsive to the conceptual shifts of the late sixteenth century, tell us what the treatises often cannot, that an alternative physiological model for blood is already available, even as the Christian and chivalric allegories of blood are under revision by the theological, economic, and social changes that are transforming European and transatlantic societies.

While the theory of blood as a fluid that makes a circuit of the body, a liquid organ, was anticipated by several sixteenth-century anatomists, it was finally announced in Michael Servetus's *Christianismi Restitutio* (Restoration of Christianity) of 1553, a treatise that censures Catholics and reformers alike in its pursuit of a return to an original Christianity[23]—and that, sharply revising Galen, first describes the lesser circulation through the lungs, completing the hemodynamic path through the entire body.[24] A literalist in theological as well as scientific matters, the Iberian scholar Servetus might be the presiding genius of the late-century turn to blood itself. His zeal for counterposing the observation of plain fact to received knowledge led him into remaking several of the conceptual envelopes of the time. For instance, he edited Ptolemy's *Geography* in 1535 and, determined to bring the classical and contemporary worlds together, took pains to identify the places mentioned there with their modern names. He studied anatomy in Paris alongside Andreas Vesalius, who was to contradict Galen and reinvent the discipline in *De Humani Corporis Fabrica* (1543). Servetus's literalist reading of the Bible prompted him to preach and publish Unitarian heresies concerning infant baptism and the nature of God. Finally, with the appearance of *Christianismi Restitutio* and at Calvin's instigation, he was burned at the stake in 1553. On the question of blood, Servetus revised Galen to conform to biblical passages about blood and *anima* (spirit) as well as his own anatomical observations.[25] His turn to sheer material fact as a counterweight to outmoded allegory marks the reconception of blood in a liminal moment, as a material connected to private, individual experience, to singular as opposed to collective identity, that briefly stands apart from one parcel of received allegory before being subsumed into another. Particular to the later sixteenth century, this is an alternative *cri du sang*—a call for attention to blood as itself.

Perhaps this episode is suspended between the emerging literalism of the sixteenth century, according to which many disciplines are reoriented toward anatomies, observations, and collections, and the vitalism of the mid-seventeenth century, by which matter is imagined by scientists and philosophers as self-moving, self-governing, and possessed of an inherent agency, energy, and spirit. Seventeenth-century vitalism lays a foundation for the rise of liberalism, it has been argued, conceiving the material body of creation in terms of "moral choice, independent action, and free association," much as political philosophers would envision the body politic, making vitalism a threshold in early modern thought.[26] In the interval between these programs, the culture rediscovers blood itself, in the welter of its often contradictory senses in this period, perhaps as prologue to rethinking matter in general, and refashions the conceptual envelope around the term *blood* to accommodate new principles for science and politics together. For vitalism, for example, William Harvey is a prompting figure, especially during the era framed by his two major treatises on circulation, *De motu cordis* of 1628 and *De circulatione sanguinis* of 1649;[27] but the earlier moment I am tracing concludes with *De motu cordis*, which provides a conceit—the principle of circulation—that reframes the discussion of blood's ontology and agency that had been passed on from the sixteenth century.

Blood

115

Of course many artists and scholars remained constitutionally attached to the doctrine of the humors during this period and after. The forty or so years spanning the later sixteenth and earlier seventeenth centuries saw a spate of treatises and poems on moral philosophy that adjusted the Galenic doctrine of humors, generally toward a more abstract account of mental states and a less prominent role for blood itself.[28] Ben Jonson is the chief example of a playwright who operates within this doctrine, although without looking very far one sees in plays such as *Bartholomew Fair* (1614) a fraying of the conceptual envelope that held the humors intact as theory and perhaps Jonson's contradictory desire both to rehabilitate this doctrine and to get beyond it.[29]

Moreover, there were any number of poets whose conception of blood was resolutely historical and climactic, perhaps because the events they wished to tell demand an unbroken atmosphere of legend. Such are the Earl of Surrey in England and Luis de Camões in Portugal. For Surrey, blood is the emblem of heroes and martyrs (as in the poems "London, hast thow accused me" and "Dyvers thy death doo dyverslye bemone") and the index of fear or arousal ("So crewell prison! Howe could betyde, alas!");[30] the latter conceit grounds Surrey's most famous poem ("Love that doth raine and liue within my thought"), an adaptation of Petrarch's *Canzoniere* 140 that is the graft from which English Petrarchism grows.[31] Camões' *Lusiads* depicts several battles between the Portuguese and the Moors in which rivers of "sangue desparzido" (spilt blood) enrich the ground on which a nation and empire were established.[32] Yet even here, among these conventional understandings of blood, the unfinished business of the present appears. While *Canzoniere* 140 accepts a conceit of blood as the ensign (Petrarch's "insegna") of emotion, we should ask why both Surrey and Thomas Wyatt are drawn to translating a poem that narrates the movement of blood from the breast to the face and then back to the heart.[33] For Camões, blood often has the aura of a substance clinically observed as much as allegorically invoked. Even Edmund Spenser, in an allegorical episode representing the defeat of the Spanish Armada, includes a wounding of the English hero Prince Arthur (he "opened . . . the welspring of his blood") that has little traction with the historical event and much to do with the contemporary attention to blood as substance.[34] All of these are bloods in the process of becoming private, self-referential, modern.

The shrewdest writers see this challenge of moving between envelopes as an invitation, as Philip Sidney does in the *Arcadia* when he shows an exchange between the duplicitous Clinias and Basilius, the prince of Arcadia, whom Clinias opposes. Supposing him an ally, Basilius asks Clinias to account for a rebellion against his rule, and Clinias, who was injured in the battle by a sword to the face, "purposing indeed to tell him the truth of all, saving what did touch himself . . . , first dipping his hand in the blood of his wound, 'Now by this blood,' said he, 'which is more dear to me, than all the rest that is in my body, since it is spent for your safety, this tongue (perchance unfortunate, but never false) shall not now begin to lie unto my prince, of me most beloved.'"[35] In one sweeping gesture, Sidney here encircles most of the elements his contemporaries choose among: the blood of heroism, the everyday blood that remains "in [the] body" unavailable to interpretation, and the question of blood's "truth." In spite of his pretensions of heroism, Clinias lives by the opposed notion of blood—we might call it the clinical—according to which the entirely quotidian substance can be manipulated to evoke what remains of its former symbolic and metaphysical meanings. The last thing such a clinician wants is to shed real blood for a cause. Later Clinias finds himself at blows with the not very formidable herdsman Dametas and begins "with lamentable eyes to see his own blood come out in many places—and before he had lost half an ounce, . . . he yielded."[36]

Across the sixteenth century, then, I am interested in those episodes in which we can see a modern relation between blood and the everyday being worked out; in which the humoral, historical, and Christian senses of blood are accommodating something that as yet has little discourse of its own; in which poets search out ways of addressing a public audience about private experience; and in which we can see the becoming material of this already figurative and ideal substance. How do poets turn the ideal into the material? Nearly all poetic theory of the period, like Sidney's in his *Apology for Poetry*, is oriented toward the opposite motion, so the reconception of blood in this fashion occurs in an unacknowledged space in poetics. And instead of converting established doctrine into poetry as they do in many other instances (such as religion and philosophy), several of the poets, playwrights, and fiction writers who reimagine blood do so by probing the limits of conventional notions. Four episodes from the interval when blood's conceptual envelope was under revision will show literary works anticipating what the wider culture would soon confront.

One of the century's most ambitious collections of prose fiction, Marguerite de Navarre's *L'Heptaméron des Nouvelles* appeared in two editions in 1558 and 1559. The presumed author, Marguerite, was the late Queen of Navarre, sister of Francis I, and patron of Rabelais and Marot. Modern readers incline to classify the *Heptaméron* as a collection of short stories, but one might justly see it as something more complex, a zone of social and religious exploration in a medium, prose, in which fiction was still unconstrained by the historical and cultural pressures on poetry. Particularly in the last decades before the development of the novel, prose fictions such as Marguerite's stories maintain a franchise to reframe, counterpose, and creatively distort the topics of the present, not glancingly as poetry often does, but with unblinking attention.

The tenth story of *L'Heptaméron* has come under acute discussion in recent years. It tells of a turbulent, unconsummated love affair between Amadour, a young minor nobleman, a Castilian who seems more like a Catalan, famous for his exploits in the army of the Viceroy of Catalonia, and Floride, the brilliant and lovely daughter of the Countess of Aranda. As Marguerite tells it, the tenth story is an indoor epic, elaborating the intrigues and surprises of its main characters, all of whom, except Floride, have established reputations, and even some considerable fame, in the public world. The plot goes as follows. Amadour conceives a passion for Floride and contrives to be near her, first by marrying a woman in her society whom he arranges to have join her household. Floride in turn marries someone else, and after a while Amadour confesses his love to her in the fashion of a courtly romance. Everything, it seems, points toward the fiction's evoking a conventional model for romance that is already moribund in the mid-sixteenth century—we imagine that Amadour and Floride will conduct a doomed love affair—until Marguerite interjects some considerations that propel the story forward into a more complicated and contemporary world. For one thing, it becomes evident early on that these characters cannot be contained within romance, even though no other convention has arisen to take its place. Amadour is entirely unscrupulous in his attempts to gratify his desires, which eventually include a near rape of Floride, while she experiences feelings too unruly to allow her to enact the role of courtly lady. The drift of the story is to show us the daily negotiations of two people who are living out a mode that no longer makes sense in the increasingly modern society of Latin Europe. We see, often in painful narrative close-up, how Amadour and Floride meet, gather themselves emotionally, resolve to handle their feelings one way or another, meet again, gather themselves again, and so on. Often years pass between these meetings, but Marguerite's narrator gives almost no attention to the public world. The story takes place entirely within the houses, and the minds, of the unfulfilled lovers. It is a resolutely modern tale fashioned out of the workings of older, all but obsolete romance fiction in which the gaps and misprisions among the principals are vastly more important than what succeeds at bringing them together.

Among those gaps, certain refusals stand out. Marguerite virtually neutralizes two received, historical senses of blood that one might expect to find in a conventional romance: the public blood of heroism and the familial blood of lineage. On the one hand, the narrator openly declines to talk about the presumably bloody events that make Amadour famous, "for to tell all of his deeds," she writes, "would take an entire day."[37] He is a war hero whose triumphs are imagined as if from a housebound standpoint, with the results noted but no guts or gore visible. On the other hand, blood as family currency is neutralized in that Amadour is an upstart whose good looks and manner endear him to everyone, especially Floride and her mother, the countess. He voices the fear that "you would consider it vainglory that I, an ordinary nobleman, should address myself to a place too high for my rank," but even in saying so he is literally the only one who mentions this evidently outworn consideration.[38] A strict attention to blood in either of these traditional senses would change this story profoundly. An Amadour drenched in the blood of battle would amount to something more than a smooth-talking seducer—would have a public, martial dimension that the feminine narrator of the story, Marguerite's stand-in, Parlamente, can scarcely imagine—while

Blood

a consciousness of his bloodlines by the female characters would keep his seductions in check and render unthinkable the idea of his and Floride's becoming lovers. Marguerite represents here a world in the act of casting off received notions of many things, including blood in its several received senses, and a narrative in the process of questioning an interlocking array of abstractions—such as blood, honor, and chastity—that do not mean much anymore.

In this setting, then, two curious episodes seem to indicate that Marguerite is displacing blood from its usual senses and relocating it in a fresh context—as private, concrete, and material. At the midpoint of the narrative, Floride, already committed to the son of the Aragonese nobleman L'Infant Fortuné and unofficially but ardently in love with Amadour (who is now a prisoner of the King of Tunis), becomes betrothed at her mother's insistence to a third suitor, the Duke of Cardona.

> Et pour la réjouir de tant de malheurs, entendit que l'Infant Fortuné était malade à la mort. Mais jamais, devant sa mère ni nul autre, n'en fit un seul semblant, et se contraignit si fort que les larmes, par force retirées en son cœur, firent sortir le sang par le nez en telle abondance que la vie fut en danger de s'en aller quand et quand. Et pour la restaurer épousa celui qu'elle eût volontiers changé à la mort.[39]

> (To crown all her sorrows, she then heard that the son of the Infante of Fortune had fallen sick and was close to death. But never once in the presence of her mother, or of anyone else, did she show any sign of how she felt. So hard indeed did she repress her feelings that her tears, having been held back in her heart by force, caused violent bleeding from the nose which threatened her life. And all the cure she got was marriage to a man she would gladly have exchanged for death.)[40]

With this, and strikingly in the absence of blood in other senses, Marguerite stakes her representation of a blood that is the direct outcome of passion. Figuratively rich in other contexts, blood here indexes the state of the private mind, and means what the narrator openly says it means, its abstractions emphatically kept away. The narrator, Parlamente, suggests that the irruption of blood is caused by Floride's holding back her feelings, but we might say that this blood is the outcome of the fiction's relocation as much as her repression: a blood that might have been visible or problematic at several other junctures has been displaced into a strictly private realm, as though to announce that private and public have exchanged places, that here the bloodiest battles take place between lovers and with oneself. Marguerite transposes the import of public blood—its "force," its "danger"—into the domestic world and will put blood nowhere else. She reorients the term.

But it remains for Floride herself to reorient the term still further. Shortly after the preceding episode, Amadour is paroled from captivity and returns to Barcelona, where Floride and her family are staying. The two would-be lovers are about to commit to each other—despite Floride's having married the duke—when Amadour's wife dies in an accident, and in his guilt and grief he decides to take Floride sexually, by persuasion or by force. She resists him, reminding him somewhat incongruously of their supposed devotion to virtue. He departs for a three-year service to the king in war and resolves to return and take her by force in any case. He has become an embodiment of desire without scruples; she has become the personification of tortured, ambivalent resistance. When he is finally in the house and about to attack her,

[Floride] pensa que souvent Amadour l'avait louée de sa beauté, laquelle n'était point diminuée nonobstant qu'elle eût été longuement malade. Parquoi, aimant mieux faire tort à sa beauté en la diminuant que de souffrir par elle le cœur d'un si honnête homme brûler d'un si méchant feu, prit une pierre qui était en la chapelle, et s'en donna par le visage si grand coup que la bouche, le nez et les yeux étaient tout difformés. Et afin qu'on ne soupçonnât qu'elle l'eût fait, quand la comtesse l'envoya quérir, se laissa tomber en sortant de la chapelle, le visage contre terre et en criant bien haut. Arriva la comtesse qui la trouva en ce piteux état, et incontinent fut pansée et bandée par tout le visage.[41]

(remembering that Amadour had often praised her beauty, which in spite of long sickness had in no way diminished, [Floride] could not bear the thought that this beauty of hers should kindle so base a fire in the heart of a man who was so worthy and so good. Rather than that she would disfigure herself, impair her beauty. She seized a stone that lay on the chapel floor, and struck herself in the face with great force, severely injuring her mouth, nose and eyes. Then, so that no one would suspect her when she was summoned, she deliberately threw herself against a [large piece of stone] as she left the chapel. She lay with her face to the ground, screaming, and was found in this appalling state by the Countess, who immediately had her wounds dressed and her face swathed in bandages.)[42]

We might see this episode as true to Marguerite's exchange of public and private worlds—again, the most horrific wounds are dealt in battles of the heart, not of the sword. The climax of their passion, the episode nonetheless seals their affair as unconsummated. Amadour's response to her disfigurement—"[I will not] be deterred because you've disfigured your face! I'm quite sure you did it yourself, of your own volition. No! If all I could get were your bare bones, still I should want to hold them close!"—shows his desire for what it is, a will to power regardless of its object, much as Floride's self-mutilation reveals the vanity that has driven her participation in this affair all along. From this point to the impending conclusion of the story, the two lovers stand exposed, and their peculiar liaison cannot be rendered whole again. And yet it is hard not to notice that blood is implied but not mentioned in this scene, just as at several places in the story it is suggested but not depicted in scenes of war. (Narrating Amadour's three years of martial adventures, Parlamente again holds out against particulars: "Amadour did so many lovely deeds that all the paper in Spain could not hold them."[43]) It is as though Parlamente and Marguerite do not see blood where it must be expected and record its least probable appearances instead. At the end of a fiction of wars, accidents, and traumas, the only visible blood comes from a nosebleed—a seeming illogic that reveals something about how blood is imagined in the world of this fiction and beyond. While an account of private and material blood is largely missing in midcentury European thought, this story is arranged to allow for nothing else; and wherever the blood of private experience is about to be transformed into public signage, as in Floride's disfigurement, it becomes invisible. Like Surrey and other contemporaries, Marguerite seems intrigued by the involuntary display of blood as an ensign of passion. In a memorable passage, she recounts how Floride sees Amadour, maddened by lust, with his face and eyes "so changed that the most beautiful face in the world became red like fire, and a sweet and kind expression so horrible and furious that it seemed a raging fire burned in his heart and his face."[44] This showing forth of blood is recognized by many of the lyric poets of the age. As a writer of narrative fiction, however, Marguerite is obliged to throw this tableau into motion, applying it to the wider world of action besides feeling, and she does so by refusing to join in the conventional narrative values around blood. It is not idealized: her characters see blood, have blood, in connection with their deepest selves, but it cannot stand in for heroism or martyrdom. It is not volitional: blood appears not where they summon it by their deeds, but only where it is unexpected and inexplicable. Most important, it is oblique to human purposes. However Marguerite's characters live with blood, they cannot write in it. It cannot be disposed to make reputations, consolidate power, or tell stories. In the interval between conceptual regimes, while the theory of humors is not yet replaced by the theory of circulation, sixteenth-century observers explore the matter of blood's secret life as a substance that belongs to no system and no power but is part of quotidian life. Marguerite's tenth story forces blood and private experience together.

Some twenty years later, George Gascoigne published the two editions of his prose fiction *The Adventures of Master F. J.*, another courtly tale in which two lovers, F. J. and Elinor, carry out a passionate but inconclusive love affair until it dissolves in mutual recriminations. While Marguerite's story is told from a female perspective, Gascoigne's is emphatically male; in each story one sex is represented as natural in its inclinations, while the other is mysterious, volatile, illegible. Early on in Gascoigne's story, when the two principal characters are newly acquainted, F. J. conveys his desire to Elinor by means of an amateurish love poem that ends with this envoy: "To you these few suffice, your wits be quick and good, / You can conject by change of hue what humours feed my blood." While the literature of the middle sixteenth century and after is saturated with such allusions to

the humors, they often weigh little alongside the striking figures—of
blush, rage, pulse—that are everywhere in this period, evoking blood
as everyday matter and an index of private feeling. Having made a
perfunctory gesture toward the received notion of blood as humor,
Gascoigne propels *The Adventures of Master F. J.* into the uncertainties
of its era. After an exchange of flirtatious letters and conversation,
Elinor provokes one of the critical episodes in the fiction:

> The Dame (whether it were by sodain chaunge, or of wonted cus-
> tome) fell one day into a great bleeding at the nose. For which accident
> the said *F. J.* amongst other prety conceits, had a present remedy,
> wherby he tooke occasion (when they of the house had all in vayne
> sought many ways to stop hir bleeding) to worke his feate in this
> wyse: First he pleaded ignorance, as though he knewe not hir name,
> and therefore demaunded the same of one other Gentlewoman in the
> house, whose name was Mistres Frances, who when shee had to him
> declared that hir name was *Elinor*, he said these wordes or very lyke
> in effect: If I thought I should not offend Mystres *Elynor*, I would
> not doubt to stop hir bleeding, without eyther payne or difficulty. . . .
>
> *F. J.* repayred to the chamber of his desired: and finding hir sette
> in a chayre, leaning on the one side over a silver bason: After his
> due reverence, hee layd his hand on hir temples, and privily round-
> ing hir in hir eare, desired hir to commaund a Hazell sticke and a
> knyfe: the which being brought, hee delivered unto hir, saying on
> this wyse. Mystres I will speak certen words in secret to my selfe, and
> doe require no more: but when you heare me saie openly this word
> *Amen*, that you with this knyfe will make a nycke uppon this hasell
> stycke: and when you have made fyve nickes, commaunde mee also
> to cease. The Dame partly of good wil to the knight, and partly to
> be stenched of hir bleeding, commaunded hir mayd, and required
> the other gentils, somewhat to stand asyde, which done, he began his
> oraisons, wherein he had not long muttered before he pronounced
> *Amen*, wherewith the Lady made a nyck on the stick with hir knyfe.
> The said *F. J.* continued to an other *Amen*, when the Lady having
> made an other nyck felt hir bleeding, began to steynch: and so by the
> third *Amen* throughly steinched. *F. J.* then chaunging his prayers into
> private talk, said softly unto hir. Mystres, I am glad that I am hereby

enabled to do you some service, and as the staunching of your own bloud may some way recomfort you, so if the shedding of my bloud may any way content you, I beseech you commaund it, for it shalbe evermore readily employed in your service, and therwithal with a loud voyce pronounced *Amen*: wherwith the good Lady making a nyck did secretly answere thus. Good servaunt (quod shee) I must needs think my self right happy to have gained your service and good will, and be you sure, that although ther be in me no such desert as may draw you into this depth of affection, yet such as I am, I shalbe alwayes be glad to shewe my self thankfull unto you, and now, if you think your self assured, that I shall bleede no more, doe then pronounce your fifth *Amen*, the which pronounced, shee made also hir fifth nicke, and held up hir head, calling the company unto hir, and declaring unto them, that hir bleeding was throughly steinched.[45]

Continuing where Marguerite's story left off, Gascoigne's *The Adventures of Master F. J.* imagines, in Elinor's nosebleed, a private blood that signifies passion and intimacy but nonetheless is amenable to interpretation and regulation. Where Marguerite removed blood from the public to the private world and left it as a product of Floride's frustration, a cipher, a sign of uncertain reference, Gascoigne further circumscribes his story in a rarified world of great houses and seignorial estates, allowing his lovers to treat blood there as a vehicle of communication, of a private language or sign system. And where Marguerite erased blood from the settings of war and patrimony and showed its meanings to be equivocal where it did explicitly or otherwise appear, Gascoigne represents his lovers in seemingly perfect communication through blood; only the denouement of the story will reveal that this exchange is an illusion, that blood remains an illegible, ungovernable substance. Marguerite and Gascoigne are among the writers—including Sidney, Shakespeare, Lodge, Nashe, Deloney, Ford, Webster, and many others—who treat the epistaxis or nosebleed "on the sudden" and "by chance" as the bodily sign of the age, an index of passion that cannot be transposed into ritual or language, a reminder of blood's irruptions into everyday bodily experience, and a souvenir of the fact that its motions and appearances are poorly explained in received thought.[46] Where we find nosebleeds in the context of a multivalent literary account of blood—as humor, as metonym for lineage or virtue, as sign of passion—we encounter a late episode in the discussion that runs across the latter half of the sixteenth century.

Twenty years after Gascoigne, Shakespeare's *The Merchant of Venice* offers an extended commentary in several voices on the problem of treating blood as a medium of private experience. For several of the issues that animate the play, such as religion, family, and social class, blood is already a metonym by custom. For others, such as commerce and justice, the play borrows blood as an arbitrary device, a boundary beyond which Shylock's confiscation must not go. Or is it arbitrary? Nearly all of the characters subscribe to understandings of blood that accommodate their outlooks on more urgent matters; when their conflicts arrive at a crisis, the incompatibilities among these different bloods stand exposed, a semantic metric for the jagged differences that drive the play. Meanwhile, one received understanding of blood supposedly in force at this time, that of the humors, is probably the least adequate outlook—as Shylock himself demonstrates when he mocks those who would ask why he chooses flesh over ducats: "I'll not answer that; / But say it is my humor, is it answer'd?"[47] The implication here and throughout the play is that neither the established doctrine of the humors nor the debased senses of the term (as "whim") current in the 1590s suffices to explain the feelings abroad in this world, whether Shylock's willful distortion of the capitalist ethos, Antonio's sadness, or Portia's weariness. Most of the main characters live by urges and emotions that overgo the available explanations, and the theory of humors holds a particular office—indispensable as intellectual background, but inadequate to this densely textured reality. How, the play asks, can blood be limited to any single model? If it belongs to all of them and none of them, then we are invited to cast new attention on blood itself as itself— the substance not only of human life but of many worldviews. *The Merchant of Venice* deposits us in Shakespeare's distinctive moment of a multivalent blood whose material reality is more intriguing than any allegory.

In the play's contest of bloods, on the one side is the unreflective Gratiano, who counsels Antonio in the play's first scene with exhortations and stale bromides:

> Let me play the fool,
> With mirth and laughter let old wrinkles come,
> And let my liver rather heat with wine
> Than my heart cool with mortifying groans.
> Why should a man, whose blood is warm within,
> Sit like his grandsire cut in alablaster?
> Sleep when he wakes? and creep into the jaundies
> By being peevish?
> (1.1.79–86)

Here is one version of the state of the humors in Shakespeare's time: a reference point that has ceased to move anyone or explain anything, especially Antonio's melancholy. Likelier but still insufficient is the outward-looking materialist perspective of Salerio, who sees the origin of Antonio's sadness in the hazards of navigation and commerce rather than in the motions of the humors—the "tossing" of one fluid instead of another. Where blood is concerned, another obsolete but vestigial notion is that familial relations determine the nature of the individual. Launcelot Gobbo's father is the first to articulate this assumption in terms of possession ("if thou be Launcelot, thou art mine own flesh and blood"), and even his son, the least refined figure in the play, resists such an identification—he wants to cultivate the "confusions" of identity that come with not being the son—before he concedes who he is (2.2.92–93, 37). Likewise, Shylock reacts to Jessica's flight in act 3, scene 1 with a statement of this assumption, answered by Solanio, who (pretending or not) overliteralizes what Shylock means by "flesh and blood," until Salerio openly rejects Shylock's correspondence of bloods:

SHYLOCK.   My own flesh and blood to rebel!
SOLANIO.   Out upon it, old carrion, rebels it at these years?
SHYLOCK.   I say, my daughter is my flesh and blood.
SALERIO.   There is more difference between thy flesh and
           hers than between jet and ivory, more between
           your bloods than there is between red wine and
           Rhenish. But tell us, do you hear whether Antonio
           have had any loss at sea or no?
           (3.1.34–43)

Blood

127

Has "flesh and blood" as consanguinity lost its meaning in this society? Or rather in the contest among marginalized groups that is Shakespeare's Venice, has the pull of "flesh and blood" become a last refuge for groups and persons lacking any other claim on power?[48] The denial of such ties to the next group down the ladder is a stock means of domination. Jessica herself, in planning her escape, seems well rehearsed in the adjustment of consanguinity, from a law of identity to a kind of social fiction that can be put aside:

> Alack, what heinous sin is it in me
> To be ashamed to be my father's child!
> But though I am a daughter to his blood,
> I am not to his manners.
> (2.3.16–19)

Whatever Jessica believes, however, her flight and conversion activate a logic that will be played out two acts later in the trial scene: "for the loss of his daughter—his own flesh and blood—he will take the flesh and blood of Antonio."[49]

These speeches condition our understanding of Shylock's soliloquy, only a few moments after his exchange with Solanio and Salerio, in which he asks: "Hath not a Jew eyes? Hath not a Jew hands, organs, dimensions, senses, affections, passions; fed with the same food, hurt with the same weapons, subject to the same diseases, heal'd by the same means, warm'd and cool'd by the same winter and summer, as a Christian is? If you prick us, do we not bleed?" (3.1.59–64). Undercut by the construction of blood as family, religion, and destiny that Shylock and the Venetians endorse alike, this seeming appeal to common humanity sends a message that not even Shylock himself believes in. Where blood is concerned, Shylock's preferred ideal is consanguinity or the pull of family: one astute interpretation tracks his hope and desolation through act 3, scene 1 against the problem of Jessica's elopement, which directly threatens what blood means to him.[50] He does not normally accept a view of blood as the common substance of humanity rather than family, but here he is thinking aloud, considering the several bloods that are imaginatively available to him and choosing an emergent sense that will allow him, before the speech is over, to make a fresh case for revenge against the Christians. Readers and audiences given to Romantic notions of Shylock have often treated this speech as entirely modern, while materialist critics have seen it as a rhetorical strike against the ideological differences between himself and Christian Venice.[51] The speech is better seen, I think, as an emotional exploitation of blood's instability in this time and place, an erotesis or rhetorical questioning that avoids inquiring into how concepts such as selfhood, humanity, and blood are connected to one another. In this sense, Shylock's speech cynically masks his own complex views of what blood allows. But it also anticipates the climactic feat by which Portia will force Shylock to accept what is really the modern view of blood in the play, as a simply material substance that cannot be exchanged and belongs entirely to each human being. For rhetorical purposes he implies he believes that view here, though it contradicts his beliefs elsewhere in the play. He will soon be obliged to take that position more seriously than he imagines.

Yet another received notion of blood—entangled with these, yet embodied apart—is that it represents superior quality in breeding or virtue, as though better blood makes a better man. The Prince of Morocco, Portia's first suitor, speaks to this view when he urges Portia to "let us make incision for your love, / To prove whose blood is reddest, [a rival's] or mine" (2.1.6–7).[52] The play even mentions a nosebleed, though parodically in the voice of the clown, Launcelot Gobbo, as he predicts a masque while the masquers are already filling the street (2.5.22–27). As the play unfolds, then, many of the conventional attachments of blood, measured against everyday experience, are shown to be wanting. Will Jessica's love and faith be determined by her bloodline? Will Portia choose a husband whose blood is reddest? Even the nosebleed, which a generation or two earlier was an untidy, unexplained appearance of blood in the quotidian, has come to seem laughably portentous—but of what? The available notions of blood are both heavy with accumulated meanings and light of real significance. Perhaps the same is true of the play's larger beliefs: the Christianity of the Venetians, for instance, weighs little alongside the more urgent imperatives of commerce and friendship that drive their everyday behaviors, while Shylock's Judaism, likely warped by his oppression, is reactive and unreflective. Friction is the ground note of this society—between communities, between ideals and practices, between friends and within families.[53]

In this atmosphere of friction, the resolution of the comedy demands an accommodation. As the agent of that resolution, Portia knows better than anyone among the dramatis personae that principles always fall short of practice: "If to do were as easy as to know what were good to do, chapels had been churches, and poor men's cottages princes' palaces. It is a good divine that follows his own instructions; I can easier teach twenty what were good to be done, than to be one of the twenty to follow mine own teaching. The brain may devise laws for the blood, but a hot temper leaps o'er a cold decree" (1.2.12–19). Blood here is the name of a quality that makes persons act in unruly, unpredictable fashion. Together with Bassanio's self-assessments,

> Madam, you have bereft me of all words,
> Only my blood speaks to you in my veins,
> And there is such confusion in my powers . . .
> . . . .
> When I did first impart my love to you,
> I freely told you all the wealth I had
> Ran in my veins: I was a gentleman;
> And then I told you true,
> (3.2.175–77, 253–56)

this invocation of blood casts Portia and Bassanio as the characters least encumbered by the outworn notion that virtue is ensured by family, nobility, or the past or that happiness is a property of the unseen motions of humors. Rather, for them, when blood speaks, it tells of the individual; virtue is the outcome of a struggle within a particular person; and happiness is the result of a negotiation between oneself and the world. And blood for Portia and Bassanio, scarcely a vehicle for abstractions, is emphatically material and everyday, as though they recognize one another by how they treat the concept.

Bassanio's framing of his statement after the arrival of word from Venice allows us to anticipate that he will say something else—that his wealth is his family name, his nobility, his valor—so that when he asserts "I [am] a gentleman," a statement that nearly every Venetian Christian man in the play can make, we are obliged to realize that his blood is simply his blood, a token of honor and integrity that every figure, even one born female and Jewish like Jessica, can claim. "Gentleman" is the commonest social category in Shakespeare's plays; since gentility is defined less by blood than by property, the blood of a gentleman is a blood empty of extraordinary value but redolent merely of human worth and possibility.[54] A hundred years earlier, Bassanio's statement that the blood of a gentleman is a kind of wealth would have been virtually a catachresis, a figure of speech that seemingly goes astray because one of its elements is misapplied (the blood of a gentleman instead of a nobleman; wealth in place of common currency) but still makes sense. A hundred years after Shakespeare, when the term "gentleman" has become widely applicable, a marker of class mobility, the statement would be unremarkable. But in Shakespeare's moment, Bassanio's self-assertion shows the making of a new conceptual envelope for blood from the fabric of an older one. In the new order that only Portia and Bassanio fully inhabit in the play, blood is what it will be for Servetus and Harvey, the substance of life that is everywhere in the body at all times, that belongs as much to the commonplace as to crisis, and that, more present and recognizable than the other humors, lives beyond the limit of the Hippocratic and Galenic systems.

In the climactic trial scene, then, Bassanio and Portia unknowingly echo each other a hundred lines apart, both insisting that blood must be part of the resolution between Antonio and Shylock that puts the former out of danger. When after Shylock's refusal of six thousand ducats Bassanio insists to Antonio that "the Jew shall have my flesh, blood, bones, and all, / Ere thou shalt lose for me one drop of blood" (4.1.112–13), he unwittingly envisions an outcome in which blood figures as both a metaphysical element—signifying a bond between friends—and a material token representing only itself, with a value that cannot be measured or paid out. Adapting one recent discussion of *The Merchant of Venice* in economic terms, we might say that while blood stands for many things in the play, this scene demonstrates what becomes ever more evident through the sixteenth century, that the question of value around blood—we might frame it as use-value in relation to exchange-value—has reached a crisis, and accordingly blood cannot be exchanged, equated, or even quantified. It is only itself, a "short-circuiting" of the value-relation.[55] Speaking in the idealist register of friendship, Bassanio outlines a resolution in the commercial register of barter, much as the Duke of Venice anticipates another part of the resolution when he asks Shylock, "How shalt thou hope for mercy, rend'ring none?" (4.1.88). Antonio, perhaps the most commercially minded figure in the play, nonetheless operates within an older worldview where blood is concerned, and he barely hears the pledge:

> I am a tainted wether of the flock,
> Meetest for death; the weakest kind of fruit
> Drops earliest to the ground, and so let me.
> (4.1.114–16)

It hardly occurs to him or any of the other Venetians that blood has a place in their inventory of commodities; the claim that Bassanio will preserve Antonio's blood must be heard on the Rialto as commendable but hollow bravado implicating their friendship on the one hand and Antonio's person on the other—but not his blood itself, because blood means so many things in *The Merchant of Venice* that it is unthinkable as only itself.[56]

Portia, in the role of Doctor Balthazar, exploits the distance between a panoply of voices within the play who speak to waning notions of blood and the emergent perspective in (and especially out of) the play that favors a literal, mechanical understanding of it. When her injunction for mercy is refused by Shylock, she is obliged (and encouraged by him) to enforce the most literal reading of the bond:

PORTIA.	Have by some surgeon, Shylock, on your charge,
	To stop his wounds, lest he do bleed to death.
SHYLOCK.	Is it so nominated in the bond?
PORTIA.	It is not so expressed, but what of that?
	'Twere good you do so much for charity.
SHYLOCK.	I cannot find it, 'tis not in the bond.
	(4.1.257-62)

Here occurs unheralded the insight that gives the scene its denouement. Portia sees blood as an object with which to exert leverage over

Shylock's literalism. The position that she and Bassanio represent, that blood is a token only of quiddity and a substance unto itself, confronts Shylock's determination to read the bond strictly:

PORTIA. Tarry a little, there is something else.
This bond doth give thee here no jot of blood;
The words expressly are "a pound of flesh."
Take then thy bond, take thou thy pound of flesh,
But in the cutting of it, if thou dost shed
One drop of Christian blood, thy lands and goods
Are by the laws of Venice confiscate
Unto the state of Venice.
(4.1.305–12)

The power of the scene comes in Portia's resolving not only Antonio's mortal danger but the condition of blood as a vehicle for many of the values that the play puts into contradiction. She grafts Shylock's literalism onto the question of blood's nature, rendering Antonio's "Christian blood" an object—not the carrier of virtue or power, but property—that falls under the legal terms of the bond; the abstractions that envelop blood at many points in the play are dispelled in favor of a starkly materialist position, barely attenuated by the adjective "Christian." Interpreting the bond in this fashion, and of course severing "flesh" from "blood" in her injunction, Portia plays out in forensic terms what she and Bassanio have understood all along—the self-sufficiency of blood. Moreover, her echo of the covenant of Genesis 9, where Yahweh enjoins humankind from eating the flesh of animals in which blood flows, casts her emphatically modern understanding of blood as a restatement of the law. She reminds us that before blood was anything else to Jews and Christians, on the threshold of its allegorization through Yahweh's connecting it to the "image of God," blood was nothing more or less than the medium of life, apart from all abstractions.[57] Shylock, his sense of blood neither the oldest nor the newest, is stranded here. Not merely denied access to blood, he is blocked from its symbolic meanings that have been accumulating in the play, and offered too much access to blood as a thing that cannot be handled, counted, or equated—and it is the irreconcilability of these bloods that defeats him.[58] It might also be said that Shylock's inability to carry out the injunction argues for the inseparability of flesh and blood, but that inseparability is a relearned lesson that depends on attention to blood as itself, not the truism it has been for Shylock and others.

The exhilaration of the denouement comes when the dramatic resolution coincides with a recalibration of the concept of blood. Shylock and we are obliged to notice an emergent early modern blood at the expense of the retreating senses of the term. While the motif of the bond redeemed by flesh but not blood has a long life among the play's antecedents from the thirteenth-century *Gesta Romanorum* forward, Shakespeare alone sees in it the outcome of a cultural problem that has been voiced from several angles.[59] Even a close antecedent such as Anthony Munday's prose fiction *Zelauto: The Fountain of Fame* (1580) invokes blood only in the trial scene as a substance not to be spilled, but hardly as an object of semantic and cultural transformation throughout the fiction.[60] Portia's disguise and feat of casuistry—which also figure in the version in the *Gesta Romanorum* and in *Zelauto*—find an entirely new context in the later sixteenth century, when several of the most vivid *cris du sang* concern women such as Floride or Elinor, whose blood is the mute, uninflected sign of private experience. Portia as Doctor Balthazar resolves public and private matters together through blood in that she not only settles Antonio's debt but speaks to Bassanio in a register he and she understand best. The trial scene is a kind of love letter passed between these two modern observers of Venetian society. Adrift in a new order in which blood is not always tied to lineage, heroism, religion, or the cosmos, Shylock is no less a casualty of this new concept than he was before—there is something tyrannical about calling Antonio's thoroughly material blood "Christian" even when Shylock is denied the possibility of maintaining his own Jewish bloodline. But then neither conceptual envelope is fair to the part of Shylock that remains a proverbial Elizabethan Jew, and the final imperative of this resolution is to enforce at all costs the authority of the Christian Venetians. As one astute critic argues, in the resolution "Venetian society is able to have it both ways," convicting Shylock not because of his Jewishness—that would flout the city-state's well-known tolerance—but because he is "an alien" who has sought "the life of [a] citizen" (4.1.349, 351), a crime that then calls up a punishment particularly adapted to his religion, namely, conversion.[61] The contradiction of reifying blood as merely material and then invoking its "Christian" character belongs to this display of inspired hypocrisy. For that matter, Antonio, as "the only unmarried figure on stage at the end,"[62] becomes an object lesson in blood's self-sufficiency. His life is spared, but he has no further claim on the central couple, as though the feat of logic that preserved him also established that his businessman's blood is a closed circuit with no outlet in marriage, children, or combat. Portia advances an entirely modern agenda for blood, except when she reaches back enough to provide the play with a supposedly satisfying comic ending—and herself with a marriage, since she has vowed to marry Bassanio only if Antonio is spared.[63] Despite the inconsistency, and in the face of implicit tragedy, Portia—unlike the inarticulate heroines of Marguerite and Gascoigne who speak by mutilating themselves or simply bleeding—manages to make the emergent conception of blood seem fresh and necessary. The word itself becomes a metric of where one stands in the early modern world.[64]

For my purposes, the last word will belong to Cervantes, for whom both the received and emergent senses of blood are open to burlesque in *Don Quijote*. Spanish society enters early modernity saturated with idealist meanings of blood, and Cervantes has perhaps an unusual measure of interest in proposing, like Portia, a counteridealist representation of blood that will compel attention to the substance itself. For one thing, no less than in *The Merchant of Venice*, blood is a metric here. It distills into one concrete emblem the obsolescent values of the protagonist, who represents "an entire social class whose reason for being has disappeared, that finds itself in a kind of limbo waiting for new institutions and new social structures to develop where there will be a place and a role for them."[65] Like *L'Heptaméron*, *Don Quijote* registers the heat of not only social tension but intellectual ferment; the energies accumulating behind blood are too much to ignore. Accordingly, Cervantes advances the project shared by Marguerite, Gascoigne, and many others to the point that anything other than a literal understanding of blood is made to seem absurd. Like Shakespeare, he recognizes blood as a concept under revision and registers that revision for a less learned, more diverse audience than an earlier generation of writers had.

Blood in *Don Quijote* appears through a single word, *sangre*, that opens onto several conceptual planes with starkly different relations to the world at large. One of these is the heroic blood of romance, which encompasses the idealist abstractions of Shakespeare's Duke of Morocco. While Quijote himself sees this blood throughout the novel, the reader does not, for its power depends in part on scarcity and indirection. It is evoked in prospect and retrospect, as when Quijote sees an icon of Santiago Matamoros with a bloody sword or when he prepares for battle with the Knight of the Wood: "The knights woke [the squires] and ordered them to ready the horses, because as soon as the sun rose, the two of them would have to engage in bloody, single, and unequaled combat."[66] This sort of blood cannot be shed in the here and now of the novel, since the valor it signifies belongs to an inaccessible past and an unlikely future, but never to the present. Another part of the same conceptual envelope belongs to the clinical blood of late Renaissance science, which flows copiously from the wounds given and received by the men of this world. Frustrated on his errand to Dulcinea, Sancho Panza even pummels his own head and draws this blood from himself.[67] Subject to human disposition, such blood resists abstract meanings in favor of a matter-of-fact quality. And a third element is particular to Spain and its territories, namely, the *sangre* that is judged for *limpieza* or purity by statute and custom, betokening lineage as a *cristiano viejo* (old Christian), *converso*, or *morisco* (Jewish or Muslim convert).

One might ask of the novel the same question we ask of the Renaissance at large: Is this all the same blood? When a master and servant fall to blows in the confusion of a dark inn, or when a carrier thrashes Don Quijote in his bed, is the blood that gushes forth the same as the blood that signifies valor or that can be pure or impure? The contradictions of early modern blood are brought to crisis here, rendering the concept not only semantically open but—what we have not noticed elsewhere—illegible to the characters themselves, who cannot know how to connect a bloody mouth to the distinctions they maintain in principle or why a largely abstract concept should flow so freely that it makes the room a lake.[68] Cervantes stages this illegibility much as

Shakespeare does, by compelling attention to the material substance of blood, as if to suggest that the reality controls all of these abstractions. But he goes further, insisting on blood's condition as a fluid available to human agency. Where people make their own blood and control its appearances, the received abstractions will be in danger of collapse. I will look briefly at two episodes from part 1 of *Don Quijote* and another from part 2.

A little more than halfway through part 1, starting in chapter 33, the main plot of the novel is interrupted by the priest's reading aloud a tale in a manuscript, "El curioso impertinente" (The curious fool), to the other characters. The story concerns a husband, Anselmo, who decides to test the strength of his happy marriage to Camila by encouraging his best friend Lotario to seduce her; Camila and Lotario begin an affair, and complications ensue. At the tale's climax, determined to restore her reputation with Anselmo but continue her affair with Lotario, Camila mounts a scene, witnessed by her husband, in which she pretends to attack her lover with a dagger, he fends her off, and she plunges the instrument into her body in such a way that she seems to injure herself:

La cual tan vivamente fingía aquel estraño embuste y falsedad, que por dalle color de verdad la quiso matizar con su misma sangre; porque, viendo que no podía haber a Lotario, . . . y haciendo fuerza para soltar la mano de la daga, que Lotario la tenía asida, la sacó y, guiando su punta por parte que pudiese herir no profundamente, se la entró y escondió por más arriba de la islilla del lado izquierdo, junto al hombro, y luego se dejó caer en el suelo, como desmayada.

Estaban Leonela [su doncella] y Lotario suspensos y atónitos de tal suceso, y todavía dudaban de la verdad de aquel hecho, viendo a Camila tendida en tierra y bañada en su sangre. Acudió Lotario con mucha presteza, despavorido y sin aliento, a sacar la daga, y en ver la pequeña herida salió del temor que hasta entonces tenía y de nuevo se admiró de la sagacidad, prudencia y mucha discreción de la hermosa Camila. . . .

Leonela tomó, como se ha dicho, la sangre a su señora, que no era más de aquello que bastó para acreditar su embuste, y, lavando con un poco de vino la herida, se la ató lo mejor que supo, diciendo tales razones en tanto que la curaba, que, aunque no hubieran precedido otras, bastaran a hacer creer a Anselmo que tenía en Camila un simulacro de la honestidad.[69]

([Camila] was acting out that strange deception and lie so vividly that in order to give it the appearance of truth, she tried to color it with her own blood; seeing that she could not reach Lothario, . . . and struggling to free from Lothario's grasp the hand that held the dagger, she finally succeeded, aimed the point at a part of her body that she could wound, but not deeply, and plunged it in above her left armpit, near the shoulder; then she dropped to the floor as if she had fallen in a faint.

Leonela [her maid] and Lothario were dumbfounded, astonished at what had just happened and still doubting its reality although Camila lay on the floor, bathed in blood. Lothario, horrified and breathless, rushed over to her to pull out the dagger, and when he saw how small the wound was, he stopped being afraid and once again marveled at the great sagacity, prudence, and intelligence of the beautiful Camila. . . .

Leonela stanched her mistress's blood, which was no more than what was necessary to make the lie believable, and washing the wound with a little wine, she bandaged it the best she could, and as she treated her she said words that would have been enough, even if nothing had been said before, to persuade Anselmo that he had in Camila the very image and example of virtue.)[70]

While in the denouement of *The Merchant of Venice* blood is revealed afresh as material substance and property, in this scene Cervantes goes further by entertaining the faulty connections between its material appearance and the abstractions of virtue and heroism. We see here what we never see in Shakespeare, an Anselmo who, witnessing actual blood, sees truth where we recognize deception. Instead of Portia's suspension of abstractions, this tale turns on Camila's shrewdness in summoning a host of them with a few drops of real blood. But this is only one in a train of such episodes.

Part 1, chapter 35 interrupts "The Curious Fool" with an interlude in which Quijote, asleep in the inn where the story is being read,

dreams that he is in battle against the giant who menaces the Princess
Micomicona. Sancho Panza witnesses the start of this struggle and
calls the priest, the barber, and the innkeeper from the reading of the
tale, saying

—Acudid, señores, presto y socorred a mi señor, que anda envuelto
en la más reñida y trabada batalla que mis ojos han visto. ¡Vive Dios
que ha dado una cuchillada al gigante enemigo de la señora princesa
Micomicona, que le ha tajado la cabeza cercen a cercen, como si fuera
un nabo! . . .

En esto oyeron un gran ruido en el aposento y que don Quijote
decía a voces:

—¡Tente, ladrón, malandrín, follón, que aquí te tengo y no te ha
de valer tu cimitarra!

Y parecía que daba grandes cuchilladas por las paredes. Y dijo
Sancho:

—No tienen que pararse a escuchar, sino entren a despartir la
pelea o a ayudar a mi amo; aunque ya no será menester, porque sin
duda alguna el gigante está ya muerto y dando cuenta a Dios de su
pasada y mala vida, que yo vi correr la sangre por el suelo, y la cabeza
cortada y caída a un lado, que es tamaña como un gran cuero de vino.

—Que me maten—dijo a esta sazón el ventero—si don Quijote
o don diablo no ha dado alguna cuchillada en alguno de los cueros de
vino tinto que a su cabecera estaban llenos, y el vino derramado debe
de ser lo que le parece sangre a este buen hombre.[71]

("Come, Señores, come quickly and help my master, who's in-
volved in the fiercest, most awful battle my eyes have ever seen! By
God, what a thrust he gave to the giant, the enemy of the Princess
Micomicona, when he cut his head right off, like a turnip! . . .

Just then they heard a loud noise in the garret and the sound of
Don Quijote shouting:

"Hold, thief, scoundrel, coward! I have you now, and your scimitar
will be of little use to you!" And he seemed to be slashing at the walls
with his sword. Sancho said: "Don't stand and listen, go in and stop
the fight or help my master, though that won't be necessary because,
no doubt about it, the giant must be dead by now and giving an

accounting to God of his sinful life; I saw his blood running along the floor, and his head cut off and fallen to one side, a head the size of a big wineskin."

"Strike me dead," said the innkeeper, "if Don Quixote, or Don Devil, hasn't slashed one of the skins of red wine hanging at the head of his bed; the spilled wine must be what this good man thinks is blood.")[72]

As the narrator goes on, "He had slashed the wineskins so many times with his sword, thinking he was slashing the giant, that the entire room was covered in wine." The innkeeper, furious at the loss of the wine, begins to beat Quijote much more fiercely than anyone would beat him if the room were awash with blood. Quijote's heroic "blood"—that which can never really be shown in the novel—is replaced by an even more prosaic and literal fluid, but one that has greater exchange-value in the quotidian order of this provincial inn. This is to parody the problem of articulating a discourse of blood as part of the everyday, because at one stroke Quijote seemingly accomplishes a virtual enactment of the early modern project around blood. But he only appears to carry blood over from legend and symbol into material reality: in fact this episode confirms that the blood of his chivalric fantasies has no place in the emergent modern world, that its parodic equivalent might be wine but that there will be no rivers of heroic or monstrous blood in this inn. While Quijote, with eyes of romance, sees all blood as heroic, even he would notice that there is too much of it here—but he is asleep throughout this episode, and after sleepwalking through the battle with the wineskins, is taken to bed without awakening.

Finally, these episodes are answered by another, in chapter 21 of part 2, in which yet another seeming irruption of blood changes the course of the plot. The rich farmer Camacho is about to marry Quiteria, the most beautiful girl in a neighboring village. Since childhood she has loved the poor shepherd Basilio, but out of covetousness and despite Basilio's many natural gifts, Quiteria's father has arranged the marriage to Camacho. Quijote and Sancho attend the wedding, and at the moment that Camacho and Quiteria appear, Basilio announces his prior claim on Quiteria and then theatrically impales himself on his dagger. On the edge of death, "bathed in his own blood," Basilio asks Quiteria to marry him since he is about to die anyway. Camacho, he observes bitterly, will be delayed only a little in claiming her as his bride. She and Camacho agree, the marriage is carried out, and then Basilio

> con presta ligereza se levantó en pie, y con no vista desenvoltura se sacó el estoque, a quien servía de vaina su cuerpo. Quedaron todos los circunstantes admirados, y algunos dellos, más simples que curiosos, en altas voces comenzaron a decir:
> —¡Milagro, milagro!
> Pero Basilio replicó:
> —No ¡milagro, milagro, sino industria, industria!
> El cura, desatentado y atónito, acudió con ambas manos a tentar la herida, y halló que la cuchilla había pasado, no por la carne y costillas de Basilio, sino por un cañón hueco de hierro que, lleno de sangre, en aquel lugar bien acomodado tenía, preparada la sangre, según después se supo, de modo que no se helase.[73]

> (leaped with great agility to his feet and with remarkable ease pulled out the sword that had been sheathed in his body. All the onlookers were astonished, and some of them, more simple-minded than inquisitive, began to shout: "A miracle, a miracle!" But Basilio replied: "Not 'a miracle, a miracle,' but industry, industry!" The priest, confused and bewildered, hurried to touch the wound with both hands, and he discovered that the blade has passed not through the flesh and ribs of Basilio, but through a hollow metal tube filled with blood, which he had carefully placed there; as it was later learned, he had prepared the blood so it would not congeal.)[74]

Having established that the blood of romance is unavailable here, Cervantes goes further than perhaps any contemporaneous writer of fiction in representing blood as what it has never been before this era, a substance whose ideality is pure illusion. Basilio's cry "industry, industry!" is the refrain of this shift. For blood in this episode is made aggressively literal, figuring itself but remaining an inert, instrumental fluid; and in the triptych of episodes beginning with "The Curious Fool," Cervantes shows there is no natural correspondence between the appearance of blood and the conclusions drawn by its observers, that counterfeit blood evokes the same values as real—and that where early modern blood is concerned, there is no place for the heroic or the miraculous. The reflection on a quotidian blood, imagined since the early sixteenth century and dramatized by writers such as Marguerite and Gascoigne, is realized here at the expense of the received abstractions. The cry "industry, industry!" seals the changes that have been under way throughout the century.

One is obliged to ask, as a concluding grace note, how a writer who has imagined the multifarious but always highly material bloods of *Don Quijote* could then conceive a story like *La fuerza de la sangre*, in which, as I noted, the *cri du sang* can appear to retain its force. Perhaps the convention might be understood as a superstitious tribute to a moribund system of beliefs, or a return by Cervantes to the kind of idealisms he mocks in the novel.[75] Or perhaps like Pierre Menard's *Don Quijote*, the *cri du sang* reproduced in the era of an individual, industrial blood may evoke a different set of assumptions and values through exactly the same conventions. Thus the boy's blood spilt at the center of the tale is only itself a liquid whose appearance provokes a series of social acts that end by reestablishing consanguinity, reconstituting by coincidence something that has otherwise lost its force—but the object of the tale is blood, not consanguinity. The power of this blood is the power not of the received *cri du sang* nor of superstition, but of its distinctive moment, between allegories. An envelope—or so the lexicographer Thomas Blount has it in his *Glossographia* (1661)—involves not only the act of enclosure but the possibility that an enclosed object is encumbered, burdened, even embarrassed by its wrapping. Shakespeare and Cervantes show blood both inhabiting a received conceptual envelope and remaking that enclosure from the inside out.

WORLD

In the later 1550s, the Scottish polymath George Buchanan launched a strident attack in verse on the Portuguese colonial enterprise in Brazil and less directly on the entire apparatus of European empire. The poem, written like all of Buchanan's poetry in Latin, is titled "In colonias brasilienses":

> Pars ista mundi, quam sibi propriam
>   Sedem dicavit mollis amœnitas
> Luxusque, sub fœdis colonis
>   Servitium tolerat pudendum. . . .
>
> Ignota rostris verrimus æquora,
>   Gentes quietas sollicitavimus
> Terrore belli, orbisque pacem
>   Miscuimus misero tumultu.
>
> Per ferrum et ignes et mare naufragum
>   Secreta rerum claustra refregimus,
> Ne deesset impuris cinædis
>   Prostibulum Veneris nefandæ.

Gens illa nullos mitis in hospites,
    Et ora victu assueta nefario,
Portenta conspexit Cyclopum
    Sanguineâ dape fœdiora.

Nunc Scylla, sævos exsere nunc canes,
    Nunc nunc, Charybdis, vortice spumeo
Convolve fluctus, et carinas
    Flagitiis gravidas resorbe.

Aut hisce tellus in patulos specus,
    Ætherve flammis perde sequacibus
Turpes colonos, Christianæ
    Dedecus opprobriumque terræ.

(That part of the world which a gentle and temperate exuberance
    Has consecrated as its own seat and proper place,
Suffers a shameful servitude
    Under the rule of these disgusting settlers. . . .

We swept unknown waters with our prows;
    We went after peaceful peoples
With the terror of war, and we stirred
    Misery and tumult into the peace of the world.

Through iron and fire and a sea of shipwrecks,
    We have broken down the secret bar of things,
So that no place will be free of the unspeakable lust
    Perpetrated by the filthy perverts.

Those people hospitable to no guests,
    And shores accustomed to an unspeakable diet,
Have looked upon sights more disgraceful
    Than the bloody feasts of the Cyclops.

Now Scylla, let out your raging dogs,
    Now Charybdis, make your stream

World

A spumy whirlpool, and swallow ships
    Laden with disgraces.

Or split open, earth, in gaping caves,
    And destroy, heavens, with resistless flames
The foul colonists, the shame and dishonor
    Of Christian lands.)[1]

Poet, republican theorist, historian, and playwright, Buchanan was perhaps the most worldly Scotsman of the sixteenth century. Over the course of his career, he went from being an admirer of the empire of the king of Spain and Holy Roman emperor Charles V and, after 1547, of the Portuguese empire of John III, for whom he worked at Coimbra as a professor of Greek, to being one of the most ardent critics of those empires. Buchanan wore many ideologies at the same time, including Calvinism, anticlericalism, and the theory of resistance, and during his extended periods of living in England, France, and Portugal, he was often in trouble with the church authorities; in 1550 he was arrested by the Inquisition in Portugal and held for two years, after which he emerged to write bitter dissections of the same imperial projects he had earlier celebrated. Much of Buchanan's criticism was concentrated on Brazil, which as he saw it took the Portuguese out of their natural place and into a steep moral decline brought about by expanding clerical authority and commercial desire. His attacks on the enterprise of Brazil, as in this poem, often take a semantic and rhetorical approach that is available in the period for many critical and speculative uses. He asks not only whether empire is justified in the usual spiritual and political senses but how it affects the understanding of the world for himself and his contemporaries. What is a world? What was a world to the ancients? And how has the arrival of modernity inflected the received understandings of the concept and compelled a making of new horizons? Anything but abstract, these questions belong to a problem of definition that is not limited to one term, *world*, but unfolds across the entire vocabulary of singularity and totality, the human and the divine, the subjective as well as the corporate. Further, the answers change over the period, as successive early modern generations rethink the nature of worlds and worldmaking for themselves.

The episode of *world* recapitulates the larger story of early modernity, but it enters the period inconspicuously. An anecdote might go as follows. Medieval observers of the *world* as a concept tended to conceive it as singular and unitary in the service of intellectual projects that depended on such a construction, whether the preservation of received and cartographic knowledge in a mappa mundi or the philosophical position of antipathy for worldly concerns known as *contemptus mundi*. Moreover, while the *terra* or physical earth could be an object of empirical interest, the world as *mundus* or *orbis*—partly physical, partly conceptual, always elusive—was often conceived with suspicion and disdain.[2] Petrarch was among the first to intervene in this conventional outlook with perspectives adapted from Cicero, Seneca, and other classical models.[3] For him and his early humanist successors, the world must be an integer, distinct from the nature and opposed to the interests of the self; but its parts and properties are identified so that they can be lent back to the self in an act that is not only imaginative but ethical, demonstrating the self's desire to turn away from worldly things. Instead of being forsworn, worldliness and worldmaking are annexed to the purposes of self-making. The *Secretum*, Petrarch's dialogue with Augustine, shows this kind of transaction: "See what snares the world holds out to you, how many vain hopes encircle you, how many empty cares oppress you."[4] In the Petrarchan project here and elsewhere to shore up the self as an object of knowledge, one "sees" the world to learn about the self, and when the transaction is completed, as Augustine prompts Francesco to assess his own outlook, it is the self that changes, has compartments, and is the subject of comparisons, while the world, singular and totalized again, stands apart.[5] Or observe how in the proem to Petrarch's *Canzoniere*, the *mondo* lurks in the final line ("what pleases in the world is a brief dream"), countering the foregoing thirteen lines of self-analysis, weighing almost as much as they do.[6] The arrival of Neoplatonism brought philosophers such as Marsilio Ficino and Giovanni Pico della Mirandola to consider the sensible world by the light of Plato, Plotinus, and others as the image of a superintending World created by God, a projection of the Good into the realm of the heavenly and the earthly, and a part of the orderly universe.[7] But by program Ficino, Pico, and their contemporaries are more interested in the world as a container for nature and a stage for love and desire than in its worldliness or the process of worldmaking; and their attention often turns away from the term *world* in favor of human concerns such as reason and beauty. In the first phase of the humanist enterprise from about 1400 to 1500, then, the self is the site of considerable imaginative energy while the world remains its antithesis but also its context. But then something happens, a shift in the reality that underlies the vocabulary, and the terms that stand counter to the self—*world, mondo, mundo*—come to be revisited under the pressure of events, a project that will continue across the sixteenth century in writing of every sort. Near the end of this first phase, when the first wave of humanism is about to disperse into a more searching and open-ended conversation after 1500, the signs of a reweighing of self and world together are everywhere.

The epitaph that was composed for Christopher Columbus's tomb early in the sixteenth century,

> A Castilla y a León,
> Nuevo mundo dió Colón
>
> (To Castile and Leon,
> Columbus gave a new world),[8]

confirmed a new commonplace in European and transatlantic ideas—that the imperial enterprise changed the nature of "the world" as the late Middle Ages had known it.[9] Exploration, conquest, and trade literally disclosed new territories to European observers but also contributed empirically to a general problem of the sixteenth century, namely, how to conceive the world under the pressures of the new knowledges brought forward by humanism. Accordingly, in a coincident but also succeeding phase, say from 1450 to 1600, "the world" comes into importance as a concept in several dimensions of geopolitics, science, and poetics, from Machiavelli to Sidney to Galileo. For my present purposes, the salient fact is that the increasing complexity of the world as a concept comes to inflect the original project of conceiving selfhood so that at the end of this period, it is not easy sometimes to disentangle self from world, and a statement about one can often be taken as about the other. This episode is not exactly a neglected chapter of early modern intellectual history. But it has too seldom been transposed out of platitude and into the workshop of literary history, especially for the richly expanded Renaissance of the past generation or two. The scholarly discussion has been rightly preoccupied with selfhood and its developing relation to nature, the earth, and some-times the world.[10] But the world itself—abstract, inchoate, often more epithet than concept—is the more challenging problem for a critical semantics.[11] Selves are fashioned in ways that we can narrate, but worlds are made and unmade across many settings by many agents.

The ground plan of this episode is established under early humanism, when philosophers such as Nicholas of Cusa take as funda-mental the mutual definition of self and world. One of the first early modern figures to think comprehensively about these two concepts together, Cusanus proposed several figures with which to bring the relation into scrutiny, including man as god and world as game.[12] In an often remarked statement, for instance, Cusanus argues that the human mind "is a divine seed that comprehends in its simple es-sence the totality of everything knowable" but that "must be planted in the soil of the sensible world."[13] For much of the next phase of early modern European individualism, a major preoccupation is the making of adjustments to that foundational idea: imagining how the mind or self can be embedded in the world, elaborating one term or the other, resolving the dialectical tensions between them in various ways.[14] From about 1450 on, the self and the world were found in a reciprocal, mutually defining state of relation, and the concept of the world, which had been singular and totalizing, was proving to be multiple and partial. It is as though the repertory of descriptive models for selfhood developed under the humanist program in its first phase was made to accommodate a new but complementary purpose, addressing the world in terms that had been reserved for the self. With that adjustment, new genres such as the picaresque—where the complexity of the observed world is often greater than that of the observing self—become thinkable, ethnography becomes as rich in potential as hagiography or autobiography, and a literature of empire, as opposed to mere travel writing, comes into existence for the first time.[15] In the thought of Cusanus, Columbus, and many others, as well as in the empirical acts of geographers, explorers, and rulers, we witness a characteristic humanist attraction toward the inherent liabilities in the term itself, for *world* is a term and a concept they (and we) cannot do without, but the dimensions of which can scarcely be agreed on. In this period, then, every instance of *world* is potentially the taking of a position as to what is a world, what is a self in relation to a world, and how the term *world* either suffices or fails to serve. Is there one "world"—"the region of all regions," the sum of everything that exists—or many?[16] If worlds are plural, how do we find access to one or another? What is the politics of their relations to one another? Recalling Vieira's observation that the discovery of new worlds had changed language, how do the several kinds of knowledge—philosophy, legal theory, theology, aesthetics—address the realization that this term no longer names something everyone agrees on, let alone the stable horizon of reality itself? And how do poets, from the early humanists to the artificers of the Baroque, reconceive their roles as not only makers but worldmakers?[17] In this final chapter, I will investigate the discussion around *world* not in view of some other concept but for itself. As I will argue, *world* is a semantic engine. The parts of the engine entail a scheme of imagined properties that are combined to make new figures for the nature of the world, including two (the "global I" and the world as island) that I will anatomize in detail. The power and mystery of this marker *world* is one of the most vivid problems of the age.

In Buchanan's "In colonias brasilienses," he narrates the arrival of the Portuguese in Brazil as precisely a breakdown of the ontological distinctions between one and many, whole and part, as an effect of empire. A Brazil that is legible as "part of the world" before the establishment of the Portuguese settlement becomes broken and partial afterward, the explorers and colonists having stirred confusion and misery into "the peace of the world." Most striking, Buchanan indicts the Portuguese and by implication all European imperialists for transgressing the "secret bar of things" ("secreta rerum claustra")—in strictly empirical terms an ocean, but in ontological terms a boundary between states of unity and sufficiency and their undoing. By this view, the disclosure of a new world often attributed to Columbus is not the doubling of available reality for European designs, the most benign interpretation of the Columbian project in early modern terms, but the fracturing of an ideal integrity, a breach that cannot be repaired. In this argument, Buchanan resorts to a notion of the world as singular that proves highly resilient throughout the sixteenth century and is often invoked in polemics against the drift of several activities that define the knowledge of the era, from natural philosophy to imperialism. If worlds may be plural and even multiple, how are new worlds found or established? Besides the capacity of human invention, what are the limits on worldmaking? And when the coincidence of the telluric and the conceptual is broken—when the natural earth is no longer coextensive with the concept of "the world"—what are the consequences? Buchanan imagines an earth and world cracked wide ("aut hisce tellus in patulos specus") by the annulment of this coincidence, where ships returning from Brazil actually sail into the imponderable space opened by imperialism.

The zenith of Buchanan's attacks on empire is his cosmological long poem *De Sphæra* (Of the spheres), a polemic both behind and ahead of its time—a defense of the Ptolemaic universe and an attack on imperialism—in which the Portuguese (and Spanish, and other) imperial projects are criticized as reaching, through vicious motives and unreliable means, the insight that should have come through reason alone:

> Quærensque viam per devia mundi,
> Dum nihil occultum, dum nil sibi linquit inausum,
> Quod ratio longis nisa est extundere seclis,
> Illa oculis hominum ostendit, terramque fretumque
> Aeraque et gremio cœli versatile templum
> Cætera complexum tumidos se cogere in orbes:
> Et mundi effigiem per singula membra rotundam,
> Pendentemque suo et libratam pondere terram
> In media mediam mundi regione locatam:
> Et circumfusos cunctis e partibus orbes
> Ætheris, in medium toto procumbere nisu,
> Inque globum cogi nitendo, in seque volutos
> Nectere perpetuis redeuntia secula seclis.

(Seeking a way through the trackless regions of the world,
Fearing nothing hidden, nothing unventured,
Avarice showed to men's eyes what reason had done its best
To hammer out over the long course of centuries:
This is the fact that earth, sea, and air taken together,
And the turning temple in the bosom of the heavens
Which embraces everything—that they have a spherical shape;
And that the earth, hanging and balanced by its own weight,
Is the veritable image, in each and every part, of the universal
    whole,
The midpoint situated in the midst of the macrocosm.)[18]

For Buchanan, the exploration that moves to undo the unity and singularity of the pre-1492 world seems to pull that world apart into
incommensurable pieces. By descrying the spherical shape of the globe,
the Iberian explorers and their successors only enable us to identify a
larger whole of which those old and new worlds are properly parts,
the celestial spheres from which imperial exertions look paltry and
inconsequential. Greed is therefore a caricature of reason that nonetheless arrives at the same end, if we resist the temptation to see empire
on its own terms and instead render it partial. This is Buchanan's cor-
rosively ironic way of reimagining the period's figure of geopolitical
entirety and sufficiency, empire itself, as a process leading to a more
encompassing kind of knowledge. What an imperial perspective does
to the indigenous and local, the celestial does to the imperial, and
the singularity and integrity of the world is reestablished, although
through a detour into the preoccupations for multiplicity and partiality
over which many of Buchanan's contemporaries obsess.

As Buchanan's *De Sphæra* discloses, early modern writers tended
to think about the world as a concept by entering into an intellectual
scheme that is articulated nowhere in full but nonetheless informs
many of the period's assumptions, not to mention its critical investigations of worlding by figures such as Buchanan, Giordano Bruno,
and Galileo. Such poets, philosophers, and geographers often pose
alternative conditions—such as the states of wholeness and disintegra-
tion implied in Buchanan's observation that exploration and conquest
divided a once integral world into confused segments—and then insist

that the world exists, simply "is," in one of these conditions. As the alternatives are often posed, the world is

Entire	or	Partial
Singular	or	Multiple
Corporeal	or	Abstract
Natural	or	Constructed

The left column accords with received ideas of the world out of Aristotelian and Ptolemaic cosmology, while the right represents the cracks in this classical consensus that were to open across philosophy, theology, astronomy, and fiction from the sixteenth to the middle seventeenth century. For the earliest humanists, such as Petrarch and Coluccio Salutati, the Aristotelian and Ptolemaic cosmos allowed too little scope for human freedom, and thus while they tend to envision a unitary, singular world, they propose one that accommodates human action in its making.[19] A century later, Giovanni Pontano's cosmological poem *Urania* celebrated both God's creation of the earth and humankind's invention of something like the world of culture, leaving little doubt that he conceived the celestial world by analogy with the earthly, material one.[20] With the publication of Nicholas Copernicus's *De Revolutionibus Orbium Caelestium* (On the revolutions of the celestial spheres) in 1543, a more radical question became unavoidable: Was the earth one planet among many circling one sun among many, or was it the unique center of creation?[21]

For the succeeding two or three generations, the word and concept of *world* seemed in play everywhere. And when in the seventeenth century Galileo's *Dialogo sopra i due massimi sistemi del mondo* (Dialogue concerning the two chief world systems [1632]) summarizes the state of advanced thinking, he addresses many of the alternatives through the voices of his dialogists as they argue over the motion of the planets, the corruptibility of the celestial spheres, and ultimately the nature of the earth as one of the planets that circles the sun.[22] For the semantics of *world*, the setting of Galileo's dialogue in its era of observational science puts into relief two events that were always latent in the humanist project: the unsettling of the term *world* from both of the related terms to which it sometimes corresponds, namely, *earth* and *universe*, and the loosening of its range of application between the terrestrial and the cosmological. No longer necessarily the *oikoumene* (the inhabited world) or the *kosmos*, ambiguated by possibilities such as partiality and multiplicity, the *world* as concept comes to float free of its stock meanings.[23] After the revisions to the term by seven generations of early modern thinkers, it remains for the post-Copernican, post-Galilean philosophers and artists to reinvest *world* with new senses.

While each of the columns implies a consistent set of values, it is not only possible but commonplace for a given iteration of "the world" to join elements from both, reflecting the complexity of the topic at the risk of incoherence. For many early modern thinkers, the first issue is singularity versus plurality. Is there, perhaps by definition, one world, as today we might say there is necessarily one universe, or are there several, or many?[24] The antiquity of a notion of plural worlds is well known: Alexander the Great's lament ("Is it not worthy of tears" that "when the number of worlds is infinite, we have not yet become lords of a single one?") was a familiar dictum in the Renaissance.[25] To many observers of the period, astronomy and geographical exploration seemed to lend new promise to an exhilarating sense of multiple worlds.[26] A complementary issue, as we see in *De Sphaera*, is that of entirety versus partiality. Is a given world entire and self-sufficient or a part of something larger? The integrity of a putative world can often be ascertained by the enumeration of its parts, many of which might seem to threaten to break into discrete worlds; and the same parts that assemble a totality can, with a shift of perspective, pull that totality apart. Some of the figures with whom I am concerned see the most pressing issues of worlding in terms like these, making urgent the promise and danger of partiality.

Singularity versus plurality on the one side and entirety versus partiality on the other: the coincidence of these two sets of questions does not amount to their identity. On the contrary, the configurations of thought that occupy early modern speculations about worlding—conceiving, say, a plurality of entire, self-sufficient worlds or a singular world that is fully constructed rather than natural—often draw on parts of this scheme with divergent, potentially contradictory implications. The scheme provides for any number of possible conditions that make the concept of the world thinkable. These conditions provide a principal basis, in society and politics, for ideologies, and in literature, for genres or modes—in other words, fundamental stances on what makes worlds possible or desirable. A writer who envisions "the world" as constituted in conditions of singularity and entirety, like Spenser, is reactionary for the times.[27] At the other extreme, a writer who sees multiple worlds and all of them entire, like Sidney, or all of them partial, such as Cervantes, is probably interested in exploring literary models that allow for a progressive decentering of power and knowledge. Spenser's unfinished epic all but avoids using *world* in the plural, as though maintaining a rearguard stance against the emerging fascination with plurality and difference. Sidney and Cervantes, by contrast, turned out sequels to their own prose fictions in which the closed world of the first is decisively, sometimes vertiginously opened in the second.

Of course, the implicit scheme that holds the properties of *world* depends on certain figures and conceits to give them body, rendering them not only imaginable but rich with implications. Early modern writers develop many figures for the world: the body, the poem, the moon.[28] One of the common figures of the sixteenth century is the kind of statement that might be called the "global I." This figure includes propositions, questions, and exclamations that join *I* and *the world* to emphasize the friction of these terms and often to improvise a startling utterance as the only available way of their inhabiting the same sentence. We hear an early instance of the "global I" in the soliloquy by the heartbroken father Pleberio at the end of *La Celestina*:

> ¡O vida de congoxas llena, de miserias acompañada! ¡O mundo, mundo! Muchos mucho de ti dixeron, muchos en tus qualidades metieron la mano; a diversas cosas por oýdas te compararon; yo por triste esperiencia lo contaré, como a quien las ventas y compras de tu engañosa feria no prósperamente sucedieron. . . .
>
> Yo pensava en mi más tierna edad que eras y eran tus hechos regidos por alguna orden; agora, visto el pro y la contra de tus bien-andanças, me pareces un labirinto de errores, un desierto espantable, una morada de fieras, juego de hombres que andan en corro, laguna llena de cieno, región llena de espinas, monte alto, campo pedregoso, prado lleno de serpientes, huerto florido y sin fruto, fuente de cuy-

dados, río de lágrimas, mar de miserias, trabajo sin provecho, dulce ponçoña, vana esperança, falsa alegría, verdadero dolor.[29]

(Oh life, full of troubles and misery! Oh world, world! Many have written of its practices and compared it with many things, but they spoke from hearsay. I will describe the world as one who has been cheated in its false marketplaces. . . .

When I was young I thought the world was ruled by order. I know better now! It is a labyrinth of errors, a frightful desert, a den of wild beasts, a game in which men run in circles, a lake of mud, a thorny thicket, a dense forest, a stony field, a meadow full of serpents, a river of tears, a sea of miseries, effort without profit, a flowering but barren orchard, a running spring of cares, a sweet poison, a vain hope, a false joy, and a true pain.)[30]

Even here, where the speech seems to honor the notion of a singular world as absolute horizon with the apostrophe ("¡O mundo, mundo!"), Pleberio evokes a unitary world in the process of becoming plural, a collection of epithets that are all but impossible to hold together in a single conception. The idea of the singular, totalized world is broken and reimagined to reveal unexplored depths of deceit and human misery; and the idea becomes dynamic as the speech continues, one depiction shading into the next and the chain of them suggesting a number of possible narratives. It is hard not to see, as the passage winds down, that what was presumed to be a single world "ruled by order" is about to become, for Pleberio and his post-Columbian audience, many worlds of human experience, opening into infinity. In some ways, of course, Pleberio's lament is merely an expression of personal disillusionment recast as a statement about the world itself, but I believe it is also an effect of period style—an observation about the changing understanding of the world in this era put into the terms of subjective experience.[31]

Another notable instance occurs in *The Comedy of Errors*, in what might be the earliest moment in the Shakespearean canon in which a character speaks in soliloquy. Alone onstage, Antipholus of Syracuse voices his feelings as a separated twin, a Syracusan abroad, and a sixteenth-century Englishman in Hellenistic disguise:

I to the world am like a drop of water,
That in the ocean seeks another drop,
Who, falling there to find his fellow forth
(Unseen, inquisitive), confounds himself.
So I, to find a mother and a brother,
In quest of them (unhappy), ah, lose myself.[32]

Like Pleberio's soliloquy, this statement imagines a relation between
the singular person and the world as an entirety. Once introduced here,
this measurement of the subjective against the global becomes indispensable to the worldmaking of the play, as though every standpoint
must be marked against the horizon, or as Luciana, sister-in-law of
Antipholus of Ephesus, puts it, "There's nothing situate under heaven's
eye / But hath his bound in earth, in sea, in sky" (2.1.16–17). It is the
nature of the "global I" that, as a statement, it makes either no sense
or too much sense; it is either a disorienting conjunction of literally
disparate terms or a kind of world picture that convinces entirely.
The power of the topos here is sealed through parody, when Dromio
of Syracuse celebrates his kitchen wench Nell by measuring himself
against her as world: she is "no longer from head to foot than from
hip to hip; she is spherical, like a globe; I could find out countries in
her," he says (3.2.113–15), and goes on to identify Scotland, France, and
the rest as regions of her body—"the global I" embodied, by groping.

The "global I" is only one of several such figures for the world
in this period. When sixteenth-century thinkers conceive multiple
and partial worlds, the island may operate as a figure for this sort
of fragmentary, extensible worlding. Islands are multiple—they are
proverbially infinite in number, a convention depicted in Bartolomeo
dalli Sonetti's *Isolario*, an inventory of islands in the form of a portolan
atlas published at Venice in 1485.[33] Islands are partial—every island
exists in relation to some mainland, as in the structure of Thomas
More's *Utopia*, where we encounter the island Utopia in a discrete
book 2, apposite to the Europe of book 1.[34] Islands are constructed—
a fact dramatized in the same book, where King Utopus fashions an
island out of a peninsula. How many fiction writers from Rabelais
to Margaret Cavendish have an island book in their repertory? How
many historians from Oviedo to Guicciardini to Stow have an island

episode in their histories? Each of these is a safety valve, letting off pressure within and around the idea of unitary, self-contained worlds and prompting reflection on the terms of worldmaking itself. Islands make possible the observation of their own constructedness, and the constructedness of other measures of the world, because they enforce a certain clarity: they have definable borders, they are conceptually distinguishable from the world at large, and they promote attention to the conditions of indigeneity and importation. In this latter dimension especially, islands often undermine some of the mystifications of money and power. Suddenly, in the light of insularity or what I call "island logic," the exertions with which capital fashions a world according to its own unquestioned values are exposed as exertions, we are encouraged to notice the trail of investment that furnishes the island with people and materials, and those whose power is untraceable and natural elsewhere are more easily questioned. We are encouraged to ask, on an island as nowhere else, not only what is native and what is not, but how these categories are established and whether what is naturalized by history and capital might be unmasked as constructed, imported, or interested. Island logic offers a vantage point from which the conditions of multiple and partial worlds are taken to their most unsettling extremes.

But for many of the most intriguing intellectual brokers of the sixteenth and seventeenth centuries, the variables of this scheme produce an equivocal outcome: a view, for instance, that there are multiple worlds while each of them is integral and entire to itself, or the position—which amounts to existential doubt for this period, and whose examples might include Christopher Marlowe and Walter Ralegh—that while there is a singular world, it is yet not sufficient to itself but riddled with signs of its being part of an incomprehensible, perhaps nonexistent, whole. The shadings among these positions are the most compelling not only for their implications but because of the philosophical reach of the works in which they figure, such as Marlowe's plays and Ralegh's *History of the World*.

The semantic possibilities within the concept of *world* operate as a set of moving parts, and together make an intellectual engine. By *engine* here I mean something different again from the other conceits I have advanced in the preceding chapters, such as the conceptual envelope around *blood* or the pendents of *tongue* and *language*. An engine is a moving object that produces motion in another object. Accordingly, a semantic engine generates effects not only in its near set of corresponding terms but across a cultural terrain. Having once held in conjunction meanings such as *kosmos*, *mundus*, and *aion* that evoked both time and space, the term *world* entered the sixteenth century with two alternating, coincident senses, more or less: the absolute horizon of being, what comes to be known as the universe, and the scene of human events. Much as it does in Pleberio's speech, the first sense of *world* as universe had all but fallen away toward the end of the sixteenth century. What had been the mortal, experiential sense was augmented by a still more personal and quotidian one, which might be called the scene not only of human events generally but of a unique human story. How any writer or thinker responds to these changes is often deeply significant for an array of other terms and concepts, many of which appear remote from the concept of the world. *Self* (as in the "global I"), *nature*, *age*, *space*, *land*: as *world* moves and changes, it moves and changes all of these words, concepts, and assumptions. From the cosmological to the quotidian, the concept operates on several levels of observation and experience. Its effects can be so diffuse that they may appear to name or imply "how things are," an incontrovertible reality, rather than a negotiated outcome among semantic possibilities. And yet across the long sixteenth century, every reader notices that More's parallel worlds, joined by the conceit of embassy that carries Europeans to Utopia and back, are imagined in a way strikingly different from Samuel Daniel's immanentist notion of England as "a world within a world standing alone"; and both of those are in turn different again from the incommensurable worlds of much speculative and fictional writing of the seventeenth century.[35] More than a word or an idea under pressure, a semantic engine absorbs but also catalyzes intellectual developments. It reflects changes in a network of related ideas but also changes those ideas by occasioning rethinkings. We should not be surprised to see *world* everywhere in the period, often in the thick of observations and arguments on the making of reality itself.

As I have mentioned, Cervantes tends to favor a position that holds for the multiplicity and partiality of worlds. After all, he is the author of perhaps the greatest island fiction of the seventeenth century, the episode in part 2 of *Don Quijote* in which Sancho Panza becomes governor of his island in fulfillment of the promises Quijote has made since early in part 1; and Cervantes uses this episode to respond vigorously to island books such as *Utopia* that depict their insular worlds as entire to themselves rather than damaged or incomplete. If, as I have noticed, islands are often figures for both worlds and fictions, the episode of Sancho's island gives us the last of the novel's many fictions within the fiction, and the most self-reflexive. Because a visitor does not cross a body of water to get there, we know that Sancho's island is in the most literal sense both constructed and insufficient. It is a village that has been renamed an island for the imaginative purposes of the duke and the duchess, the wealthy aficionados of the first part of *Don Quijote* who undertake to bring aspects of that novel to life in a kind of theme-park environment. And the episode of the island shows emphatically that the conditions of multiplicity and partiality are not static but dynamic facts, levers that can be used to wring truths out of reality by questioning the assumptions of this and other worlds. One of the ethical imperatives of "island logic," after all, is what Quijote urges on Sancho Panza in his advice to the prospective governor, that is, to "try to discover the truth in all the promises and gifts of the rich man, as well as in the poor man's sobs and entreaties"—in other words, behind the world as you find it.[36] Perhaps the paradigmatic exercise of what I have called "island logic" is Sancho's, where as governor he resolves a dispute between two men over a debt by literally seeing through appearances, breaking open a cane to disclose money hidden inside.

But I propose to look briefly at an earlier episode in part 2, from chapter 41, in which Sancho gives his account of the world's nature and complexity in terms that help us to measure the revolutions of the intellectual engine of worlding to see that the questions of singularity and entirety that vexed the sixteenth century have taken a new shape in the seventeenth. This is the episode of the wooden horse Clavileño. The duke and duchess insist that Quijote and Sancho, with blindfolds, ride the wooden horse in order to fulfill an adventure. As in a romance, they promise facetiously, Clavileño will carry the two travelers into the ether, and to ensure the illusion they provide that henchmen will surround the earthbound horse with wind (from a bellows) and fire (from matches). When Quijote and Sancho conclude a ride that has really taken them nowhere and remove their blindfolds, the duchess interrogates Sancho about his experience. He says two things of note: from the sky he looked down and saw the earth as no bigger than a mustard seed, and the men walking on it as no bigger than hazelnuts. The duchess observes that if the earth is the size of a mustard seed, the men cannot be the size of hazelnuts, but Sancho insists. Moreover, he says,

> —Así es verdad—respondió Sancho—, pero, con todo eso, la descubrí por un ladito, y la vi toda.
> —Mirad, Sancho—dijo la duquesa—, que por un ladito no se vee el todo de lo que se mira.
> —Yo no sé esas miradas—replicó Sancho—: sólo sé que será bien que vuestra señoría entienda que, pues volábamos por encantamento, por encantamento podía yo ver toda la tierra y todos los hombres por doquiera que los mirara.[37]

> ("That's true," responded Sancho, "but even so, I lifted up the blindfold just a little on one side, and I saw all of it."
> "Look, Sancho," said the duchess, "from just one side you can't see all of whatever you may be looking at."
> "I don't know about those lookings," replied Sancho. "All I know is that it would be nice if your ladyship would understand that since we were flying by enchantment, by enchantment I could see all the earth and all the men no matter how I looked at them.")[38]

If one were looking for a decisive instance of the rise of the Baroque, one might choose this conversation, in which Sancho—in a parody of the urge of many early modern humanists, explorers, and cosmographers—has seen the world, not merely the earth, and insists that it is the product of incommensurability, the sum of an earth on one scale and men on another. He insists that the proper answer to the question of whether the world is entire or partial is yes (to render his statement literally, "I saw it from one little side, and I saw everything"). The questions about worlding remain largely the same, but the answers to them, and the atmosphere in which they are asked and answered, feel entirely different from a hundred years earlier. In part this is a consequence of the change in intellectual and aesthetic climate. The Baroque is artifice's revenge against the humanist habits of mind that domesticated incongruity, disproportion, and anachronism, and its specimens tend to enable readers and viewers to step out of their historical circumstances and participate in "a marvelous theater of sensations."[39] The oversize utterances, curved forms, and unsubordinated detail of the Baroque represent a liberation of the senses that imagines alternative pasts, presents, and even futures in answer to the gathering regimentation of the real present. To the reader or spectator, the Baroque exchanges social and intellectual uncertainty for fictional and sensory liberation, an uneven bargain that nonetheless found considerable appeal in the transition from the sixteenth to the seventeenth centuries.

In artistic terms, the Baroque wields incommensurability as an aesthetic principle. Against a social background of increasingly ordered knowledge, articulated state power, and stratified class relations, the sensation of the incommensurable is that the elements in a structure might escape from their structuring, might resist resolution into a logic, might prove impossible to measure one against another by a single scale. The principal works of European humanism typically allow hints of incommensurability to disturb their surfaces, such as the existence of slaves in *Utopia* and the attendant potential for their experience to fashion an alternative narrative or such as the conjoining of religion and science in the *Lusiads*, where Vasco da Gama describes to the sultan of Malindi the fragile tissue of Portuguese national destiny as compounded out of providence and technology, implicitly raising the question of whether a single outlook can hold these standpoints together for much longer. The Baroque often starts from such intuitions of the incommensurable. The energies released in its process—which mark out Calderón, Margaret Cavendish, and Sor Juana Inés de la Cruz as different from Erasmus, More, and Camões—often seem to foresee the breakdown of humanist order and all its associated events, such as linear perspective, a system of value for all things human, and comparison itself. The Baroque favors logics that turn back on themselves, dynamic movement, overdeveloped figuration, and a cultivation of grotesqueness or monstrosity. In both debt and contrast to humanism, these qualities are among the forms of the incommensurable, a property that takes on a new urgency in the crease between the Renaissance and the Enlightenment. Where intellectual and social life is being ever more emphatically parceled out, the conviction that one parcel overweighs another, and might overwhelm that other in a sudden motion, becomes a vehicle for thought, an idea in the making.

In some ways, Cervantes's intervention in the discussion of worlds resembles Buchanan's. He sees the received dichotomies as inadequate to the complexities not of empire in this case but of simple experience, of which Sancho is the spokesman. For *Don Quijote*, singularity and plurality, entirety and partiality are interdependent concepts that we variously apply from our obviously partial perspective to an elusive world, and the most we can do is to leverage that partiality to get a view of these properties not in some ideal state but in the process of formation. To Cervantes and many of his generation and after, the questions become not whether the world is singular or worlds are multiple, for instance, but how the concepts of singularity and multiplicity become associated with worlds and worlding and how they relate to one another. Where Buchanan sees empire retrospectively as the cause of the instability of these terms, Cervantes treats fiction as the imaginative space in which they should be made unstable and mutually dependent.

In the last section of my argument, I will move into the later phase of early modern literary culture and suggest that an acute sense of the stresses and contradictions of worldmaking is important to the enlargement of literary and artistic concepts, in this case the appearance of the Baroque near the end of the sixteenth century. One might say that Baroque culture is predicated on a set of particularly rich and recursive responses to the questions about worlds that I have remarked in the first phase of early modernity, responses that seventeenth-century writers develop with an unusual degree of self-consciousness and play.[40] It has long been a commonplace in criticism that the Baroque is a style favored by poets who see "an indubitable connection between the emblematic image and their belief in the pervasive parallelism between macrocosmos and microcosmos, in some vast system of correspondences which can be expressed only by sensuous symbolism."[41] There is, however, a distinction to be made between, on the one hand, "the world" as invoked by a scholarship that sees it as a static term, a given, against which other terms that are thought to have richer intellectual histories play themselves out and, on the other hand, "the world" according to a criticism that sees it as one of those substantive terms.

In turning toward John Milton, Margaret Cavendish, and my conclusion, I would like to consider further how the Baroque stands for an imaginative working out of the problems attending the realization of multiple worlds. In general, as we know, Baroque artists propose to reorient that realization by capturing infinity within a circumscription, depicting limitless spaces within a frame, movement finally controlled by stasis, or plural worlds within the world. In the literary Baroque, the term *world* is an engine that not only raises provocative questions but mobilizes many representative works of the period. John Donne offers innumerable relevant examples, where his poems' worlds multiply promiscuously—so that a heart is a world, two hearts are two worlds, and every season begins yet another world—and yet everything is finally encircled by the poet's determination that there is one world after all. As though forcing the word through its early modern changes, his "Nocturnall upon S. Lucies day" exhibits three senses in the first three stanzas, namely, the totality of creation, an age within history, and finally a private zone between lovers.

If the early modern preoccupation with worlding has a tangible result in the culture at large, it must be in the concern of many thinkers and writers of the seventeenth and eighteenth centuries with how worlds are made and maintained that produces, at a remove, the novel. I will consider two cases. In Milton's *Paradise Lost*, the preeminent Baroque epic, the urgency of the questions I have been sketching is addressed both implicitly—in Milton's choice of a topic that depicts how worlds are made in Christian history—and explicitly— in the philosophical discussions that animate the epic and position its characters along the axes of extant theories of worldmaking. In a sense, the question of what constitutes worldmaking in *Paradise Lost* is a simple one. The world is what God makes in book 7, the primordial history of which is told in the body of the epic. But what is a world? In addressing this question, Milton establishes himself within not only a Baroque worldview but a certain emergent early modern understanding of dynamic space as implicated in worldmaking. For most of the principal characters must discover the nature of worlds and worldmaking as part of their education in the epic—and whether they succeed or fail in this enterprise corresponds closely with the theological and moral orders of the poem.

One episode in *Paradise Lost* seems particularly relevant. The term *world* first appears, of course, in the invocation of book 1, where it is introduced as if it will be one of the principal forces of the poem:

> Of Man's first disobedience, and the fruit
> Of that forbidden tree, whose mortal taste
> Brought death into the world, and all our woe . . . [42]

That term then recedes in importance for many readers because it does not seem as full of meaning as others, or, because abstract, it has too much meaning and is thus too hard to grasp. Still, where we see the term *world* in *Paradise Lost*, we see Milton making the kinds of discriminations on which the Baroque depends. Shortly after the first invocation, the speaker urges:

> Say first, for heaven hides nothing from thy view
> Nor the deep tract of hell, say first what cause
> Moved our grand parents in that happy state,
> Favoured of heaven so highly, to fall off
> From their creator, and transgress his will
> For one restraint, lords of the world besides? [43]

Clearly this term and concept carry some weight here, although modern readers have seldom given the question its due. That Adam and Eve were unable to maintain their stewardship over not only the Garden or the earth but "the world" raises the possibility that the uncontainability of that category might have been one of the "causes" after which the narrator inquires. Who can hold a Baroque world in hand or in mind?

But the passage I want to consider occurs toward the climax of book 1, where Satan addresses his army of infernal spirits. Milton here lays the foundation of what will come to seem a complex, often sympathetic portrayal of Satan; his speech will reach to an eloquence unmatched to this point in the poem. Facing his legions, Satan asks:

> For who can yet believe, though after loss,
> That all these puissant legions, whose exile
> Hath emptied heaven, shall fail to re-ascend
> Self-raised, and repossess their native seat?
> For me be witness all the host of heaven,
> If counsels different, or danger shunned
> By me, have lost our hopes. But he who reigns
> Monarch in heaven, till then as one secure
> Sat on his Throne, upheld by old repute,
> Consent or custom, and his regal state
> Put forth at full, but still his strength concealed,
> Which tempted our attempt, and wrought our fall.
> Henceforth his might we know, and know our own
> So as not either to provoke, or dread
> New war, provoked; our better part remains
> To work in close design, by fraud or guile
> What force effected not; that he no less
> At length from us may find, who overcomes
> By force, hath overcome but half his foe.
> Space may produce new Worlds; whereof so rife
> There went a fame in heaven that he ere long
> Intended to create, and therein plant
> A generation, whom his choice regard
> Should favour equal to the sons of heaven:
> Thither, if but to pry, shall be perhaps
> Our first eruption, thither or elsewhere:
> For this infernal pit shall never hold
> Celestial spirits in bondage, nor the abyss
> Long under darkness cover.[44]

One might think of the passage as a specimen that reflects the complexity of *resistance* in the period, but I turn instead to the shortest sentence here: "Space may produce new Worlds." Like much of what Satan says, this observation should provoke first a rush of agreement and then a more troubled reflection; with these words Milton has Satan draw from an intuition that many readers are likely to share. What does it mean? Satan foresees the creation of the earth and the establishment of humankind as the beneficiaries of God's favor at the expense of fallen angels; but he also seems to say that sheer distance from Heaven, and the illusion that he and his army control their own precincts, and the plenitude of their surrounding space, might be enough to fashion a world—that a world might be makeable from inside out as much as the other way around. The ambiguous subject—"space" rather than "God" or "we"—and the verb "produce" seem to promise that worlds might be invented or created as much as discovered, that they are indeed multiple and partial. We recognize the conviction from innumerable arguments and speculations of the sixteenth century. And yet: this is Satan speaking, and moreover he attributes this thoroughly Baroque conviction to a time before the making of what we call our world. In a disorienting stroke, Milton shows that angels in and out of heaven were probably debating the questions of worlding before our so-called world existed. Where Buchanan showed these questions to be legible in a political context, and Cervantes restored to them their experiential complexity, Milton argues that they are older than we can imagine. As a Baroque artist, Milton probably thinks that these are the kinds of questions to which art should lend substance; as a Christian, he certainly believes that God is the guarantor of a final singularity and entirety to his creation, however multiple and partial its specimens may appear to us. No less than Cervantes's episode of Clavileño but in a graver tone, this passage parodies the early modern preoccupation with worlding (are there any seventeenth-century instances that do not?) and demands that we see these questions in not only a historical but a cosmological light. Even if Satan as speculator is largely discredited, how can we be certain that in this case he does not voice a heavenly commonplace? Who is to say that God was not the first to ask the same questions that early moderns worry over?

The notion that Baroque artists who are concerned with the nature of worlds might be enacting the role of deities was widely shared in the period. Its expression is an idea that would be anathema to monists such as Spenser and would have surprised even pluralists like Sidney and Cervantes—that worlds are not only plural but fungible, highly contingent, and irreducibly personal. Perhaps the most complete expression of this assumption is the prose fiction of Margaret Cavendish, Duchess of Newcastle, titled *The Description of a New World, Called the Blazing World* (1666). Even more openly than fictions of a hundred years earlier, such as Marguerite de Navarre's *Heptaméron*, the *Blazing World* is conceived as a proving ground in narrative for ideas under development. In the prefatory note "To the Reader," which explains her publishing the *Blazing World* in a volume with her *Observations upon Experimental Philosophy*, Cavendish claims the purpose of repairing the breach between philosophy and fiction that runs through much early modern literary theory:

> The end of reason, is truth; the end of fancy, is fiction; but mistake me not, when I distinguish *fancy* from *reason*; I mean not as if fancy were not made by the rational parts of matter; but by *reason* I understand a rational search and enquiry into the causes of natural effects; and by *fancy* a voluntary creation or production of the mind, both being effects, or rather actions of the rational parts of matter; of which, as that is a more profitable and useful study than this, so it is also more laborious and difficult, and requires sometimes the help of fancy, to recreate the mind, and withdraw it from its more serious contemplations.[45]

For Cavendish, reason needs fancy to complete its work within the sphere of rational thought, and the figure for fancy's capacities is the world, understood as the "voluntary creation or production of the mind" in accord with some project of reason:

> And this is the reason, why I added this piece of fancy to my philosophical observations, and joined them as two worlds at the ends of their poles; both for my own sake, to divert my studious thoughts, which I employed in the contemplation thereof, and to delight the reader with variety, which is always pleasing. But lest my fancy should stray too much, I chose such a fiction as would be agreeable to the subject treated of in the former parts; it is a description of a new world, not such as *Lucian's*, or the *French*-man's world in the moon; but a world of my own creating, which I call the *Blazing World*: the

first part whereof is *romancical*, the second philosophical, and the third is merely *fancy*, or (as I may call it) *fantastical*, which if it add any satisfaction to you, I shall account my self a happy *creatoress*.[46]

While this striking apology has sometimes been seen in light of Cavendish's demand for authority as a female author and a royalist, it matters as much that she intends to give worldmaking a philosophical license as well as a literary justification and that she insists on authorizing not only second worlds but multiple, openly constructed worlds that respond to the fancy and the will of particular creators, who need not be poets. The figure Cavendish offers for the joining of the *Blazing World* to *Observations*—two adjacent worlds touching at the poles—is rendered into landscape in the fiction itself, where a young lady, forced by a suitor and his henchmen to sail away from her home, finds herself alone at the North Pole when her captors freeze to death:

> For they were not only driven to the very end or point of the Pole of that world, but even to another Pole of another world, which joined close to it; so that the cold having a double strength at the conjunction of those two Poles, was insupportable; at last, the boat still passing on, was forced into another world, for it is impossible to round this world's globe from Pole to Pole, so as we do from East to West; because the Poles of the other world, joining to the Poles of this, do not allow any further passage to surround the world that way; but if any one arrives to either of these Poles, he is either forced to return, or to enter into another world.[47]

With that, the lady becomes a proxy for all the early modern theorists of worldmaking who imagine moving from one world into another, as she literally does. She enters a new world populated by a ruling class of eunuchs, a general population of highly various complexions (including deep purple and grass green), and another kind of men of different "sorts, shapes, figures, dispositions, and humours," including some who look like bears, flies, and jackdaws.[48] Coming to the emperor of this new world, the lady refuses his offer to worship her as a goddess, settling instead for marrying him and obtaining "an absolute power to rule and govern all that world as she pleased."[49] The lady, now empress, begins a long interview with the inhabitants about their monarchy and monotheism, their social customs, and—what especially interests her—the phenomenal constitution of their world, such as the nature of light, wind, and heavenly bodies. The fatal step across the poles from one world to another, it begins to appear, was not the random or impulsive act of a frightened woman, but a first gesture in an investigation of worlds and worldmaking that belongs to both the lady and Cavendish herself and follows the preoccupations of late Renaissance culture. As the conversation continues, the bear-men, who are experimental scientists, produce telescopes and microscopes to show the empress their prowess at optics, but she displays her character as an unmaker of given worlds and a maker of new ones by asking for new instruments that can make great bodies even larger—a whale whose image cannot fit the glass—or much smaller. Like Sancho Panza, the empress courts disproportion and unsettles what is given. Even so, it is noted that no glass can show a vacuum, or immaterial substances, "or such as are between something and nothing."[50] The elements of our world may be visible or even knowable, Cavendish suggests, but the world itself is more recalcitrant; and a change in the semantics of *world*, allowing for worlds that are partial, multiple, abstract, or constructed, produces new conditions in everything that furnishes those worlds. Cavendish not only understands but represents, probably better than any other writer of early modern fiction, how the concept of *world* acts as an engine of early modern culture, changing (as it seems) everything in its wake. When the lady is about to arrive at the emperor's island for the first time, she encounters "a certain engine, which would draw in a great quantity of air, and shoot forth wind with a great force." The sailors of the Blazing World, she is told, employ these engines to make breaches in the waves through which "they forced their passage through," as if through rents in reality.[51] The lady herself as empress will be such an engine, questioning how worlds are made and finally making them herself.

The heart of Cavendish's investigation into worldmaking is found in the latter sections of part 1 of the *Blazing World*, where the inquiries made by the empress turn metaphysical. Convening immaterial spirits as her interlocutors, she asks at length about the nature of the Cabbala or Kabbalah, the esoteric corpus of knowledge in Jewish thought that discloses the nature of the creation, particularly what we know as the world. She pursues a number of cabbalistic questions about the boundaries between perception and reality, not least how the concept of world coincides with what we recognize as real:

> The Empress desired the spirits to inform her where the Paradise was, whether it was in the midst of the world as a centre of pleasure? Or whether it was the whole world, or a peculiar world by itself, as a world of life, and not of matter; or whether it was mixed, as a world of living animal creatures? . . .
>
> . . . The Empress asked them further, whether there was not a world of spirits, as well as there is of material creatures? No, answered they; for the word world implies a quantity or multitude of corporeal creatures, but we being immaterial, can make no world of spirits. . . .
>
> . . . The Empress asked further, whether animal life came out of the spiritual world, and did return thither again? The spirits answered, they could not exactly tell; but if it were so, then certainly animal lives must leave their bodies behind them, otherwise the bodies would make the spiritual world a mixed world, that is, partly material, partly immaterial; but the truth is, said they, spirits being immaterial, cannot properly make a world; for a world belongs to material, not to immaterial creatures. If this be so, replied the Empress, then certainly there can be no world of lives and forms without matter?[52]

What makes a world? As the empress inquires further, she proposes to make a Cabbala of her own that would decode the mysteries of the material world in which she finds herself and to enlist a renowned writer as her scribe—a Galileo, a Gassendi, or a Descartes. Every reader of the Baroque era notices that the empress identifies herself with thinkers on physics, biology, astronomy, and other branches of science whose speculations concerned the nature of the world as such. Descartes is exemplary in this respect: his unfinished book *Le Monde* began as an investigation of parhelia or multiple suns, then became a treatise on meteorology, then turned to physics. As the project approached a comprehensive argument about the making of the world, Descartes was stopped by the Roman Catholic Church's condemnation of Galileo's *Dialogo* and decided to leave *Le Monde* in parts touching light and physiology; the two parts were published posthumously in 1664 and 1666.[53] Like many Baroque thinkers from Ralegh to Sor Juana, Descartes was tantalized by the notion of explaining what makes the world, but then retreated from it under political and intellectual pressure.

Cavendish's contribution to this discussion is both a surrender and a victory: to redefine, perhaps for the first time explicitly, the nature of a world away from materiality and mechanism and toward all of the properties considered revolutionary in early modern thought, such as partiality, multiplicity, abstraction, and constructedness. At last the empress settles on the Duchess of Newcastle as her scribe, and together the two ladies imagine several modes of worldmaking familiar to early modern Europeans, including discovery, conquest, and experiment. Informed by the spirits that material worlds are infinite in number, the duchess considers annexing one, the sort of colonial gesture in which Buchanan and the Inca Garcilaso de la Vega found much to criticize. She and the empress are struck, however, by the realization that as material creatures they have the capacity to make an immaterial world "within the compass of the head or scull." Every human being, they decide, "may create a world of what fashion and government he will, and give the creatures thereof such motions, figures, forms, colours, perceptions, etc., as he pleases, and make whirlpools, lights, pressures and reactions, etc. as he thinks best." The duchess imagines new worlds according to the principles of Epicurus, Descartes, Hobbes, and other world makers, but resolves to invent her own, "so curious and full of variety that it cannot possibly be expressed by words, nor the delight and pleasure which the Duchess took in making this world of her own."[54]

Cavendish here represents as a growing awareness within the duchess and the empress what occurred by stages to European and transatlantic culture at large, namely, that worlds under construction are engines that produce change and motion across a wide field. Since the transformative gestures of Columbus and *La Celestina*, the word *world* had developed into a principal criterion for inquiring into knowledges. In Cavendish's fiction we can see the motions of *world* as engine even in relation to the deliberately constrained vocabulary of my project. All of the five words appear in the conversations between the empress, the duchess, and the denizens of the Blazing World as they suppose how worlds are made. In investigating her new world, the empress asks about the nature of human and animal blood there, seeking its literal character; in proposing her world, the duchess affirms that it must be "of her own invention," as though invention and authority create one another; in moving among worlds, she is obliged to inquire about languages; and in conceiving the absolute government of the Blazing World, the empress confronts the fact of resistance by her worm-men and bear-men. Everything I have followed is there, written in little. It is not that these five words have a special franchise in the period; one could probably find many words of common usage under Cavendish's inquisitive glass. Rather, where the concept of *world* is under revision it carries a great deal more in its wake, and the emergent modernity of the other four words—or any words—can often be found in proximity to that of the most complex one, *world* itself. The mobility of these five concepts stands for the general transfigurations of culture in words that Cavendish registers and answers.

Every moment, every period has its engine-words, and when we identify these we see the semantic and conceptual histories of many other terms crossing them in turn. The literary history of any language or period owes a little acknowledged debt to the story of those words that work as engines to throw off change across a wide semantic range. When we identify major authors or works, the coming and going of periods, and vivid thresholds in literary history, we ought to be concerned at the same time with words, not only in the sense of etymology or philology but according to the expansive view that sees *world* and other engine-words as fundamental to literary and intellectual culture. Of course words are hard to grasp critically, even as authors and works are naturally followed, explained, and rendered as protagonists and objects of attention. All but invisible according to much conventional interpretation, the fortunes of *world* and other engine-words invite us to imagine different stories of how literature works in society.

AFTERWORD

"Wordes tho / That hadden pris"—value or significance—"now wonder nice and strange / Us thinketh them, and yet they spake [them] so."[1] When Geoffrey Chaucer made this observation about semantic change in *Troilus and Criseyde*, he spoke for the sixteenth century as well as his era two hundred years earlier. Across both languages and time, Renaissance thinkers were preoccupied with words as vessels of change. Montaigne complained that words estrange us from reality—"when you hear people talk about metonymy, metaphor, allegory, and other such names in grammar, doesn't it seem that they mean some rare and exotic form of language?"—but knew that they make reality. "I am not speaking of actions, I am speaking of words."[2] A European and transatlantic culture saturated in texts and realities both old and new had a wealth of ways to imagine the power of words, from palimpsests to engines. In this book, I have tried to re-create some of those imaginings.

Five Words appears in the era of five hundred billion words, when digital resources make it possible to scan corpuses of published writings of the past for the contours of how words change. The resources made available through Google—recently enlisted for a project of cultural investigation based on the frequency of words in English, French, Spanish, German, and other languages between 1500 and

2010—allow us to see in schematic fashion how words rise and decline.[3] *Blood* in English spikes from 1580 and 1590 and again about 1640. *Resistance* sees two phases of interest, a burst of attention in the 1570s and then a durable presence in the lexicon of the seventeenth century, especially from about 1630 to the end of the English Civil War in 1651. *Langage* in French, *language* in English, and especially *lenguaje* in Spanish become highly visible in the 1560s and remain so into the new century.

It seems that these resources enable us to do in seconds what scholars have accomplished over lifetimes, to develop a sense of the rhythms of semantic motion. But a two-dimensional graph based on a computational analysis of five million books indicates only what it is not, a picture of change in three dimensions. I want to account for how *wit* evolves in a crowded semantic field and how *region* emerges out of the Latin *regere* to mean a place in which history and politics are rendered as landscape, a frozen story for the reader or visitor to discover, as in *The Faerie Queene* and *Paradise Lost*. Throughout the sixteenth and seventeenth centuries, *fancy* is inscribed on a semantic palimpsest that collates meanings such as "fantasy," "illusion," "imagination," and "invention." One wonders about *change*, a word that appears everywhere in the period but is seldom confronted directly. My approach to this challenge to criticism has been to make my argument inhabit a set of conceits that are themselves part of the imaginative apparatus of the sixteenth century. The nature of such conceits is not as important as how they respond to the challenges of situating semantics among other representational processes and locating literature among other discourses.

The kind of graph that we can extract from digital resources has two or three illustrative purposes. It can instigate attention to the fortunes of words, rendering in a stark drawing what can otherwise only be paraphrased. The suggestive power of such a drawing is considerable. Still, it puts us only at the beginning of a process of reading and sifting. It leaves us to distinguish important usages from trivial ones or to discern concepts in the absence of the words themselves. It does nothing to discriminate literary usages—as I have argued, often the most transformative—from instrumental or prosaic ones. And in the middle of a project of critical semantics, a graph can corroborate ideas coming into visibility, telling us where we need to know more. Such graphs represent not semantics, much less culture, but only a notion in the mind of the critic. They are hieratic. Between the intuition that draws up a query for a search and the intelligence that reads widely to gather context around the result, there is only the critic herself or himself. When we see such two-dimensional graphs we are looking at our own notions of the past, schematically or perhaps prospectively, and we confront the ethical imperative to give substance to a mere line, to build models of explanation and extrapolation. Only the critic can make such a line into something real.

What I have called here *critical semantics* responds to a long tradition of writing about literature and language according to words. In the end, the luminous term in the phrase is not *semantics*, but *critical*. Critical semantics is a critic's job of work, to adapt R. P. Blackmur's dictum, and the emergence of digital resources makes the social role of the critic even more vital. The critic of sixty or seventy years ago, a figure with a prominent (though hardly uncontested) role in the culture, stood between a circumscribed canon of past literature and a fairly elite class of professional writers in the present and explained all of that to a general audience of readers. Today the critic stands in a different zone, between the expanding body of past works made available digitally and an even larger production in the present. Even as newly accessible writings of the past often trouble the categories of literature, much new writing resists the conventional ministrations of criticism. I believe we need criticism as much as ever. But we have to revise the cultural economy that has lent value to our work. Or rather: that economy has already changed around us, and we must respond to it.

Much classic literary criticism was based on the premise that the ground of its discipline—the object of its attention, the source of its significance—was the literary work itself. Through the debates over methods that persisted throughout the last century, this was the article of faith that joined formalists, poststructuralists, and historicists. I have written elsewhere about the critical convention that I call the "in Shakespeare" problem, in which real-world issues are portrayed as finding their beginning and end in canonical authors: political thought in Shakespeare, the environment in Shakespeare, race and ethnicity in

Afterword

Shakespeare.[4] I call this a misplaced horizon, in which social, historical, and intellectual issues are located entirely within literature, rather than literature's being emplaced in the multifarious and unruly discourses of society and culture. The so-called New Historicism of a generation ago, which ostensibly considered literature in its most ample contexts, sometimes foreshortened horizons to produce arguments that really concerned a handful of canonical literary figures.

A critical semantics is the kind of approach that, instead of reducing the empirical world to a perspective within a literary horizon, puts literature among other kinds of writing and thinking. Perhaps we hesitate before such a method because it might reveal literature as a minor factor in some questions; perhaps we feel competent or comfortable only when we can see race or science or economics in the shadow box of literature alone. But I am convinced that we have gained local, disciplinary validation at the expense of a tangible link to the rest of the humanities and, of course, to readers. Shakespeare, Cervantes, and other major authors are among the many voices whose investments in five words deserve attention, but they are not the final horizons of this project—only the words are. The literary power of these figures is distinctly seen when literature makes its way among other discourses. This is to invite literary criticism to operate within a wider economy than it has often done before and to abandon some of its insular conventions in exchange for a less certain office on a larger intellectual stage. Most of all, a critical semantics displays what only criticism can do—to speak of literary representation as a powerful, indispensable factor in the culture.

Every period, in every language, for every critic, has its five words, the ordinary semantic integers that seem ubiquitous and even unremarkable but tell a story about a vanished world.

Introduction

1.   Leo Spitzer, *Essays in Historical Semantics* (New York: Russell and Russell, 1948), was perhaps the first modern exponent of a semantic history apart from what he calls "idea-histories" or the study of corresponding words (e.g., *Renaissance, romanticism, civilization*). William Empson, *The Structure of Complex Words* (London: Chatto and Windus, 1951), came to words as combinations of emotions, senses, implications, and moods out of his earlier work on ambiguity. Raymond Williams, *Keywords: A Vocabulary of Culture and Society*, rev. ed. (New York: Oxford University Press, 1983), more or less invented the approach to the past through a cluster of terms; a related approach is found in Martin Jay, *Cultural Semantics: Keywords of Our Time* (Amherst: University of Massachusetts Press, 1998). Reinhart Koselleck's influential work on conceptual history (*Begriffsgeschichte*) is available in English in *The Practice of Conceptual History: Timing History, Spacing Concepts*, trans. Todd Samuel Presner et al. (Stanford, CA: Stanford University Press, 2002), and *Futures Past: On the Semantics of Historical Time*, trans. Keith Tribe (New York: Columbia University Press, 2004). Theodor Adorno's classic essay "Words from Abroad" is translated in *Notes to Literature*, ed. Rolf Tiedemann, trans. Shierry Weber Nicholsen, 2 vols. (New York: Co-

lumbia University Press, 1991), 1:185–99. Perhaps the least systematic of the major approaches to semantic history is C. S. Lewis, *Studies in Words*, 2nd ed. (Cambridge: Cambridge University Press, 1967). At a further remove, and less relevant to my project, are the influential studies of concepts, metaphors, and images by Giorgio Agamben, Walter Benjamin, Hans Blumenberg, Carl Schmitt, and others.

2. There are any number of relevant accounts, but one that resonates with my approach is J. G. A. Pocock, *The Ancient Constitution and the Feudal Law: A Study of English Historical Thought in the Seventeenth Century* (Cambridge: Cambridge University Press, 1957), 2–6.

3. Juan de Castellanos, *Elegías de varones ilustres de Indias*, ed. Gerardo Rivas Moreno (Bogotá: Gerardo Rivas Moreno, 1997), 9–10.

4. Edmundo O'Gorman, *The Invention of America: An Inquiry into the Historical Nature of the New World and the Meaning of Its History* (Westport, CT: Greenwood Press, 1961).

5. I have been influenced by Stanley Cavell's conviction that "we learn language and learn the world *together*, that they become elaborated and distorted together, and in the same places." *Must We Mean What We Say? A Book of Essays*, rev. ed. (Cambridge: Cambridge University Press, 2002), 19.

6. For example, Lynn Hunt, "The Rhetoric of Revolution," in *Politics, Culture, and Class in the French Revolution* (Berkeley: University of California Press, 1984), 19–51; Donald R. Kelley, "'Second Nature': The Idea of Custom in European Law, Society, and Culture," in *The Transmission of Culture in Early Modern Europe*, ed. Anthony Grafton and Ann Blair (Philadelphia: University of Pennsylvania Press, 1990), 131–72; Jens Bartelson, *A Genealogy of Sovereignty* (Cambridge: Cambridge University Press, 1995); John Martin, "Inventing Sincerity, Refashioning Prudence: The Discovery of the Individual in Renaissance Europe," *American Historical Review* 102 (1997): 1304–42; Peter Harrison, "Curiosity, Forbidden Knowledge, and the Reformation of Natural Philosophy in Early Modern England," *Isis* 92 (2001): 265–90; and Anne Ferry, *"Anonymous:* The Literary History of a Word," *New Literary History* 3 (2002): 193–214.

7. I borrow the term "equipment for living" from Kenneth Burke, "Literature as Equipment for Living," in *The Philosophy of Literary Form: Studies in Symbolic Action,* 3rd ed. (Berkeley: University of California Press, 1973), 293–304, without sharing his idea of a sociological criticism.

8. Edward Phillips, *The New World of English Words* (London, 1658), Kk3i^v, L1^r, Nn3i^v.

9. On *history* as a semantic engine, see Anthony Grafton, *What Was History? The Art of History in Early Modern Europe* (Cambridge: Cambridge University Press, 2007).

10. Thus Sigmund Freud in "A Note upon the 'Mystic Writing-Pad,'" trans. James Strachey, in *Complete Psychological Works*, ed. James Strachey et al., 24 vols. (London: Hogarth Press and Institute of Psycho-analysis, 1956–74), 19:227–32, treats means of writing as representations of the structure of the psyche, a possibility developed further by Jacques Derrida in *Writing and Difference*, trans. Alan Bass (Chicago: University of Chicago Press, 1978), 196–231.

11. For instance, see the human geographer Clarence K. Glacken, *Traces on the Rhodian Shore: Nature and Culture in Western Thought from Ancient Times to the End of the Eighteenth Century* (Berkeley: University of California Press, 1967); the historicist John Danby, *Shakespeare's Doctrine of Nature: A Study of* King Lear (London: Faber and Faber, 1961); the new historicist Stephen Greenblatt, *Shakespearean Negotiations: The Circulation of Social Energy in Renaissance England* (Berkeley: University of California Press, 1988)—and many more studies like these. Danby considers *nature* and its meanings "the moving parts of Shakespeare's world" but does not reflect on or develop the conceit.

12. To cite only a few representative examples: for *conquest*, Inga Clendinnen, "'Fierce and Unnatural Cruelty': Cortés and the Conquest of Mexico," *Representations* 33 (1991): 65–100; for *matter*, Jonathan Goldberg, *Writing Matter: From the Hands of the English Renaissance* (Stanford, CA: Stanford University Press, 1991); for *imagination*, Murray W. Bundy, "'Invention' and 'Imagination' in the Renaissance," *Journal of English and Germanic Philology* 29 (1930): 535–45; for *rebellion*, Andrew Hadfield, "Treason and Rebellion," in *A Concise Companion to English Renaissance Literature*, ed. Donna B. Hamilton (Oxford: Blackwell, 2006), and Rebecca Lemon, *Treason by Words: Literature, Law, and Rebellion in Shakespeare's England* (Ithaca, NY: Cornell University Press, 2006); and for *experience*, Charles B. Schmitt, "Experience and Experiment: A Comparison of Zabarella's View with Galileo's in *De motu*," *Studies in the Renaissance* 16 (1969): 80–138, repr. in his *Studies in Renaissance Philosophy and Science* (London: Variorum, 1981), unpaginated; and Jay, *Cultural Semantics*, 62–78.

13. Gertrude Stein, *Lectures in America* (London: Virago Press, 1988), 157.

Invention

1. François Rabelais, *Le Tiers Livre*, ed. M. A. Screech (Geneva: Droz, 1964), 327.

2. François Rigolot, "Rabelais's Laurel for Glory: A Further Study of the 'Pantagruelion,'" *Renaissance Quarterly* 42 (1989): 60–77.

3. Rabelais, *Le Tiers Livre*, 342–44.

4. François Rabelais, *The Histories of Gargantua and Pantagruel*, trans. J. M. Cohen (London: Penguin Books, 1955), 427–28.

5. Charles Trinkaus, *The Scope of Renaissance Humanism* (Ann Arbor: University of Michigan Press, 1983), 364–85, addresses the backgrounds of this tradition.

6. Rabelais, *Le Tiers Livre*, 338.

7. François Rabelais, *Œuvres complètes*, ed. Guy Demerson, rev. ed. (Paris: Éditions du Seuil, 1995), 51.

8. These two factors are often called by the terms *res* and *verba*, or "thing" and "word," but I prefer to draw the contrast more broadly. See Brian Vickers, "'Words and Things'—or 'Words, Concepts, and Things'? Rhetorical and Linguistic Categories in the Renaissance," in *Res and Verba in der Renaissance*, ed. Eckhard Kessler and Ian Maclean (Wiesbaden, Germany: Harrassowitz, 2002), 287–336.

9. Rita Copeland, *Rhetoric, Hermeneutics, and Translation in the Middle Ages: Academic Traditions and Vernacular Texts* (Cambridge: Cambridge University Press, 1991), 151–78.

10. Murray W. Bundy, "'Invention' and 'Imagination' in the Renaissance," *Journal of English and Germanic Philology* 29 (1930): 535–45, rehearses a stock account of the making of invention. A diffuse but illuminating picture of invention in the Renaissance may be assembled from the fine discussion across several chapters of Grahame Castor, *Pléiade Poetics: A Study in Sixteenth-Century Thought and Terminology* (Cambridge: Cambridge University Press, 1964), 86–136, 168–83; the essays in *The Cambridge History of Literary Criticism*, vol. 3, *The Renaissance*, ed. Glyn P. Norton (Cambridge: Cambridge University Press, 1999), esp. Ulrich Langer, "Invention," 136–44; and Rayna Kalas, *Frame, Glass, Verse: The Technology of Poetic Invention in the English Renaissance* (Ithaca, NY: Cornell University Press, 2007), esp. 54–81.

11. Mario Biagioli, *Galileo's Instruments of Credit: Telescopes, Images, Secrecy*

(Chicago: University of Chicago Press, 2006), provides a stimulating discussion of discovery and invention in their relation through Galileo's career.

12. Thomas Sébillet, *Art poétique français* (1548), in *Traités de poétique et de rhétorique de la Renaissance*, ed. Francis Goyet (Paris: Livre de Poche, 1990), 58; Pierre de Ronsard, *Abrégé de l'Art poétique français* (1565), in the same volume, 435.

13. Thomas Wilson, *Arte of Rhetorique*, ed. Thomas J. Derrick, Renaissance Imagination 1 (New York: Garland, 1982), 31.

14. Among many treatments of this shift, three especially engaging studies are Timothy Hampton, *Writing from History: The Rhetoric of Exemplarity in Renaissance Literature* (Ithaca, NY: Cornell University Press, 1990); Anthony Grafton, *What Was History? The Art of History in Early Modern Europe* (Cambridge: Cambridge University Press, 2007); and Grafton, *Worlds Made by Words: Scholarship and Community in the Modern West* (Cambridge, MA: Harvard University Press, 2009), 35–55.

15. Jerrold E. Seigel, *Rhetoric and Philosophy in Renaissance Humanism: The Union of Eloquence and Wisdom, Petrarch to Valla* (Princeton, NJ: Princeton University Press, 1968), 3–30, follows Cicero's philosophy; Victoria Kahn, *Rhetoric, Prudence, and Skepticism in the Renaissance* (Ithaca, NY: Cornell University Press, 1985), intermittently narrates his reception in the period.

16. Cicero, *De Inventione*, trans. H. M. Hubbell (Cambridge, MA: Harvard University Press, 1949), 15–17. I have altered the translation for my purposes.

17. Aristotle, *Rhetoric*, trans. John Henry Freese (Cambridge, MA: Harvard University Press, 1975), 15, 1355b.

18. Quintilian, *The Orator's Education*, trans. Donald A. Russell, 4 vols. (Cambridge, MA: Harvard University Press, 2001), 3:150–51, 1:406–17.

19. Cicero, *De Inventione*, 18–20. I have altered the translation. Compare *Rhetorica ad Herennium*, trans. Harry Caplan (Cambridge, MA: Harvard University Press, 1954), 6.

20. Roger Ascham, *The Scholemaster*, in *English Works*, ed. William Aldis Wright (Cambridge: Cambridge University Press, 1904), 249.

21. Jerónimo Osório, *Carta à Rainha da Inglaterra*, ed. Sebastião de Pinho (Lisbon: Biblioteca Nacional, 1981), 166; the translation is titled *An Epistle of the Reuerend Father in God Hieronimus Osorius Bishop of Arcoburge in Portugale, to the most excellent Princesse Elizabeth by the grace of God Quene of England, Fraunce, and Ireland*, trans. Richard Shacklock (Antwerp, Belgium, 1565), 27r.

22. Osório, *Carta*, 220, 176; *Epistle*, 67r, 34v.

23. Ascham, *Scholemaster*, 259.

24. Ibid., 261.

25. Ibid.

26. George Gascoigne, "Certayne Notes of Instruction," in *A Hundreth Sundrie Flowres*, ed. G. W. Pigman (New York: Oxford University Press, 2001), 454–55.

27. Ascham, *Scholemaster*, 269.

28. Ibid., 264.

29. Gascoigne, "Certayne Notes," 455.

30. Ibid., 458.

31. Juan Luis Vives, *Introduction to Wisdome*, trans. Richard Morison (London, 1575), x.

32. George Puttenham, *The Art of English Poesy*, ed. Frank A. Whigham and Wayne Rebhorn (Ithaca, NY: Cornell University Press, 2007), 109.

33. Philip Sidney, *Poems*, ed. William A. Ringler Jr. (Oxford: Clarendon Press, 1962), 165.

34. Ibid., 459.

35. Philip Sidney, *An Apology for Poetry*, in *Elizabethan Critical Essays*, ed. G. Gregory Smith, 2 vols. (Oxford: Clarendon Press, 1904), 1:177.

36. Michel de Montaigne, *Essais*, ed. Alexandre Micha, 3 vols. (Paris: Flammarion, 1969–79), 3:283; Michel de Montaigne, *Complete Works*, trans. Donald M. Frame (1943; repr., New York: Alfred A. Knopf, 2003), 1000.

37. Montaigne, *Essais*, 3:284; *Complete Works*, 1001.

38. Montaigne, *Essais*, 1:35; Michel de Montaigne, *Essayes*, trans. John Florio (New York: Modern Library, 1933), xxvii.

39. Roland Greene, *Unrequited Conquests: Love and Empire in the Colonial Americas* (Chicago: University of Chicago Press, 1999), 171–93.

40. Copeland, *Rhetoric, Hermeneutics, and Translation*, 154–58.

41. Anne Lock, *Meditation of a Penitent Sinner*, in *Collected Works*, ed. Susan M. Felch, Medieval and Renaissance Texts and Studies 185 (Tempe: Arizona Center for Medieval and Renaissance Studies, 1999), 65. The most illuminating recent discussion of Lock's sequence appears in Christopher Warley, *Sonnet Sequences and Social Distinction in Renaissance England* (Cambridge: Cambridge University Press, 2005), 45–71.

42. Ascham, *Scholemaster*, 248.

43. Barbara Kiefer Lewalski, *Protestant Poetics and the Seventeenth-Century*

Religious Lyric (Princeton, NJ: Princeton University Press, 1979), 213–50, esp. 227.

44. Henry Lok, *Ecclesiastes, otherwise called the preacher, abridged, and dilated in English poesie* (London, 1597), av^r.

45. Henry Lok, *Sundry Christian Passions* (London, 1597), ii^v. On *Sundry Christian Passions*, see Lewalski, *Protestant Poetics*, 239–40.

46. Ascham, *Scholemaster*, 265.

47. Montaigne, *Complete Works*, 993.

Language

1. Antônio Vieira, *Sermões*, ed. Frederico Ozanam Pessoa de Barros, 21 vols. (São Paulo, Brazil: Editôra das Américas, 1957), 7:13. Insightful accounts of Vieira and his milieu include António Saraiva, *O discurso engenhoso: estudos sobre Vieira e outros autores barrocos* (São Paulo, Brazil: Perspectivas, 1980); Margarida Vieira Mendes, *A oratória barroca de Vieira* (Lisbon: Caminho, 1989); Alcyr Pécora, *Teatro do sacramento: a unidade teológico-retórico-político dos sermões de Antonio Vieira* (Campinas, Brazil: Editora da UNICAMP, 1994); and Miguel Real, *Padre António Vieira e a cultura portuguesa* (Matosinhos, Portugal: QuidNovi, 2008).

2. Vieira, *Sermões*, 7:17–18.

3. Ibid., 26.

4. Ibid.

5. Joachim Du Bellay, *La Déffence, et illustration de la langue francoyse*, ed. Francis Goyet and Olivier Millet, in *Œuvres Complètes*, ed. Olivier Millet et al., 2 vols. (Paris: Honoré Champion, 2003), 1:19.

6. Timothy Hampton, *Literature and Nation in the Sixteenth Century: Inventing Renaissance France* (Ithaca, NY: Cornell University Press, 2001), 1–34, assembles in national terms much of the context around Du Bellay's treatise. Richard Helgerson, *Forms of Nationhood: The Elizabethan Writing of England* (Chicago: University of Chicago Press, 1992), especially 25–40, does the same for the later period in England.

7. Du Bellay, *Déffence*, 1:20.

8. Herbert E. Brekle, ed., *Grammaire générale et raisonée ou La Grammaire de Port-Royal*, 2 vols. (Stuttgart-Bad Cannstatt, Germany: Friedrich Frommann, 1966); a translation was published as Antoine Arnauld and Claude

Lancelot, *General and Rational Grammar: The Port-Royal Grammar*, ed. Jacques Rieux and Bernard E. Rollin (The Hague: Mouton, 1975). Hans Aarsleff, *The Study of Language in England, 1780–1860* (1967; Minneapolis: University of Minnesota Press, 1983), tells the history of philology that begins with Port-Royal. See also the essays in his *From Locke to Saussure: Essays on the Study of Language and Intellectual History* (Minneapolis: University of Minnesota Press, 1982).

9.   Joseph T. Shipley, *The Origins of English Words: A Discursive Dictionary of Indo-European Roots* (Baltimore: Johns Hopkins University Press, 1984), 72. See the detailed list of cognates in the *Oxford English Dictionary*, 2nd ed., s.v. "tongue."

10. Desiderius Erasmus, *Lingva*, ed. F. Schalk, in *Opera Omnia*, ed. J. H. Waszink et al., 9 vols. (Amsterdam: North-Holland, 1969–74), 4 (pt. 1): 241. See the translation in *Lingua*, ed. Elaine Fantham and Erika Rummel, in *Collected Works of Erasmus*, ed. R. J. Schoeck et al., 86 vols. (Toronto: University of Toronto Press, 1974–), 29:265.

11. Erasmus, *Lingva*, 4 (pt. 1): 242; *Collected Works*, 29:265. Carla Mazzio, "Sins of the Tongue," in *The Body in Parts: Fantasies of Corporeality in Early Modern Europe* (New York: Routledge, 1997), 53–79, reproduces a great deal of early modern commentary on the organ.

12. John Calvin, *Sermons on Deuteronomy* (Edinburgh: Banner of Truth Trust, 1987), 240.

13. Erasmus, *Lingva*, 4 (pt. 1): 244; *Collected Works*, 29:267. On nonsemantic sounds of various kinds in relation to early modern language theory, see Carla Mazzio, *The Inarticulate Renaissance: Language Trouble in an Age of Eloquence* (Philadelphia: University of Pennsylvania Press, 2009).

14. Leo Spitzer, "Muttersprache und Muttererziehung," in *Essays in Historical Semantics* (New York: Russell and Russell, 1948),15–65, explores the historical semantics of *mother tongue*.

15. Erasmus, *Lingva*, 4 (pt. 1): 331; I use the translation in *Collected Works*, 29:366. See Shane Gasbarra, "Lingua Quo Vadis? Language and Community in Erasmus's *Lingua*," *Viator* 22 (1991): 343–55.

16. Nicole Oresme, *Le Livre de Ethiques d'Aristote*, ed. Albert Douglas Menut (New York: G. E. Stechert, 1940), 128.

17. Richard Mulcaster, *The First Part of the Elementary* (London, 1582), 55.

18. Margreta de Grazia, "The Secularization of Language in the Seventeenth Century," *Journal of the History of Ideas* 41 (1980): 319–29, treats the chang-

ing conception of language as imperfect and removed from both God and nature.

19. Giorgio Agamben, *The End of the Poem: Studies in Poetics*, trans. Daniel Heller-Roazen (Stanford, CA: Stanford University Press, 1999), 53–54. The two aspects are defined in Dante Alighieri, *Convivio*, ed. Franca Brambilla Ageno, 3 vols. (Florence: Le Lettere, 1995), 2:20–23, translated in *Il Convivio (The Banquet)*, trans. Richard H. Lansing (New York: Garland, 1990), 12–14, and at length in *De Vulgari Eloquentia*, ed. Pier Vincenzo Mengaldo, 2 vols. (Padua, Italy: Antenore, 1968), 1:3, translated in *De Vulgari Eloquentia*, trans. Steven Botterill, Cambridge Medieval Classics 5 (Cambridge: Cambridge University Press, 1996), 3.

20. Du Bellay, *Déffence*, 1:31–32.

21. Ibid., 25.

22. Ibid.

23. Ibid., 26.

24. Ibid., 34, 37.

25. Ibid., 37–38.

26. Peter Burke, *Languages and Communities in Early Modern Europe* (Cambridge: Cambridge University Press, 2004), 15–42.

27. Jonathan Hope, "Shakespeare and Language: An Introduction," in *Shakespeare and Language*, ed. Catherine M. S. Alexander (Cambridge: Cambridge University Press, 2004), 3, notes the prevalence of *tongue* over *language* in the titles of English books between 1500 and 1700.

28. William Wood, *New England's Prospect*, ed. Alden T. Vaughan (Amherst: University of Massachusetts Press, 1977), 110.

29. Juan de Valdés, *Diálogo de la lengua*, ed. Juan M. Lope Blanch (Madrid: Castalia, 1969), 43.

30. Ibid., 52–53.

31. Ibid., 57.

32. Ibid., 60.

33. João de Barros, *Diálogo em Louvor da Nossa Linguagem*, ed. Luciana Stegagno Picchio, Testi e Manuali 45 (Modena, Italy: Instituto di Filologia Romanza dell' Università di Roma, 1959), 72.

34. Ibid., 74.

35. Ibid., 74–75.

36. Miguel de Cervantes, *Novelas Ejemplares*, ed. Juan Bautista Avalle-Arce, 3 vols. (Madrid: Castalia, 1982), 3:248, 272.

37. William Shakespeare, *The Tempest*, in *The Riverside Shakespeare*, ed. G. Blakemore Evans et al., 2nd ed. (Boston: Houghton Mifflin, 1997), 1.2.363–65, 1666.

38. Ibid., 1.2.429–31, 1667.

39. Antonio de Nebrija, *Gramática de la lengua castellana*, ed. Antonio Quilis (Madrid: Editora Nacional, 1980), 97.

40. Ibid., 100.

41. Pero de Magalhães Gandavo, *Tratado da Terra do Brasil e História da Província Santa Cruz*, Coleção Reconquista do Brasil, n.s., 12 (São Paulo, Brazil: Editora Itatiaia, 1980), 52. Gandavo is the author of *Dialogo em Defensam da Lingua Portuguesa* (1574), an edition of which by Edwin B. Williams appears in *PMLA* 51 (1936): 636–42.

42. Edmund Spenser, "A View of the Present State of Ireland," in *Works: A Variorum Edition*, ed. Edwin Greenlaw et al., 10 vols. (Baltimore: Johns Hopkins Press, 1932–49), 10:118–19.

43. Jean de Léry, *Histoire d'un Voyage fait en la Terre du Brésil, 1557*, ed. Frank Lestringant (Montpellier, France: Max Chaleil, 1992), 174; *History of a Voyage to the Land of Brazil*, trans. Janet Whatley, Latin American Literature and Culture 12 (Berkeley: University of California Press, 1990), 162.

44. Frank Lestringant, *Jean de Léry ou l'invention du sauvage*, 2nd ed. (Paris: Honoré Champion, 2005), 31.

45. Barbara Kiefer Lewalski, *The Life of John Milton: A Critical Biography*, rev. ed. (Malden, MA: Blackwell, 2003), 285.

46. Roger Williams, *Complete Writings*, ed. J. Hammond Trumbull et al., 7 vols. (New York: Russell and Russell, 1963), 1:24, 78; Léry, *Histoire d'un Voyage*, 196; *History of a Voyage*, 188.

47. Williams, *Complete Writings*, 1:25, 38, 47.

48. Ibid., 20.

49. Two studies that examine speculations and practices around language in colonial and early national North America are Michael P. Kramer, *Imagining Language in America: From the Revolution to the Civil War* (Princeton, NJ: Princeton University Press, 1992), and, more expansively, Edward G. Gray, *New World Babel: Languages and Nations in Early America* (Princeton, NJ: Princeton University Press, 1999).

50. The standard account of language in the *Comentarios* is Margarita Zamora, *Language, Authority, and Indigenous History in the* Comentarios reales de los Incas (Cambridge: Cambridge University Press, 1988).

51. Inca Garcilaso de la Vega, *Comentarios reales de los Incas*, ed. Aurelio Miró Quesada, 2 vols. (Caracas, Venezuela: Biblioteca Ayacucho, 1976), 1:7.

52. Garcilaso de la Vega, El Inca, *Royal Commentaries of the Incas and General History of Peru, Part One*, trans. Harold V. Livermore (Austin: University of Texas Press, 1966), 5. I have altered the translation for my purposes.

53. Garcilaso, *Comentarios reales*, 1:7.

54. Garcilaso, *Royal Commentaries*, 5.

55. Garcilaso, *Comentarios reales*, 1:8.

56. Garcilaso, *Royal Commentaries*, 6.

57. Garcilaso, *Comentarios reales*, 2:87.

58. Ibid.

59. Thomas M. Cohen, *The Fire of Tongues: António Vieira and the Missionary Church in Brazil and Portugal* (Stanford, CA: Stanford University Press, 1998), is an informative study of the Jesuit enterprise in Brazil.

60. Vieira, *Sermões*, 2:102.

61. Ibid., 2:118.

62. Ibid., 15:79.

63. Ibid., 15:82.

64. Cohen, *Fire of Tongues*, 240.

Resistance

1. Fernando de Rojas, *La Celestina: Comedia o Tragicomedia de Calisto y Melibea*, ed. Peter E. Russell (Madrid: Castalia, 1991), 259. I suppress the brackets that indicate the editor's interpolations.

2. Perhaps the most influential such study is Stephen Greenblatt, "Murdering Peasants: Status, Genre, and the Representation of Rebellion," *Representations* 1 (1983): 1–29, repr. in *Representing the English Renaissance*, ed. Greenblatt (Berkeley: University of California Press, 1988), 1–29. It includes a brilliant analysis of the passage from Sidney's *Arcadia* discussed here.

3. Donald R. Kelley, "Ideas of Resistance before Elizabeth," in *The Historical Renaissance: New Essays on Tudor and Stuart Literature and Culture*, ed. Heather Dubrow and Richard Strier (Chicago: University of Chicago Press, 1988), 48–76, sensitively distinguishes the stages in the emergence of resistance theory with attention to language.

4. See Robert M. Kingdon, "Calvinism and Resistance Theory, 1550–1580," in *The Cambridge History of Political Thought, 1450–1700,* ed. J. H. Burns

(Cambridge: Cambridge University Press, 1991), 193–218; J. H. M. Salmon, "Catholic Resistance Theory, Ultramontanism, and the Royalist Response, 1580–1620," in *Cambridge History of Political Thought*, 219–53; and Richard Strier, *Resistant Structures: Particularity, Radicalism, and Renaissance Texts*, New Historicism 34 (Berkeley: University of California Press, 1995), esp. 165–202.

5. Romans 13:2, Douay-Rheims Version.

6. Marsilius of Padua, *The Defender of the Peace*, ed. and trans. Annabel Brett (Cambridge: Cambridge University Press, 2005); William of Ockham, *A Short Discourse on Tyrannical Government*, ed. Arthur Stephen McGrade, trans. John Kilcullen (Cambridge: Cambridge University Press, 1992), 64.

7. Edmund Spenser, "A View of the Present State of Ireland," in *Works: A Variorum Edition*, ed. Edwin Greenlaw et al., 10 vols. (Baltimore: Johns Hopkins Press, 1932–49), 10:52.

8. Richard L. Kagan, *Lucrecia's Dreams: Politics and Prophecy in Sixteenth-Century Spain* (Baltimore: Johns Hopkins University Press, 1990), recovers a politically charged dream vision; Kagan and Abigail Dyer, eds., *Inquisitorial Inquiries: Brief Lives of Secret Jews and Other Heretics* (Baltimore: Johns Hopkins University Press, 2004), includes several testimonies by people caught up in the Inquisition.

9. Giorgio Vasari, *Lives of the Painters, Sculptors, and Architects,* trans. Gaston du C. de Vere, 2 vols. (New York: Alfred A. Knopf, 1996), 1:21.

10. *Biblia*, trans. Miles Coverdale (Antwerp, 1535).

11. *The Geneva Bible: A Facsimile of the 1560 Edition*, ed. Lloyd E. Berry (Madison: University of Wisconsin Press, 1969), 278^{r-v}.

12. Holy Bible, King James Version (Oxford: Oxford University Press, n.d.), 574.

13. Greenblatt, "Murdering Peasants," 19–23, is persuasive.

14. Quentin Skinner, *Liberty before Liberalism* (Cambridge: Cambridge University Press, 1998), follows the concept to its outcome in the eighteenth and nineteenth centuries.

15. Luís de Camões, *Os Lusíadas*, ed. Emanuel Paulo Ramos (Porto, Portugal: Porto Editora, [1987?]), 95 (1.93.2–4). Numbers in parentheses in these citations refer to canto, stanza, and line numbers. I suppress the italics in Ramos's text.

16. Luís de Camões, *The Lusíads*, trans. Landeg White (Oxford: Oxford University Press, 1997), 21. I have altered the translation for my purposes.

17. Camões, *Os Lusíadas*, 116 (2.69.7–8).

18. Ibid., 138 (3.36).

19. Ibid., 144 (3.61.1–4).

20. Ibid., 148 (3.79.7–8).

21. Ibid., 324 (10.29.5–6).

22. Ibid., 258–59 (7.55.3–7, 56).

23. Camões, *The Lusíads*, 150.

24. David Quint, *Epic and Empire* (Princeton, NJ: Princeton University Press, 1993), 114–25, discusses the African resistance to the Portuguese in the *Lusiads* in view of how the latter are authorized to see themselves in the former. Josiah Blackmore, "Africa and the Epic Imagination of Camões," *Portuguese Literary and Cultural Studies* 9 (2003): 107–15, compounds the issue by considering the estrangement of the Africans a kind of identity with the Portuguese mediated by melancholy.

25. Camões, *Os Lusíadas*, 333 (10.66).

26. Camões, *The Lusíads*, 210.

27. Camões, *Os Lusíadas*, 333–34 (10.67–68).

28. Camões, *The Lusíads*, 210.

29. Gavin Alexander, *Writing after Sidney: The Literary Response to Sir Philip Sidney, 1586–1640* (Oxford: Oxford University Press, 2006), xx–xxvii, summarizes the facts.

30. Edward Berry, *The Making of Sir Philip Sidney* (Toronto: University of Toronto Press, 1998), 28–48, covers the friendship with Languet; Katherine Duncan-Jones, *Sir Philip Sidney: Courtier Poet* (New Haven, CT: Yale University Press, 1991), 80–81, discusses Duplessis-Mornay; and James E. Phillips, "George Buchanan and the Sidney Circle," *Huntington Library Quarterly* 12 (1948): 23–55, treats Buchanan.

31. Philip Sidney, *The Countess of Pembroke's Arcadia (The Old Arcadia)*, ed. Jean Robertson (Oxford: Clarendon Press, 1973), 254; Blair Worden, *The Sound of Virtue: Philip Sidney's* Arcadia *and Elizabethan Politics* (New Haven, CT: Yale University Press, 1996), gives the definitive account of this eclogue in a chapter titled "Resistance." Alan Sinfield, "Power and Ideology: An Outline Theory and Sidney's *Arcadia*," *ELH* 52 (1985): 259–77, discusses the eclogue in terms of Sidney's class position and his views of aristocratic resistance to absolutism.

32. Sidney, *Old Arcadia*, 255.

33. Ibid., 259.

34. Ibid.

35. Richard C. McCoy, *Sir Philip Sidney: Rebellion in Arcadia* (New Brunswick, NJ: Rutgers University Press, 1979), 38–41, and Richard M. Berrong, "Changing Depictions of Popular Revolt in Sixteenth-Century England: The Case of Sidney's Two *Arcadias*," *Journal of Medieval and Renaissance Studies* 19 (1989): 15–33, discuss the ambivalent treatment of resistance in the *Arcadia*.

36. Sidney, *Old Arcadia*, 370.

37. Philip Sidney, *The Countess of Pembroke's Arcadia (The New Arcadia)*, ed. Victor Skretkowicz (Oxford: Clarendon Press, 1987), 280, 282.

38. Ibid., 283.

39. Ibid., 79.

40. Ibid., 372–73.

41. Ibid., 373, 375, 377.

42. McCoy, *Sir Philip Sidney*, 124.

43. Inca Garcilaso de la Vega, *Comentarios reales de los Incas*, ed. Aurelio Miró Quesada, 2 vols. (Caracas, Venezuela: Biblioteca Ayacucho, 1976), 1:16; Garcilaso de la Vega, El Inca, *Royal Commentaries of the Incas, Part One*, trans. Harold V. Livermore (Austin: University of Texas Press, 1966), 16. I have altered the translation for my purposes.

44. On Tahuantinsuyu, see María Rostworowski de Diez Canseco, *History of the Inca Realm*, trans. Harry B. Iceland (Cambridge: Cambridge University Press, 1999), x. The notion that the Inca realm was an empire in anything like the European sense is highly debatable, but because the Inca Garcilaso treated it as such, I will be more concerned with his representations than with the historical reality.

45. Margarita Zamora, *Language, Authority, and Indigenous History in the* Comentarios reales de los Incas (Cambridge: Cambridge University Press, 1988), offers an authoritative reading of the multiple layers of narrative and the challenge they present to Spanish historiography. Zamora tends to situate the *Comentarios* in continental Renaissance traditions. Her counterpart, who locates the history in Andean contexts, is José Antonio Mazzotti, *Coros mestizos del Inca Garcilaso: Resonancias andinas* (Mexico City: Fondo de Cultura Económica, 1996).

46. His version of this theme is much disputed by modern historians. On the matter of royal genealogy, Catherine Julien, *Reading Inca History* (Iowa City: University of Iowa Press, 2000), 3–22, gives a useful overview of these

disputes. Rostworowski, *History of the Inca Realm*, synthesizes many sources into an account of the domestic and imperial practice of the Incas.

47. Garcilaso, *Comentarios reales,* 2:86–87.
48. Garcilaso, *Royal Commentaries,* 402–3.
49. Garcilaso, *Comentarios reales,* 2:229.
50. Garcilaso, *Royal Commentaries,* 565–66.
51. Garcilaso, *Comentarios reales,* 2:229.
52. Garcilaso, *Royal Commentaries,* 566.
53. Garcilaso, *Comentarios reales,* 2:230.
54. Garcilaso, *Royal Commentaries,* 566–67.
55. Garcilaso, *Comentarios reales,* 2:239.
56. Garcilaso, *Royal Commentaries,* 577.
57. Garcilaso, *Comentarios reales,* 2:239–40,
58. Garcilaso, *Royal Commentaries,* 578.

Blood

1. *A Warning for Fair Women: A Critical Edition*, ed. Charles Dale Cannon (The Hague: Mouton, 1975), 142.
2. Miguel de Cervantes, *Novelas Ejemplares*, ed. Juan Bautista Avalle-Arce, 3 vols. (Madrid: Castalia, 1982), 2:171.
3. Two convincing accounts of the story are Ruth S. El Saffar, *Novel to Romance: A Study of Cervantes's* Novelas ejemplares (Baltimore: Johns Hopkins University Press, 1974), 128–38, and R. P. Calcraft, "Structure, Symbol and Meaning in Cervantes's *La fuerza de la sangre*," *Bulletin of Hispanic Studies* 58 (1981): 197–204.
4. M. C. Bradbrook, *Themes and Conventions of Elizabethan Tragedy* (Cambridge: Cambridge University Press, 1935), 18–19, treats conventions such as the banquet. The scholarship concerning blood that speaks is endless, but for recent instances see Kenneth Gross, *Shakespeare's Noise* (Chicago: University of Chicago Press, 2001), 143–44, and Lowell Gallagher, "Faustus's Blood and the (Messianic) Question of Ethics," *ELH* 73 (2006): 1–29.
5. Historians of science have not often considered the work of Galen and his successors as allegories, although such an understanding scarcely contradicts the picture of Galenism in, for example, Owsei Temkin, *Galenism: Rise and Decline of a Medical Philosophy* (Ithaca, NY: Cornell University Press,

1973), and Nancy G. Siraisi, *Medieval and Early Renaissance Medicine: An Introduction to Knowledge and Practice* (Chicago: University of Chicago Press, 1990). But see Peter Heath, *Allegory and Philosophy in Avicenna (Ibn Sînâ)* (Philadelphia: University of Pennsylvania Press, 1992).

6. Uli Linke, *Blood and Nation: The European Aesthetics of Race* (Philadelphia: University of Pennsylvania Press, 1999), 65–96, and Bettina Bildhauer, *Medieval Blood* (Cardiff: University of Wales Press, 2006), discuss the semiotic, ritual, and social functions of blood before 1500.

7. Rebecca Zorach, *Blood, Milk, Ink, Gold: Abundance and Excess in the French Renaissance* (Chicago: University of Chicago Press, 2005), 33–81, addresses the theme of abundance in the iconography of blood through a detailed study of the Galerie François Premier in the château of Fontainebleau.

8. Ibid., 19–20, reflects on this question from an art historian's vantage. Dympna Callaghan, *Shakespeare without Women: Representing Gender and Race on the Renaissance Stage* (London: Routledge, 2000), 28–30, considers recent usages of "materialism."

9. Kenneth Burke, *A Grammar of Motives* (1945; Berkeley: University of California Press, 1969), 506.

10. Michel Foucault, *The History of Sexuality*, vol. 1, *An Introduction*, trans. Robert Hurley (New York: Vintage Books, 1980), 147–50, approaches this point differently, arguing that since the seventeenth century in the West, sexuality has replaced blood as a medium of control; power that once spoke through blood came to speak of, and to, sexuality.

11. Thomas S. Kuhn, *The Structure of Scientific Revolutions,* 3rd ed. (Chicago: University of Chicago Press, 1996), 24.

12. Peggy McCracken, *The Curse of Eve, the Wound of the Hero: Blood, Gender, and Medieval Literature* (Philadelphia: University of Pennsylvania Press, 2003), treats the gendering of blood.

13. Dennis J. McCarthy, "Blood," in *Interpreter's Dictionary of the Bible*, ed. Keith Crim et al., 5 vols. (Nashville: Abingdon Press, 1976), suppl. 2:114–17.

14. J. Pohle, "Sacrifice," in *Catholic Encyclopedia*, 16 vols. (New York: Robert Appleton Co., 1912), 13:315.

15. Albert A. Sicroff, *Les controverses des statuts de "pureté de sang" en Espagne du XVe au XVIIe siècle* (Paris: Didier, 1960); J. H. Elliott, *Imperial Spain, 1469–1716* (New York: St. Martin's Press, 1964), 212–17; and for the context of genealogical attention leading to the statutes, as well as the responses to them after 1449, David Nirenberg, "Mass Conversion and Genealogical

Mentalities: Jews and Christians in Fifteenth-Century Spain," *Past and Present* 174 (2002): 3–41.

16. David Nirenberg, "Figures of Thought and Figures of Flesh: 'Jews' and 'Judaism' in Late-Medieval Spanish Poetry and Politics," *Speculum* 81 (2006): 418. See also Teofilo F. Ruiz, *Spanish Society, 1400–1600* (Harlow, UK: Longman, 2001).

17. Siraisi, *Medieval and Early Renaissance Medicine*, 104–6, places blood within the system of the humors. Mary Floyd-Wilson, *English Ethnicity and Race in Early Modern Drama* (Cambridge: Cambridge University Press, 2003), describes an intersection between humoral and climatic theories that she calls geohumoralism.

18. Piero Camporesi, *Juice of Life: The Symbolic and Magic Significance of Blood*, trans. Robert R. Barr (New York: Continuum, 1995), 27–28.

19. Peter Brain, *Galen on Bloodletting: A Study of the Origins, Development, and Validity of His Opinions* (Cambridge: Cambridge University Press, 1986), 1–14, introduces the Galenic system; but see Luis García-Ballester, "Galen's Medical Works in the Context of His Biography," in his *Galen and Galenism: Theory and Medical Practice from Antiquity to the European Renaissance*, ed. Jon Arrizabalaga et al. (Aldershot, UK: Ashgate, 2002), esp. 3–5, on the openness of the system. Owsei Temkin, *Hippocrates in a World of Pagans and Christians* (Baltimore: Johns Hopkins University Press, 1991), 241–46, describes the relations of Hippocrates and Galen. A typical application of Galen's thought to early modern literature is Lily B. Campbell, *Shakespeare's Tragic Heroes: Slaves of Passion* (New York: Barnes and Noble, 1952), 51–62.

20. Temkin, *Galenism*, reminds us that early modern Galenism is always twice removed from Galen himself, through the interventions of Byzantine and Arab scholars (98). Likewise Siraisi, *Medieval and Early Renaissance Medicine*, observes the gradual decline of Galenism in the sixteenth century (193) and the growing interest in anatomy (86–97); see also Andrea Carlino, *Books of the Body: Anatomical Ritual and Renaissance Learning*, trans. John Tedeschi and Anne C. Tedeschi (Chicago: University of Chicago Press, 1999), esp. 120–86. Marc Carnel, *Le Sang Embaumé des Roses: Sang et Passion dans la Poésie Amoureuse de Pierre de Ronsard* (Geneva: Droz, 2004), explores blood in lyric poetry as a "language of desire" (10).

21. The leading literary scholar who sees Galenism in this era as largely intact is Gail Kern Paster, *The Body Embarrassed: Drama and the Disciplines of Shame in Early Modern England* (Ithaca, NY: Cornell University Press, 1993),

64–112, who believes that Harvey's "discovery of the circulation eventually broke down Galenic physiology" (73), not that Galenic physiology was already in decline in the later sixteenth century. Her chapter on blood, which contains a great deal of useful information, rightly insists that the principal humor is deeply involved in the ideological system of patriarchal culture. Her *Humoring the Body: Emotions and the Shakespearean Stage* (Chicago: University of Chicago Press, 2004) emphasizes humoral subjectivity in the affective language of English drama.

22. Michael C. Schoenfeldt, *Bodies and Selves in Early Modern England: Physiology and Inwardness in Spenser, Shakespeare, Herbert, and Milton*, Cambridge Studies in Renaissance Literature and Culture 34 (Cambridge: Cambridge University Press, 1999), deftly puts aside the question of Galenism's currency as a coherent account of the body and calls it, for example, "a remarkable blend of textual authority and a near-poetic vocabulary of felt corporeal experience" (3) and "a language of inner emotion" (8). On the exchanges between the Galenic body and a humoral self, see Paster, *Humoring the Body*; on the later career of the humors, Katherine Rowe, "Humoral Knowledge and Liberal Cognition in Davenant's *Macbeth*," in *Reading the Early Modern Passions: Essays in the Cultural History of Emotion*, ed. Gail Kern Paster et al. (Philadelphia: University of Pennsylvania Press, 2004), 169–91; and on melancholy, Douglas Trevor, *The Poetics of Melancholy in Early Modern England*, Cambridge Studies in Renaissance Literature and Culture 48 (Cambridge: Cambridge University Press, 2004).

23. William Osler, "Michael Servetus," *Johns Hopkins Hospital Bulletin* 21, no. 226 (1910): 22.

24. M. Servetus, *Christianismi Restitutio* (Frankfurt, Germany: Minerva, 1966), 168–71; a translation appears in Michael Servetus, *A Translation of His Geographical, Medical and Astrological Writings*, trans. Charles Donald O'Malley (Philadelphia: American Philosophical Society, 1953), 202–8. John F. Fulton, *Michael Servetus, Humanist and Martyr* (New York: Herbert Reichner, 1953), 41–45, and André Cournand, "Air and Blood," in *Circulation of the Blood: Men and Ideas*, ed. Alfred P. Fishman and Dickinson W. Richards (Bethesda, MD: American Physiological Society, 1982), 18–25, tell the transmission of Servetus's idea. James J. Bono, "Medical Spirits and the Medieval Language of Life," *Traditio* 40 (1984): 91–130, establishes the late medieval context for similar efforts to describe "the phenomena of life and the experience of salvation within a unified conceptual framework" (99). On the late medieval

anticipation of Servetus's discovery by Ibn al-Nafis, see George Saliba, *Islamic Science and the Making of the European Renaissance* (Cambridge, MA: MIT Press, 2007), 24–25.

25. Charles Singer, *The Discovery of the Circulation of the Blood* (London: William Dawson and Sons, 1956), 29–36.

26. John Rogers, *The Matter of Revolution: Science, Poetry, and Politics in the Age of Milton* (Ithaca, NY: Cornell University Press, 1996), 13.

27. The discussion of Harvey's early and late treatises by Rogers, *Matter of Revolution*, 16–38, is essential. Robert A. Erickson, *The Language of the Heart, 1600–1750* (Philadelphia: University of Pennsylvania Press, 1997), 61–88, treats Harvey as the figure who conceived the human heart "more literally than anyone had before" (63).

28. For example, Thomas Wright, *The Passions of the Mind in General*, ed. William Webster Newbold, Renaissance Imagination 15 (New York: Garland, 1986).

29. Gail Kern Paster, *"Bartholomew Fair* and the Humoral Body," in *Early Modern English Drama: A Critical Companion*, ed. Garrett A. Sullivan Jr., Patrick Cheney, and Andrew Hadfield (New York: Oxford University Press, 2006), 260–71, treats the humors in this period as prevailing rather than waning doctrine, although the article contains several observations (e.g., the changing meaning of "humor" and the rise of "vapors") that suggest a waning. Terri Clerico, "The Politics of Blood: John Ford's *'Tis Pity She's a Whore*," *ELR* 22 (1992): 405–34, sees the decline of Galenism but attributes it entirely to Harvey.

30. Henry Howard, Earl of Surrey, *Poems*, ed. Frederick Morgan Padelford, rev. ed. (Seattle: University of Washington Press, 1928), 87, 97, 85.

31. Ibid., 57; *Tottel's Miscellany (1557–1587)*, rev. ed., ed. Hyder Edward Rollins, 2 vols. (Cambridge, MA: Harvard University Press, 1966), 1:8, 32.

32. Luis de Camões, *Os Lusíadas*, ed. Emanuel Paulo Ramos (Porto, Portugal: Porto Editora, [1987?] 142 (3.52).

33. Compare Timothy Hampton, "Strange Alteration: Physiology and Psychology from Galen to Rabelais," in *Reading the Early Modern Passions*, 286, on the "psychology" of the Renaissance lyric expressed through alteration.

34. Edmund Spenser, *The Faerie Queene*, ed. A. C. Hamilton (London: Longman, 1977), 586 (5.8.35).

35. Philip Sidney, *The Countess of Pembroke's Arcadia (The New Arcadia)*, ed. Victor Skretkowicz (Oxford: Clarendon Press, 1987), 290.

36. Ibid., 385. Leonard Tennenhouse, *Power on Display: The Politics of Shakespeare's Genres* (New York: Methuen, 1986), 20–36, develops an account of the *Arcadia* as in part a response to the uneven authority of Elizabeth I's rule through royal blood.

37. Marguerite de Navarre, *Heptaméron*, ed. Simone de Reyff (Paris: Flammarion, 1982), 107.

38. Ibid., 102.

39. Ibid., 109.

40. Marguerite de Navarre, *The Heptameron*, trans. P. A. Chilton (London: Penguin Books, 1984), 137.

41. Marguerite de Navarre, *Heptaméron*, 117–18.

42. Marguerite de Navarre, *The Heptameron*, 146.

43. Marguerite de Navarre, *Heptaméron*, 117.

44. Ibid., 118.

45. George Gascoigne, *The Adventures of Master F. J.*, in *A Hundreth Sundrie Flowres*, ed. G. W. Pigman III (Oxford: Clarendon Press, 2000), 151–52.

46. For "on the sudden," see John Ford, *Love's Sacrifice*, ed. A. T. Moore (Manchester: Manchester University Press, 2002), 147; for "by chance," see John Webster, *The Duchess of Malfi*, in *Complete Works*, ed. F. H. Lucas, 4 vols. (Boston: Houghton Mifflin, 1928), 2:61.

47. William Shakespeare, *The Merchant of Venice*, in *The Riverside Shakespeare*, ed. G. Blakemore Evans et al., 2nd ed. (Boston: Houghton Mifflin, 1997), 309 (4.1.42–43). Further citations in this chapter will appear in the main text.

48. Alan Sinfield, "How to Read *The Merchant of Venice* without Being Heterosexist," in *Alternative Shakespeares*, vol. 2, ed. Terence Hawkes (London: Routledge, 1996), 122–39, accounts for the play as a "network of enticements, obligations, and interdictions" (129).

49. Marc Shell, *Money, Language, and Thought: Literary and Philosophical Economies from the Medieval to the Modern Era* (Berkeley: University of California Press, 1982), 61. Shell's discussion of blood in the context of exchange (47–83) is definitive.

50. H. B. Charlton, *Shakespearian Comedy* (London: Methuen, 1938), 148–53.

51. The Romantic position is summarized and challenged by Elmer Edgar Stoll, *Shakespeare Studies: Historical and Comparative in Method* (New York: Macmillan, 1927), 268, and more amply by René Girard, "'To Entrap the Wisest': A Reading of *The Merchant of Venice*," in *Literature and Society*, ed.

Edward W. Said, Selected Papers from the English Institute, n.s., 3 (Baltimore: Johns Hopkins University Press, 1980), 106; the materialist view is proposed by Paster, *Body Embarrassed,* 85.

52. While I see this exhortation as a statement of Morocco's superiority, Eric S. Mallin, "Jewish Invader and the Soul of State: *The Merchant of Venice* and Science Fiction Movies," in *Shakespeare and Modernity: Early Modern to Millennium,* ed. Hugh Grady (London: Routledge, 2000), 162, sees it as a profession of equality.

53. Frank Whigham, "Ideology and Class Conduct in *The Merchant of Venice,*" *Renaissance Drama*, n.s., 10 (1979): 93–115, examines the play in terms of class conflict and courteous conduct.

54. Lawrence Stone and Jeanne C. Fawtier Stone, *An Open Elite: England, 1540–1880* (Oxford: Clarendon Press, 1984), 3–29, gives context to the changing senses of *gentleman* from the late sixteenth century.

55. Richard Halpern, *Shakespeare among the Moderns* (Ithaca, NY: Cornell University Press, 1997), 190. On the "use-value" of flesh and blood, see 203–7.

56. Lisa Freinkel, *Reading Shakespeare's Will: The Theology of Figure from Augustine to the Sonnets* (New York: Columbia University Press, 2002), 237–91, offers, in effect, a rigorous account of the conceptual envelope around the concept of "flesh" in this period. Unlike blood, flesh at this moment operates comfortably within a received set of ideas from Augustine to Luther, and Freinkel sensitively recovers the theological and allegorical freight of those ideas.

57. Kenneth Gross, *Shylock Is Shakespeare* (Chicago: University of Chicago Press, 2006), 100.

58. Mallin, "Jewish Invader," 162.

59. Geoffrey Bullough, *Narrative and Dramatic Sources of Shakespeare*, 8 vols. (London: Routledge and Kegan Paul, 1957), 1:446–54.

60. Anthony Munday, *Zelauto: The Fountaine of Fame, 1580*, ed. Jack Stillinger (Carbondale: Southern Illinois University Press, 1963), 179.

61. James Shapiro, *Shakespeare and the Jews* (New York: Columbia University Press, 1996), 188–89. See also Freinkel, *Reading Shakespeare's Will*, 286–91; Whigham, "Ideology and Class Conduct," 110; and W. H. Auden, *The Dyer's Hand* (New York: Random House, 1962), 229.

62. Janet Adelman, "Male Bonding in Shakespeare's Comedies," in *Shakespeare's "Rough Magic": Renaissance Essays in Honor of C. L. Barber* (Newark: University of Delaware Press, 1985), 80.

63. Paster, *Body Embarrassed*, 92.

64. Shell, *Money, Language, and Thought*, 74, 82–83.

65. Carroll B. Johnson, *Cervantes and the Material World* (Urbana: University of Illinois Press, 2000), 3–4.

66. Miguel de Cervantes, *Don Quixote*, trans. Edith Grossman (New York: Ecco, 2003), 834, 541. I have altered Grossman's translation for my purposes.

67. Ibid., 209.

68. Ibid., 325.

69. Miguel de Cervantes, *Don Quijote de la Mancha*, ed. Francisco Rico, 2 vols. (Barcelona: Galaxia Gutenberg y Círculo de Lectores, 2004), 1:450–52.

70. Cervantes, *Don Quixote*, 303.

71. Cervantes, *Don Quijote de la Mancha*, 1:454–55.

72. Cervantes, *Don Quixote*, 305–6.

73. Cervantes, *Don Quijote de la Mancha*, 1:879–80.

74. Cervantes, *Don Quixote*, 595.

75. Ruth Perry, "De-familiarizing the Family: Or, Writing Family History from Literary Sources," *Modern Language Quarterly* 55 (1994): 420, repr. in *Eighteenth-Century Literary History: An MLQ Reader*, ed. Marshall Brown (Durham, NC: Duke University Press, 1999), 164, asks whether the *cri du sang* speaks to the power of consanguinity or the waning of that power.

World

1. George Buchanan, *The Political Poetry*, ed. and trans. Paul J. McGinnis and Arthur H. Williamson (Edinburgh: Scottish History Society, 1995), 61–62. I have altered the translation for my purposes.

2. James S. Romm, *The Edges of the Earth in Ancient Thought: Geography, Exploration, and Fiction* (Princeton, NJ: Princeton University Press, 1992), provides a helpful account of how the ancients construed the earth and (to some degree) the world. Likewise C. S. Lewis, *The Discarded Image: An Introduction to Medieval and Renaissance Literature* (Cambridge: Cambridge University Press, 1964), assembles information about the earth and the heavens. On the world generally in medieval thought, see Jacques Le Goff, *The Medieval Imagination*, trans. Arthur Goldhammer (Chicago: University of Chicago Press, 1988), esp. 84, and several essays in *La litterature historiographique des origins à 1500*, ed. Hans Ulrich Gumbrecht et al., Grundriss der Romanischen Litteraturen des Mittelalters 11, 2 vols. (Heidelberg, Germany: Carl Winter,

1986), vol. 1; on Isidore of Seville's delineation of the world as a singular horizon, see John Henderson, *The Medieval World of Isidore of Seville: Truth from Words* (Cambridge: Cambridge University Press, 2007); on purgatory as "the other world," see Jacques Le Goff, *The Birth of Purgatory*, trans. Arthur Goldhammer (Chicago: University of Chicago Press, 1984).

3. Ronald G. Witt, *In the Footsteps of the Ancients: The Origins of Humanism from Lovato to Bruni* (Boston: Brill, 2003), 230–91.

4. Francesco Petrarca, *Secretum*, in *Prose*, ed. G. Martellotti et al., Letteratura italiana: Storia e testi 7 (Milan, Italy: Riccardo Ricciardi, 1955), 70.

5. Ernst Robert Curtius, *European Literature and the Latin Middle Ages*, trans. Willard R. Trask, Bollingen Series 36 (1953; Princeton, NJ: Princeton University Press, 1973), 122.

6. Francesco Petrarca, *Canzoniere*, ed. Marco Santagata, rev. ed. (Milan, Italy: Arnoldo Mondadori, 2004), 5.

7. Among many possible examples, see Marsilio Ficino, *Three Books on Life*, ed. and trans. Carol V. Kaske and John R. Clark, Medieval and Renaissance Texts and Studies 57 (Binghamton, NY: Medieval and Renaissance Texts and Studies, 1989), 384–85, and Giovanni Pico della Mirandola, *Commentary on a Poem of Platonic Love*, trans. Douglas Carmichael (Lanham, MD: University Press of America, 1986), 22–27.

8. *The Life of the Admiral Christopher Columbus by His Son Ferdinand*, trans. Benjamin Keen (New Brunswick, NJ: Rutgers University Press, 1959), 285.

9. Norman J. W. Thrower, *Maps and Civilization: Cartography in Culture and Society*, 3rd ed. (Chicago: University of Chicago Press, 2007), surveys this episode.

10. Stephen Greenblatt, *Renaissance Self-Fashioning: From More to Shakespeare* (Chicago: University of Chicago Press, 1980), generally subsumes the term *world* under culture and emphasizes the definition of selfhood against forces of authority and alienness. Giuseppe Mazzotta, *The Worlds of Petrarch*, Duke Monographs in Medieval and Renaissance Studies 14 (Durham, NC: Duke University Press, 1993), deliberately employs the term *world* to refer to aspects of Petrarch's thought of history and death. *World* is part of the argument in Charles Taylor, *Sources of the Self: The Making of Modern Identity* (Cambridge, MA: Harvard University Press, 1989), in places; see especially 178–82. A magisterial account of selfhood through the early modern period is Timothy J. Reiss, *Mirages of the Selfe: Patterns of Personhood in Ancient and Early Modern Europe* (Stanford, CA: Stanford University Press, 2003).

11. Studies of literature and intellectual history with degrees of attention to the world as a concept include Ernst Cassirer, *The Individual and the Cosmos in Renaissance Philosophy*, trans. Mario Domandi (Oxford: Basil Blackwell, 1963); Paul Oskar Kristeller, "The Moral Thought of Renaissance Humanism," in *Renaissance Thought and the Arts: Collected Essays* (1965; repr., Princeton, NJ: Princeton University Press, 1980), esp. 57–60; and Hans Blumenberg, *The Legitimacy of the Modern Age*, trans. Robert M. Wallace (Cambridge, MA: MIT Press, 1983).

12. See Cassirer, *Individual and the Cosmos*, 10–45, and the introduction by Pauline Moffitt Watts to Nicholas de Cusa, *De Ludo Globi / The Game of Spheres*, trans. Watts (New York: Abaris Books, 1986), 13–51.

13. Cassirer, *Individual and the Cosmos*, 45. Ronald Levao, *Renaissance Minds and Their Fictions: Cusanus, Sidney, Shakespeare* (Berkeley: University of California Press, 1985), 3–96, offers a fine analysis of Cusanus's thought. Blumenberg, *Legitimacy of the Modern Age*, 476–80, raises provocative questions about Cusanus's role at this intellectual juncture.

14. Cassirer, *Individual and the Cosmos*, 143, famously accounted for this development as producing a new concept of nature and the "whole world of objects" in which the "'object' is now something other than the mere opposite, the—so to speak—*ob-jectum* of the Ego." Rather, he argues, the object becomes the work of the subject, toward which "all the productive, all the genuinely creative forces" of the self are directed, and the outcome is a new vision of art and science, to which I add new understandings of politics and empire.

15. See Giancarlo Maiorino, *At the Margins of the Renaissance: Lazarillo de Tormes and the Picaresque Art of Survival* (University Park: Pennsylvania State University Press, 2003); Margaret T. Hodgen, *Early Anthropology in the Sixteenth and Seventeenth Centuries* (Philadelphia: University of Pennsylvania Press, 1964); J. H. Elliott, *Empires of the Atlantic World: Britain and Spain in America 1492–1830* (New Haven, CT: Yale University Press, 2006).

16. A fruitful precursor of the present chapter is the essay "World" in C. S. Lewis, *Studies in Words*, 2nd ed. (Cambridge: Cambridge University Press, 1967), 214–68, from which I adapt several formulations, such as "the region of regions" and "the scene of human events."

17. The most important work of scholarship for orienting my argument in the following pages is Harry Berger Jr., "The Renaissance Imagination: Second

World and Green World," in his *Second World and Green World: Studies in Renaissance Fiction-Making*, ed. John Patrick Lynch (Berkeley: University of California Press, 1988), 3–40.

18. Buchanan, *Political Poetry*, 68–69.

19. Witt, *In the Footsteps of the Ancients*, 292–337.

20. For a discussion of Pontano's astrology, see Charles Trinkaus, "The Astrological Cosmos and Rhetorical Culture of Giovanni Gioviano Pontano," *Renaissance Quarterly* 38 (1985): 446–72.

21. Thomas S. Kuhn, *The Copernican Revolution: Planetary Astronomy in the Development of Western Thought* (New York: Vintage Books, 1959), 134–84.

22. Ibid., 219–28. On Galileo's career, see Mario Biagioli, *Galileo Courtier: The Practice of Science in the Culture of Absolutism* (Chicago: University of Chicago Press, 1993).

23. On *oikoumene*, see Romm, *Edges of the Earth*, 37.

24. But see Brian Greene, *The Hidden Reality: Parallel Universes and the Deep Laws of the Cosmos* (New York: Alfred A. Knopf, 2011).

25. Plutarch, "On Tranquillity of Mind," in *Moralia*, trans. W. C. Helmbold, 16 vols. (Cambridge, MA: Harvard University Press, 1939), 6:176–79. See Steven J. Dick, *Plurality of Worlds: The Extraterrestrial Life Debate from Democritus to Kant* (Cambridge: Cambridge University Press, 1982), and James Warren, "Ancient Atomists on the Plurality of Worlds," *Classical Quarterly*, n.s., 54 (2004): 354–65.

26. Keith Thomas, *Man and the Natural World: Changing Attitudes in England 1500–1800* (1983; New York: Oxford University Press, 1996), 167.

27. Paul J. Alpers, *The Poetry of* The Faerie Queene (Princeton NJ: Princeton University Press, 1967), 19–35, explores the implications of Spenser's view of his poem as a world.

28. See the English-language examples in Jeffrey Knapp, *An Empire Nowhere: England, America, and Literature from* Utopia *to* The Tempest, New Historicism 16 (Berkeley: University of California Press, 1992), 243–60.

29. Fernando de Rojas, *La Celestina: Comedia o Tragicomedia de Calisto y Melibea*, ed. Peter E. Russell (Madrid: Castalia, 1991), 598–99.

30. Fernando de Rojas, *La Celestina*, trans. Lesley Byrd Simpson (Berkeley: University of California Press, 1955), 159.

31. Américo Castro, La Celestina *como contienda literaria: castas y casticismos* (Madrid: Revista de Occidente, 1965), and Stephen Gilman, *The Spain of*

Fernando de Rojas: The Intellectual and Social Landscape of La Celestina (Princeton, NJ: Princeton University Press, 1972), offer a famous account of that subjective dislocation.

32. William Shakespeare, *The Comedy of Errors*, in *The Riverside Shakespeare*, ed. G. Blakemore Evans et al., 2nd ed. (Boston: Houghton Mifflin, 1997), 117 (1.2.34–40). Further citations in this chapter will appear in the main text and refer to act, scene, and line.

33. Tom Conley, *The Self-Made Map: Cosmographic Writing in Early Modern France* (Minneapolis: University of Minnesota Press, 1996), 167–201, and Christian Jacob, *The Sovereign Map: Theoretical Approaches in Cartography throughout History*, ed. Edward H. Dahl, trans. Tom Conley (Chicago: University of Chicago Press, 2006).

34. Louis Marin, *Utopics: The Semiological Play of Textual Spaces*, trans. Robert A. Vollrath (Atlantic Highlands, NJ: Humanities Press, 1984), esp. 102–3.

35. Samuel Daniel, *Musophilus*, ed. Raymond Himelick (West Lafayette, IN: Purdue University Studies, 1965), 76. On the two versions of worldmaking mentioned here, see Roland Greene, "Fictions of Immanence, Fictions of Embassy," in *The Project of Prose in Early Modern Europe and the New World*, ed. Elizabeth Fowler and Roland Greene, Cambridge Studies in Renaissance Literature and Culture 16 (Cambridge: Cambridge University Press, 1997), 176–202.

36. Miguel de Cervantes, *Don Quixote*, trans. Edith Grossman (New York: Ecco, 2003), 731.

37. Miguel de Cervantes, *Don Quijote de la Mancha*, ed. Francisco Rico, 2 vols. (Barcelona: Galaxia Gutenberg y Círculo de Lectores, 2004), 1:1053–54.

38. Cervantes, *Don Quixote*, 726.

39. Michael Camille, "Simulacrum," in *Critical Terms for Art History*, ed. Robert S. Nelson and Richard Schiff (Chicago: University of Chicago Press, 1996), 40.

40. On its face this may seem nothing more than an elaboration of how scholars have often seen the Baroque, namely, in terms of the confrontation between human beings and the world: thus Carl Friedrich, in a two-part article in the mid-1950s, argues that "for the Baroque the decisive experience was that of man's power (including the finiteness of such power) in the face of the world"; see Friedrich, "Style as the Principle of Historical Interpretation," *Journal of Aesthetics and Art Criticism* 14 (1955): 150.

41. René Wellek, "The Concept of Baroque in Literary Scholarship," in *Concepts*

of *Criticism*, ed. Stephen G. Nichols Jr. (New Haven, CT: Yale University Press, 1963), 109.

42. John Milton, *Paradise Lost*, in *Complete Poems*, ed. John Carey and Alastair Fowler, 2 vols. (London: Longman, 1968), 1:40.

43. Ibid., 44.

44. Ibid., 80–81.

45. Margaret Cavendish, *The Description of a New World Called the Blazing World and Other Writings*, ed. Kate Lilley (New York: New York University Press, 1992), 123–24.

46. Ibid., 124.

47. Ibid., 126.

48. Ibid., 133.

49. Ibid., 132.

50. Ibid., 145.

51. Ibid., 129.

52. Ibid., 170, 174, 177.

53. René Descartes, *Oeuvres*, ed. Charles Adam and Paul Tannery, 11 vols. (Paris: J. Vrin, 1996), 1:270–71. For the context of Descartes's abandonment of *Le Monde*, see Stephen Gaukroger, *Descartes: An Intellectual Biography* (Oxford: Clarendon Press, 1995), 290–92. On Galileo's trial, see Biagioli, *Galileo Courtier*, 329–52.

54. Cavendish, *Blazing World*, 185, 188.

Afterword

1. Geoffrey Chaucer, *Troilus and Criseyde*, in *The Riverside Chaucer*, ed. Larry D. Benson, 3rd ed. (Boston: Houghton Mifflin, 1987), 489.

2. Michel de Montaigne, *Complete Works*, trans. Donald Frame (1943; repr., New York: Alfred A. Knopf, 2003), 271.

3. Jean-Baptiste Michel et al., "Quantitative Analysis of Culture Using Millions of Digitized Books," *Science*, 16 December 2010, doi:10.1126/science.1199644; see http://www.culturomics.org.

4. Roland Greene, "Misplaced Horizons in Literary Studies," *Arcade: Literature, the Humanities, and the World*, http://arcade.stanford.edu/misplaced -horizons-literary-studies.

INDEX

Wilson, Thomas, *Arte of Rhetorique*,
   21, 35
wit, 11, 12, 174
Wood, William, 54
world, 1, 5, 7, 10, 13, 21, 35, 143–73;
   as engine, 10, 149, 157–58,
   163–72; "global I," 154–56,

158; island logic, 156–57, 158,
   159–61
Wright, Thomas, *The Passions of the*
   Mind in General, 114
Wyatt, Thomas, "The longe love," 116

Zenobius, 47